The Disabled Detective

The Disabled Detective

Sleuthing Disability in Contemporary Crime Fiction

Susannah B. Mintz

BLOOMSBURY ACADEMIC
LONDON • NEW YORK • OXFORD • NEW DELHI • SYDNEY

BLOOMSBURY ACADEMIC
Bloomsbury Publishing Plc
50 Bedford Square, London, WC1B 3DP, UK
1385 Broadway, New York, NY 10018, USA
29 Earlsfort Terrace, Dublin 2, Ireland

BLOOMSBURY, BLOOMSBURY ACADEMIC and the Diana logo
are trademarks of Bloomsbury Publishing Plc

First published in Great Britain 2020
Paperback edition published 2021

Copyright © Susannah B. Mintz, 2020

Susannah B. Mintz has asserted her right under the Copyright, Designs and
Patents Act, 1988, to be identified as Author of this work.

For legal purposes the Acknowledgments on p. vi constitute an extension
of this copyright page.

Cover design: Eleanor Rose
Cover images: Detectives © akindo/Getty Images;
dog © bubaone/Getty Images

All rights reserved. No part of this publication may be reproduced or transmitted
in any form or by any means, electronic or mechanical, including photocopying,
recording, or any information storage or retrieval system, without
prior permission in writing from the publishers.

Bloomsbury Publishing Plc does not have any control over, or responsibility for, any
third-party websites referred to or in this book. All internet addresses given
in this book were correct at the time of going to press. The author and publisher
regret any inconvenience caused if addresses have changed or sites have
ceased to exist, but can accept no responsibility for any such changes.

A catalog record for this book is available from the British Library.

A catalog record for this book is available from the Library of Congress.

ISBN: HB: 978-1-4742-3822-9
PB: 978-1-3502-1543-6
ePDF: 978-1-4742-3824-3
eBook: 978-1-4742-3823-6

Typeset by Integra Software Services Pvt. Ltd.

To find out more about our authors and books visit www.bloomsbury.com
and sign up for our newsletters.

Contents

Acknowledgments		vi
1	Introduction: Sleuthing Disability	1
2	Seer Detectives	25
3	Deafness and the Penetrating Detective	61
4	The Crip Sleuths	95
5	The Missing Arm of the Law	131
6	Detection and the Mind's Private Eye	165
Epilogue		199
Works Cited		202
Index		213

Acknowledgments

I am grateful to David Avital at Bloomsbury Academic for his support of this project, and especially for his gracious extension of the deadline when unexpected life circumstances temporarily derailed my progress. To my friends who first got me thinking about a book about mystery and whose careful reading of draft chapters helped me to discover my argument, I am also deeply indebted. Though they may never encounter these pages, I want to acknowledge those participants of the past three Convivio Italy Summer Conferences who listened so attentively as I tried to explain what I was up to, and for suggesting detective series I might not otherwise have known. Indeed, thanks go to all my friends who recommended their favorite sleuths, disabled or not (I may never be forgiven for neglecting "The Singing Detective"), because every instance reassured me that there was more to be said about this popular form. I grew up on that 1960s camp classic *The Avengers*, which I watched with my mother, Beth MacKenzie, and I wanted well into adulthood to channel Emma Peel; these past years of immersion in mystery and crime have often felt like a homecoming of sorts, and it's with melancholy more than relief that I come to the end of writing this book. It's never really over, of course, where mystery's concerned, since finding out who actually done it is usually a let-down, and the best stories reward our loyalty in being just as good on the fifth read as the first. There's something meaningful to me about officially entering with this study a worldwide community of crime fiction fans. Even the most solitary writing habits are fostered by our relationships with others. My strongest gratitude goes to the people who help me to sustain this life, my colleagues and family and friends, without whom it would be impossible to keep going back to the desk, thinking it through, getting it down on paper.

1

Introduction: Sleuthing Disability

When I first told people I was writing a book about disabled detectives, a surprisingly frequent response was, "Are there any?" In fact, there are *many*—a category all their own in a genre defined by its numerous offshoots and subtypes. Since Arthur Conan Doyle's dazzlingly brilliant Sherlock Holmes first confounded Dr. Watson with his wild fluctuations of addiction and mood, the list of fictional detectives-with-disabilities has grown surprisingly long. One website lists eighty different single books or series featuring disability in some prominent way,[1] including blind and one-eyed detectives; amputee detectives; detectives impaired and shell-shocked in war; detectives with autism, Asperger's, and obsessive-compulsive disorder; detectives recovering from stroke; para- and quadriplegic detectives; deaf and hearing-impaired detectives; and at least one investigator missing a lung. Some have amnesia; others are of short stature. One detective struck by lightning can sense the location of dead people; another, violently concussed, visualizes crimes through the "eyes" of perpetrators. Three different contemporary novels concern synesthesia. Television similarly abounds with sleuths characterized by some form of physical or mental impairment, from the wheelchair-using lawyer Ironside in the 1970s to the more recent leads of *Monk* (OCD), *House* (chronic pain), *Homicide* (stroke), *Perception* (schizophrenia), and the original *CSI* (otosclerosis). "Nearly every detective character," Gary Hoppenstand and Ray B. Browne wrote in the early 1980s, "seems burdened with some sort of personal abnormality" (1).

What is the meaning of this array of disabled sleuths? What kinds of questions are authors exploring when the protagonists of their stories are disabled, given that disabled characters have rarely been the *heroes* of literature—or, as in the case of anti-heroes like Shakespeare's Richard III and

Melville's one-legged Captain Ahab, when disability has so often been used as the harbinger of undoing? In historian Paul Longmore's words, "deformity of body symbolizes deformity of soul. Physical handicaps are made the emblems of evil" (133). What then is the connection between disability, in its many forms, and the narrative form of crime and mystery? This trend, impressive in its sheer voluminousness, has largely been ignored by scholars of both detective fiction and disability literature. Hoppenstand and Browne introduced their collection of pulp magazine "defective detectives" in 1983; a year later, sociologist Irving Zola described crime-mystery as "a major perpetuator" of stereotypical images of disability and cited a lack of structural or social analysis of disability in detective fiction. Yet neither of these works initiated any concerted exploration of the phenomenon. And as the quote from Hoppenstand and Browne above suggests, interest in the trope of disabled detection may in fact betray entrenched prejudice against impairment as a "burden," an abnormality, an exotic defect or characterological quirk. A few more recent articles and websites both advertise and seek to understand the social and generic importance of the disabled detective, but the figure and its function remain something of a mystery.

The Disabled Detective: Sleuthing Disability aims to address these questions and absences. My goal is to explore the meaning of disability when aligned with criminal *prosecution* in the context of a far more common literary and narrative convention of disability as a mark of criminal *deviance*. Is the plethora of disabled detectives just "romanticized excess," as disability scholars Frederic W. Hafferty and Susan Foster complain (194), a parade of "unrealistic, distorted, or otherwise sanitized" characters (187)? Or does it indicate, especially recently, that mystery writers have been ahead of the curve in terms of disability awareness and activism? By definition, detective fiction addresses matters of social justice, (in)equality, and cultural conflict; given its basic concern with social order and the interpretation of signs and clues, primarily physical, the genre is well positioned to engage the social model of disability, which holds that the hardships of disability are produced by cultural bias and prejudice rather than being inherent in individual bodies. The detectives to be considered in this study are capable and professional, usually dependable and courageous, often extremely smart, always full of gumption. Do they then, as a group, shift the way disability is typically assessed and understood?

To some extent, the answer is disappointingly no. In "The Detective as Other," Michael Cohen declares that "mystery fiction is very fond of cultural difference," but only because "otherness" heightens narrative tension (150). Both detectives and criminals, Cohen argues, "are constructed as foreign to ordinary experience" (153): "To be a detective is to be separate because of incorruptibility or genius or an extraordinary capacity for thinking like a criminal or any number of other distinguishing mental or spiritual features. Frequently authors add distinguishing physical or behavior features to their detectives to complement the other differences" (154). Through disability, then, as Cohen implies, the "dreadful otherness" of villains is "displace[d]" onto, and "emphasiz[ed]" by, that of the detective (156), whose anomalous body or mind thus symbolizes the ability to root out evil—which is otherwise masked in people who look "just like" us (153). That Cohen does not interrogate those "distinguishing physical or behavior features" as anything more than ornaments of the detective's cognitive skill suggests that impairment works according to what disability scholars would call a prosthetic logic, helping the narrative along but insignificant in its own right.²

The classic figure of the detective is formed, of course, in the crucible of pathology, wherein crime-busting avenges the sleuth's own trauma and deductive genius assuages private pain by triumphing over lawlessness and upheaval, if not over disability. Detectives are often described as identifying with criminals precisely because they share some sense of being damaged, and they may in turn tread a thin line between lawfulness and illegality in their investigative methods. (Both Sherlock Holmes and Edgar Allan Poe's detective C. Auguste Dupin were notoriously credited for being able to think so "like" the criminals they pursued that even arch-nemeses like Moriarty and the Minister D– stood little chance of besting them.) Consider this remark from Vera Caspary's 1943 suspense classic *Laura*: "The lame, the halt, and the blind have more malice in their souls, therefore more acumen. Cherishing secret hurt, they probe for the pains and weaknesses of others. And probing is the secret of finding" (17).³ At least in part, then, the disabilities of many detectives perpetuate the metaphorical use of impairment to signify something "broken" in those characters that solving crime somehow helps to heal, rehearsing a centuries-old equivalence of body problems to problems of self—indicative of, rather than incidental to.

Disability serves a purpose, in other words, in pointing readers toward whatever is out of whack and worthy of notice. In a discussion of Poe's "The Purloined Letter" and "Murders in the Rue Morgue," the two stories credited with inaugurating modern detective fiction, Charles J. Rzepka writes that "even the most 'analytical' mind cannot identify with another's train of thought without observing his bodily movements" and that "it is impossible to achieve empathy with the criminal mind ... without paying close attention to the physical activity displayed by the body attached to that mind" (81). For Rzepka, this keen attention to corporeal detail relates to Poe's rejection, rather than his endorsement, of inductive reasoning, in that bodily clues do not readily coalesce in answers to the problem of crime without the use of "our imaginations" in thinking "*outside* the locked room of common sense" (81; my italics). Mere plodding analytics are not enough, Rzepka says of Poe's Dupin; the detective must develop more creative and empathic habits that do not rely so heavily on a positivist—read, middle-class—notion of evidence. "Ordinary" cunning, according to Dupin, did not "take into account the mind of the criminal," and would thus devolve into "mechanical calculation" (78). Physical shape and movement are understood in this formulation to be stably interpretable because the body carries out the mind's intentions: the detective gains access to what might otherwise be an incomprehensible or impenetrable criminal consciousness through the observable data of the criminal's physical acts and gestures.

The imaginative leap Dupin prized was a teleological one that emerged from a historical moment in which anatomy was increasingly enlisted in arguments about human nature and the consequences of evolutionary theory for humanity. Where Poe's Dupin privileges "the speculative potential of philosophy and poetry" over the more purely "scientific" method of Holmes, to quote Martin A. Kayman (45), both sleuths assume that corporeality is knowable—indeed, that it is significant insofar as it provides reliable information about what cannot be visually determined.[4] The one-to-one correspondence that had historically defined impairment as both cause and effect of a person's moral and temperamental state takes only slightly different shape in early crime fiction in faith in fingerprints and physiognomy (and later DNA) as the sure mark of identity. Shifting this same notion to a disabled *detective*'s body suggests that audiences are offered access to the sleuth's inimitable deductive powers through the metaphor of exaggerated corporeal difference. Reading blind sleuth Max Carrados's fingers as they absorb the meaning of newsprint ink or PI Fred Carver's limping traversal of a parking lot provides an imaginative overlay whereby physical action (whether magical or effortful) externalizes the process of the detective's thinking; marveling at the one, we glimpse the magnitude of the other. Impairment in this sense is meant to be read *past*; it may be interesting, but only because it ultimately points elsewhere, toward the detective's mental powers.

"Formula fiction," writes Sally R. Munt, entails a "regurgitation of stereotypes," "collud[ing] with dominant definitions of Others" (103). That crime is "a predictable, highly formalized genre offering pleasure and release of tension through the affirmation of received and uncontested meanings," in Munt's words (175), is taken by many scholars as a given. John Scaggs, for example, remarks that crime fiction "is in many ways a revealingly defensive and paranoid genre" that restores order "through containment of the 'other'" (75)—the "instant morality" (44) of punishing denouements (whether explicit or implied), as well as largely homogenous landscapes in which racial and gendered others are casually denigrated or from which they are unrealistically excised. Their characterization depends on stereotyped beliefs readers are assumed to have about particular impairments, so that in seeming to "overcome" a bodily adversity that is nonetheless inconvenient and ever-present, these sleuths enact, in their persons as much as in their work, a satisfying containment of upheaval.

Yet it is also a truism of crime fiction that the form can never achieve its own ends. The argument I will make in the chapters to follow is that detective fiction, even as a literary form with explicit and enduring parameters and seemingly defined by the fantasy of managing chaos, poses a serious challenge to clichés about impairment. What Andrew Pepper and Laura Marcus independently contend, that the genre is inherently "shot through" with contradiction (Pepper, 211), suggests that its very neatness—going all the way back to the classic puzzle tales of the Golden Age—betrays an inability to secure "unproblematic control and closure." A genre dependent upon the recurrence of mayhem cannot pretend to a *guarantee* of social coherence, even if some pleasure is obtained in the temporary resolution of confusion at the end of a given story. The idea that it is only in 1970s feminist and black detective fiction that the governing templates of the genre undergo significant revision assumes too much consistency across earlier works as well as too much stability within stories whose narrative worlds are by definition troubled by threat. In other words, closure has *always* been a fantasy. Even sleuths who dependably restore order in the tamest of ways (Agatha Christie's benign Jane Marple comes to mind) tend to exceed the outlines of the very normative lifestyles their sleuthing would seem designed to protect. The unmarried, geographically mobile, intellectually fierce Miss Marple, for instance, might remind us of itinerant religious women whose unmooring from roles of wife and mother disrupted the patriarchal landscape of early modern England; and how dependable is official power if its dominance is constantly evacuated by the trope of amateur, and often marginal, investigators? Not only in parodic, postmodern work by authors like Umberto Eco, Alain Robbe-Grillet, and Paul Auster, then, is ideological tension built into the form.

As Pepper argues in the context of black crime fiction, it is possible for detectives who do not occupy hegemonic subject positions to "consciously subvert the values of a dominant, white culture while simultaneously securing its not so fluid boundaries" (223). Disabled detectives, similarly, perform what Stephen Soitos names, recalling W.E.B. Dubois, "double-consciousness detection" (33–37), charged with upholding the laws and regulations of social hierarchy with bodies that by definition problematize the fundamental ableism of that structure. For most of the sleuths I will explore, in this study, that challenge is functional more than intentional—which is to say, a kind of passive resistance to ableism may be effected simply by virtue of the presence of disability in characters who have narrative power, however unattuned to disability issues an author might otherwise be. "Disability crime fiction" does not, for the most part, comprise a generic counter-*movement* in the manner of black or lesbian detective series in which the tradition is explicitly (if imperfectly) critiqued, in part because most of the novels and TV series in question are not written by people who themselves are disabled. Disabled detection nonetheless represents an important counterpoint to traditional ways of understanding the very nature of detecting, of "solution," provoking us to interrogate the normative mechanisms of knowledge that obtain in social order and relationships, in bodily and architectural spaces. As I hope to demonstrate, disabled detection is by definition a matter of integrated knowing, where cognition is an embodied process and sensory encounters with the world are inherently perceptual and therefore epistemological. As detectives with atypical bodies and minds negotiate the physical spaces of crime and the social, interpersonal, cognitive, communicative spaces of figuring it all out, they enact intriguing alternatives for how to think, inquire, and understand.

Poe's emphasis on "a new epistemological synthesis," to quote Kayman again (45), interests me for what it might mean to the relationship between a detective's disabled bodymind—the phrase is Margaret Price's—and his or her manner of processing information.[5] My claim throughout this study is not that disabled detectives are the offspring of Dupin in any direct way, but that their non-normative bodyminds manifest Dupin's intellectual flexibility in surprisingly *disabled* ways. To take Rzepka's argument further, "in making Dupin a psychic chameleon Poe also emptied out the traditionally male role of detective ... and opened the door to its gradual re-occupation, first by the strong man's non-male, and eventually by his non-white and non-Western"—to which we must add non-able—"counterparts" (88). In this new "tradition," disability becomes a mode rather than a signifier, not a noun but a verb, not proof but process. The insistent focus in scholarship on where crime stories end up, on culmination, misses the pleasure of suspension in possibility as the forward motion of solution slowly aligns with the backward motion of what happened. (The vague—or acute—sense of let-down after suspense ends, and we find out whodunit and why, will not be unfamiliar to many readers of this book.) If the genre of crime demands linearity and closure, the figure of the disabled sleuth—whose condition does not get "better"—tells us that we're fetishizing the wrong kind of resolution, or makes impossible the kind of resolution we crave. Disabled detectives literally think outside the box.

Discussions of detective fiction invariably emphasize one of two signature spatial realms whereby writers and their texts are classified: the geographical spaces where crime occurs (city or country house, public or private, work or bedroom; England or France, the United States, Latin America) and the psychological spaces where crime is solved (is the sleuth a realist, an intuitionist, a hard-boiled disillusionist, a forensic specialist?). (To these we can add the interior space of the unconscious, where the motivation for crime might be said to originate.) Robert A. Rushing writes that "there is more than one kind of space" in detective fiction; "there is always epistemological space, the space of detection" (42). As I will explore throughout the chapters to follow, space is demarcated by a sleuth's capacity to pursue perpetrators through cognitive process as well as physical investigation. Spaces both mental and architectural become meaningful insofar as they contain evidence, clues; as masters of observation and data collection, the best fictional detectives are porous figures, agents of penetration and sites of receptivity. Detecting—insofar as the investigator must visit the scenes of crime, enter criminal settings to canvass or interview, and ultimately achieve physical capture of the villain *somewhere* (locations that may be no more sinister than a cruise ship or a simulation of Mars[6])—requires both physical movement across thresholds and imaginative, verbal, performative, and intersubjective leaps of understanding.

Such refractory interpenetrations—of entities of all kinds—recall two important concepts articulated by philosophers Gilles Deleuze and Félix Guattari in *A Thousand Plateaus: The rhizome and territorialization*. A rhizome (think of the roots of woodland ferns) consists of "multiplicities," "comprised not of units but of dimensions," "laid out on a plane of consistency" with "linkages" rather than "lineages," whereby one point is connected to all other points without "beginning [or] end" (21). Rhizomatic connectedness has "multiple entranceways and exits" and exists in a state of constant modification, reversal, and metamorphosis. Territoriality, in turn, is a process whereby the forces of life converge and separate in the dynamic shaping of space; it is the productive *spatial* expression of beings both organic and inorganic. Russell West-Pavlov explains that territoriality "takes pre-existing flows, the fluid materiality of being ... and begins to make semi-formalized domains out of it" (181), domains that are impermanent and in a sense always on the brink of return to the flow of being. "The process of life itself," West-Pavlov continues, is "one of constantly changing spaces and movement generating social space." Being, for Deleuze and Guattari, is thus always and inherently becoming, but that movement toward becoming does not take place *in* space, rather it *creates* space. As they write, territory is an "act"—rather than an *a priori* location—that emerges from the places and patterns of existence (314).

Disability, in that it complicates fixed notions of how people ought to behave in space or with other persons, similarly redraws boundaries and redefines our understanding of what it means to *be* somewhere. Recent applications of "the Deleuzean project" to disability studies, most notably by Margrit Shildrik in *Dangerous Discourses*, align Deleuze and Guattari's emphasis on intercorporeality, becoming, and plenitude with a similar project of figuring disability as possibility and gain rather than diminishment and lack, as the source of border-crossing allegiances, new forms of knowledge, and more capacious attitudes toward health, beauty, social value, success, mortality, sex, work, architecture, economics, and language. In short, the "cripping" of normative paradigms along alternate pathways of meaning—by which I foreground the reclaiming of "crip" by disability activists and artists to "identify a sensibility, identity, or activity in opposition to mainstream assumptions" (Lewis, 46). When human relationships are understood to be rhizomatic rather than subject to dyadic differentials of power, the dis/ability binary might also come under scrutiny. When social spaces are understood to result from the dynamic interaction between selves embodied in all sorts of ways, including the hybrid forms of people with canes, wheelchairs, or support animals, many other kinds of boundaries might usefully relax, and questions of accessibility rise to the level of urgency rather than ableist annoyance. When we engage seriously with the fact of corporeal difference, as Shildrik argues at the outset of her book, "modernist understandings of what it is to be a subject" must be reconsidered (2–3).

My aim is not to make disability the primary subject position from which all others emanate, nor to romanticize it as metaphor for liberatory release from the strictures of conventional paradigms, a charge that has been leveled against contemporary body theorists like Judith Butler.[7] It is, however, to propose a kind of Deleuzean *cripistemology*, the term formally coined by Robert McRuer and Merri Lisa Johnson in their co-edited issues of the *Journal of Literary and Cultural Disability Studies* in 2014. "Cripistemological" analysis takes as one starting point the kinds of knowledge that derive from anomalous corporeal engagements with the world, in addition to complicating what mainstream medical and market economies claim to know about disability—both the physical condition of it and the identity that might emerge therefrom. Knowing that derives from disability encounters in and with place, then, and places defined by the kinds of knowledge and interactions that happen in them—call this crip-territoriality. And as these scenes and stories are molded by the bodyminds of atypical detectives, a certain brand of knowing *happens*: a process of discovering, understanding, connecting through bodies whose sensory habits, styles of motion, modes of thinking, and forms of communicating disrupt the presumptions of containment that undergird the very genre in which they appear.

Crip-territory works both ways. That is, spaces come into being through the behaviors, interactions, and activities that happen there, just as bodies and minds are subject to the dynamics of the spaces in which they occur—including differentials of power, attitudes about what sorts of actions or motions are appropriate, and the basics of architecture. This is what Henri Lefebvre has called the "spatial body," a body "subject to the … interactions and reciprocal actions, axes and planes, centre and peripheries" of space (195). The issue is "the co-constituting relationship between flesh and environment," as Rosemarie Garland-Thomson puts it (594), and thus of "fit"—or rather, to use her term, *misfit*: the "incongruent" (592) juxtaposition of bodies and behaviors in time and space. "Misfitting," Garland-Thomson writes, "theorize[s] disability as a way of being in an environment, as a material arrangement," and "focuses on the disjunctures that occur in the interactive dynamism of becoming" (594). The emphasis on "'shape' in the broadest sense" and on the "distinctive, dynamic thingness" of persons and spaces "as they come together" (595) makes "misfit" an ever-changing and broadly applicable process, rather than an entity: "Any of us can fit here today and misfit there tomorrow" (597). Garland-Thomson goes on to argue that misfitting "can produce subjugated knowledges from which an oppositional consciousness and politicized identity might arise" (597), as the clash between any given bodily or emotional style and an "unsustaining environment" reveals the fiction of "normalcy," the fallacy of our fiercely held conviction that we are unified, independent beings fully in charge of ourselves. We are all of us thus continually "materializ[ing] as fitting or misfitting" in "perpetual transformation" (598) given the particulars of moment and place—identity as becoming, just as Deleuze and Guattari would have it.

Crime-space seems to me quintessentially territorial in all of these ways. It becomes what it is, in a literal sense, *in the act* of crime being committed, whatever it had been before, and so always exists as palimpsest. While evidence at the scene of a crime can be hidden, cleaned, discovered, forgotten, it remains as trace, as memory, as ingredient of whatever collects above or because of it; crime-space sediments in this way, as layered potentiality (how many plots involve the actual unearthing of bones?). Crime-space then expands as detection happens, in the crossing of thresholds both physical and imaginative—the amassing of data, the arraying of suspects, and the theorizing of what happened. Such spaces can be diagrammed, paced, and scoured for clues; delimited by crime-scene tape; identified through uniforms, signage on buildings, the activity taking place; occupied by witnesses, gawkers, perps who return to the scene of the deed—but their sectors will refuse to stay put as "dangerous" or "safe," however neat the end of the tale, since solving one crime hardly assures security (solution, as it were, is soluble). Crime-space thus also exists as reemergence. It is always but never precisely a physical site. It is what happened and where, as well as the possibility of something happening and the possibility of that something being discovered, understood, and punished; it is the various ways in which that knowing happens, the modes of detecting that disability makes possible. It is the refracting energies instigated by encounter between normative and anomalous forms of motion and thought, the coming-into-being of disabled detection as sleuths provoke acknowledgment, acceptance, alteration, from their surroundings. If it begins in crime, crime-space ends by opening up, into what Garland-Thomson calls "an expedition into unknown territory" (49).

To understand the counter-tactic I hope to generate here, consider a short piece by Tod Chambers in *The Lancet*, which argues that the so-called sick detective "makes us keenly aware that if we lack certain aspects of our own character, we may also lack the ability to understand and live our plots" (54). The "autistic" Christopher Boone, for example, narrator of Mark Haddon's *The Curious Incident of the Dog in the Night-Time* (discussed in Chapter 6), can understand "plot" (the causal logic of if X, then Y) but not "character" (how X and Y connect through emotion, relation, love, desire), and thus can't solve the mystery of who killed the dog. Or Leonard Shelby in Christopher Nolan's 2001 film *Memento*, who has anterograde amnesia (also discussed below): a sleuth who can't think sequentially because he can't form new memories, and so can't solve the murder of his wife. Interpretive failures like the ones Haddon and Shelby commit prove the need, in Chambers's analysis, for normative wholeness—without it, in the presence of "lack," subjective coherence collapses and we are not ourselves; without narrative, we are somehow not "self" at all.

That Chambers invokes two amateur *sleuths* to make this point is interesting in that it seems to exploit the inherent threat of crime, the frightening chaos of worlds in which violence happens, to underscore the legitimacy of another fear, that of abnormality, the concomitant threat of disability. Characters become interesting to "us," Chambers implies, because their diminishments "make us keenly aware" of what *fullness* of self is supposed to be. The "sick detective," in this schema, becomes the negative foil for the "healthy" reader, and stories that feature such detectives are remarkable for what the detectives *cannot* achieve, rather than for the potentially compelling alternative methods of solution they might present.

Given the publication venue of Chambers's article—*The Lancet* is an international journal devoted to general medicine—its emphasis on "sick" individuals is perhaps unsurprising: this is the medical model of disability, which defines illness and impairment as problems to be solved within individual bodies, rather than a constellation of effects that happens when embodied subjects encounter (and confront) social, environmental, architectural, largely *attitudinal* situations. To think of disability in such terms—only as a defining damage that humanizes the genius, explains his or her affinity for making things "right" again, represents social collapse, or serves as contrast to spotlight the norm—is not only ableist; it also limits the analysis of disability to a unified metaphor, ignoring what else it might represent or the ways in which disability also functions structurally in narrative. As I have been arguing throughout this introduction, disabled sleuthing is a kind of thinking-through. How is knowledge—the truths of these mysteries— produced by differing interactions in and with spaces? By non-normative modes of communication, movement, and memory, I will suggest—by the fact of alternative methodologies, the embrace of unexpected connections, the possibility of translation, the shaping of atypical forms, and the crossing of boundaries.

That so much unexpected subversion occurs in genre fiction is not incidental to this discussion. Ria Cheyne has argued that understanding the workings of narrative form helps us to appreciate the ways in which some authors resist the template in their creation of impaired sleuths, and, more intriguingly, also operate *within* those generic regulations to "contradict" (187) dominant tropes of disability. The presence of disabled protagonists in a genre defined by a drive toward knowledge and interpretation might encourage us to consider what we *don't* know about disability—that is, by reading bodies carefully, we come up against the limitations and failures of what is assumed to be real and true. The reader is *not*, in this sense, a very good detective at all, and that may be a good thing. Allowing ourselves not to know can be enormously productive.

It has become customary in recent discussions of Sherlock Holmes to situate this genius of the genre on the so-called spectrum, and to explore the relationship between his cleverness and what Dr. Watson refers to as his eccentricities—obsessive cleanliness, disregard for normative social rules, hoarding, anorexia, addiction, and an interpersonal style that might these days be diagnosed as social anxiety disorder. Like his predecessor Dupin, Holmes represents a heightening of traits that crystallizes his difference from the ordinary folk around him. His powers of observation and deduction are literally marvelous, and it is precisely in this sense of being *prodigious* that Holmes may have more in common with the human oddities displayed at Victorian freak shows than with the physicians, policemen, and aristocrats—or even the foreigners and ugly criminals—who populate his stories. Holmes thus establishes an important precedent for the generations of disabled detectives who follow him. Invited to wonder at his prowess, audiences may also be repelled by what seems strange in him; we may pity even as we admire him. That simultaneity holds the emotional stakes of the Holmes stories in a kind of tension. To the degree that Holmes is at once *unnaturally* gifted and also peculiar, he guarantees a middle ground by which readers can satisfy their own obedience to physical, cognitive, and social norms.

But reading Holmes in the context of a more contemporary neurodiversity movement requires that we put pressure on stereotypes about both autism—often associated with augmented cerebral powers (think *Rain Man*, 1988)—and cognitive or psychiatric disability, more often associated with deviance and the danger of criminal "craziness." Sonya Freeman Loftis notes of Holmes that the sleuth "perfectly fits" a series of common tropes of autism: "phenomenal memory skills," an "unusually observant … observational ability," "an imprisoning interiority," and a lack of emotion, empathy, or communication skills such that the autistic person is patently inaccessible to a "normal" reader or viewer and must be *translated* for us by the more typical interpreter/sidekick—in this case, Dr. Watson. Loftis is not alone in suggesting that "the detective proves to be the true mystery of the mystery novel[s]" that feature Holmes, in which Watson is our true detective (or the freak show barker), mediating between strangeness and normalcy.⁸ If reader is the sleuth is the mystery, then Holmes's "disability" becomes a problem to be solved: normalized, recuperated, retrieved from otherness, domesticated and subdued.

Reading diagnosis back into older texts far from "proves" that the character of Sherlock Holmes was an autistic savant, however; nor does it seem meaningful to accuse the stories of perpetuating stereotypes about an identity category that would not have been operative for their author. Applying a term like "schizophrenic" to Holmes's "swings of mood," as Peter Messent does (116), plays altogether fast and loose with distinct psychiatric categories. But Messent also provocatively complicates assessments of the Holmes stories that foreground Doyle's political conservativism and read Holmes as the restorer of bourgeois British values. What seems more productive than diagnosing Holmes is to ask how his particular set of characteristics is generative of modes of thinking or forms of relationship that correlate with what is also true of the genre, as I mention above: its tendency to rebel against its own parameters. For as Messent argues, a strong undercurrent of critique and anxiety courses through the Holmes canon. "On one level," he writes in a "case study" of *The Sign of Four* (1890), "it is perfectly possible to read this novel as ideologically conservative" (125), with Holmes the "figure of supervisory power" (118) who "restores the British national body to health" (121). At the same time, repeated images of the "interpenetration" of political regimes and national identities (122), of "interdependency and similarity," "mutual interaction and interconnection," work to "undermin[e]" (123) certitude about the superiority of that body and "suggest a more critical stance toward British life, values, and imperialist practice" (126). What is quintessentially Holmesean, in this view, is not regulation of conventional morays but quite the opposite—"complexity and ambivalence" (126).

That Holmes knowingly capitalizes on accusations of eccentricity to elude rules of normative behavior—which would constrict his detecting by preventing the infiltration and crossing of boundaries—suggests what Petra Kuppers refers to as "cripping up": "the conscious and artful manipulation of one's narrative of a disabled self, a performance of selfhood in politicized storytelling" (137). What matters is not so much whether or not it's right to deem Holmes an autistic, I think, but the fact that his performance of non-normative behaviors can be read as both an advantage to his work and a form of critique of the dominant status quo—an argument quite in contrast to what Franco Moretti says of Holmes, that he was "interested only in *perpetuating* the existing order" (140; italics in original). Nor is the oddity of Holmes reliably recuperated by Dr. Watson, putative avatar for the "representative" reader, since Watson himself is displaced from respectable society by the war injury that prevents him from doctoring.[9] Woundedness makes Watson disreputable, even as it positions him as the storyteller, the dispenser of narrative detail and momentum. Messent writes that "Watson's function in the Holmes stories … is obfuscatory, and slows down narrative resolution," since Watson's inability to differentiate "essential detail from the surrounding irrelevancies" threatens to overwhelm the process of detection with which we are presumably more urgently engaged (32). But of course, "narrative delay" is precisely the point, as Messent goes on to say, for that is what establishes the gratification of postponement, without which every crime story would abruptly end. What Messent doesn't do, however, is link Watson's role in the creation of that pleasure to the doctor's status as a disabled man.

Holmes and Watson alike are atypical bodyminds whose observational, narrative, and interpersonal styles mutually participate in what Rzepka describes as detective fiction's quintessential array of possible narrative trajectories. "There is no other type of fiction," says Rzepka, "that is designed to induce the reader to invent, moment by moment, as many retrospective arrays to match the continuous emergence of new narrative information as is the classic tale of detection" (30). "What the reader of detection desires at each step of the reading process is not its end, but its immediate continuation" (27). That this process of proliferation, whereby readers are afforded "opportunities to invent" (27), might be initiated, or guided, or even controlled by the atypical persons of disabled detectives allows us to reorient another of Rzepka's claims, that "the tendency of the genre over the long run has been toward greater self-criticism, inclusiveness, and breadth of appeal" (3).

If Doyle's tales map the anxieties of pre-war Britain upon the streets of London, those of Golden Age *grande dame* Agatha Christie are more often "socially as well as spatially enclosed," in Messent's words, "representing a hierarchically ordered world and focusing especially on the upper middle classes" (128). Discussions of Christie, as Messent explains, tend to stress the conservatism of stories featuring the private, individualized crime of murder in "closeted settings" that allow readers to ignore "larger social and historical issues" (127), and detectives—the Belgian Hercule Poirot and quintessential spinster Jane Marple—who reliably restore order to their temporarily ruffled worlds. John Scaggs describes the setting of many Christie novels as a "social and historical cocoon," for example (48), and cites their "romantic resolution[s]" as emblematic of an "impulse to recover and reinstate" (47). But Christie also has a reputation as a rule-breaker who crafted her stories with a sly and knowing hand, sometimes violating the parameters of clue-puzzle mysteries—as in stories where the narrator is actually the murderer, which means that information a reader would need in order to solve the crime along with Poirot or Marple is inevitably hidden[10]—and created sleuths and plots that "suggest a certain fragility to the apparently generally well-ordered social world" she otherwise portrayed (Messent, 128). "[A] world of unnerving uncertainty," as Stephen Knight puts it (82), counteracts what can seem to be hermetically sealed, retrograde milieus, so that, for example, the very quality of characterization that many readers fault Christie for—her characters are often lambasted as two-dimensional[11]—also serves a more critical purpose of exposing the flaws of the social order those types so obviously represent.

It is in Poirot, according to some scholars, that Christie most overtly presents a challenge to traditional values. Poirot's fussy appearance (the waxed mustache, the waistcoats and patent-leather spats and galoshes[12]), his knowledge of and attention to domestic (often sartorial) detail, his emphasis on the psychology of crime rather than action or physical pursuit of criminals: these suggest a femininity that contests "stereotypical ... male heroism," in Messent's words (134), "an incipient feminist consciousness" (135) sometimes also represented in strong female characters who join Poirot in chafing against the constrictions of patriarchy. It should not surprise us that such readings do not consider Poirot as also disabled; in fact he is never cited as one of the "defective detectives" who appeared in the 1930s. And yet Poirot is surely the antecedent of television's obsessive-compulsive Adrian Monk (to whom I turn in Chapter 6)—not just foreign and effeminate, but preoccupied with orderliness in ways that go beyond a precise style of detecting. Poirot sees dust where it isn't, gets distracted by a spot of grease on his suit, easily espies "two minute strands of feather scarf" left on his couch by a client ("Cornish Mystery," 36), instructs Captain Hastings that a tie clip must be worn "in the exact centre of [his] tie" rather than "a sixteenth of an inch too much to the right" ("Johnnie Waverly," 53), aligns objects on desks and paintings on walls in absolute straight lines, finds beauty only in symmetry, is "'absolutely punctual'" (*Hallowe'en Party*, 47) and "very sensitive" to sounds ("How Does Your Garden Grow," 212), and so on. Christie herself described him as "meticulous, very tidy … A tidy little man. … a tidy little man, always arranging things, liking things in pairs."[13]

To take Poirot's distinctive behaviors only as signs of gendered or national otherness[14] is to miss disability as a structuring factor in these stories. Though moments like the ones just quoted are slight, or perhaps precisely *because* they seem slight—momentary deviations from Poirot's steady progress toward the revelation of truth—they cue readers to the sleuth's insistent observations, not, I think, simply to highlight more important clues, but to call attention to paying attention in a range of sensory ways. References to Poirot's obsessiveness tend to undercut the blustery masculinity and pre-emptive conclusion-making that characterize many of the men with whom he works, especially sidekick Captain Hastings. The effect is less to show up Poirot as dandified than to repeatedly startle us (both readers and, often, characters within the stories themselves) into wonderment about what might matter. Neither digressions nor false leads, such moments broaden the scope of our awareness; they do not interrupt the story; they are signs of engaging with one's surroundings *differently* from the norm. It is nowhere suggested that Poirot is a great detective *because* he is also obsessive; the two simply coexist. Moreover, Poirot is forever encouraging others to acquire something of his own habits to facilitate the production of knowledge. "'You might have seen something—'" he says to the woman who turns out to be the murderer in *Hallowe'en Party*, "'something quite small and unimportant but which on reflection might seem more significant to you, perhaps, than it had done at first'" (149). "Everything noticeable is worth remembering" (96).

It must be said that Christie did also deploy unhealthiness as a convenient trope of victimhood and criminality. Invalids are killed off to amplify the depravity of the villain and mental illness is often invoked to explain the prevalence of such deeds.[15] But between those poles, Poirot with his scrupulousness—along with his European air, the un-English effeminacy—conducts his investigations with gestures that implicitly quell his anxieties and overtly augment his archive of possible clues—or, simply, help him to do what he needs to do in order to work. We associate great detecting with thinking, as will become evident in the chapters to follow, and as suggested by the titular inspector's ironic remark in one episode of *Lewis*: "As a means of solving crime, it can prove useful" ("Counter Culture Blues," 2009; 3.4). Poirot does too, obviously—"there is only one thing to do—think" (*Three Act Tragedy*, 198). But he also protests to Hastings in *Dumb Witness* that he "[does] *not* 'think'" of "ingenious" things (my italics); rather, "'they are *there*—plain for anyone to see'" (448; italics in original). Poirot is alert to ambiguity, as good sleuths must be; and he is an unexpectedly corporeal detective—looking, listening, touching, tasting, sensory in every way—intuitive if also exact, his solutions borne by his compulsive bodymind.

Some scholars of crime fiction cite the Oedipus myth as the origin of all modern detective writing. Oedipus initiates the dual detective/criminal figure—"a device more common in detective fiction than one might expect," writes Rzepka (16)—by solving the crimes of unlawful desire and familial competitiveness that lie at the heart of Freudian subjectivity. Blindness in this "case" serves as the outward mark of criminality, thus prefiguring many later criminals delineated by their physical differences; it is also the sign of Oedipus's privileged status as the decipherer, in turn inaugurating the symbolically disabled sleuth. In *Oedipus Rex*, Oedipus enters the play as the detective, charged by the Apollonian oracle to find the murderer of Laius. The solution of the crime is known from the start of the story, however; this is not so much a *whodunit* as a *howdunit*. Oedipus is instructed by the Chorus to consult with Tiresias, who functions as both a guide toward discovery and a disseminator of obscure "truths" that Oedipus cannot initially understand—call them clues. Tiresias himself is thus also a precursor of later detectives, both blind and mystically genius ones.

If the mystery at the heart of the story is "how it happened," then, why does blindness frame the process of discovery, from the preternaturally insightful Tiresias to the tragically self-deluded Oedipus? Martha L. Edwards explains that in the ancient Greek world, "the meaning of physical disability depended on the community's understanding of people's roles … the criteria of physical disability rested not on one's ability to function as an individual but on one's functional ability within the community" (35). In this context, Oedipus is functional as a detective precisely *because* he is disabled—because the limp that results from a pin shot through his ankle as a baby anchors Oedipus to his own past and so leads eventually to the core of the puzzle, to his role in unraveling the riddle. "Swollen-footed" Oedipus is Oedipus-the-sleuth, his very body the locus of crime-solving clues. Detective-Oedipus can only uncover criminal-Oedipus by attending to bodily signs (lameness); Oedipus as the upholder of law can only punish Oedipus as breaker of laws by wreaking havoc on that same body in the moment of blinding himself. Once crime has infiltrated the community, disability becomes the hyperlegible sign of immorality and guilt, repentance and restitution, in the over-determined Oedipal body of criminal-detective.

Oedipus is in fact a trebled figure: disabled because violence has been done *to* him, he also occupies the position of victim—by parents obsessed with eluding the oracle. His limp in this context signifies parental error (the hubris of presuming to defeat the gods), exactly as disability would continue to do through any number of early modern dramas featuring monarchs whose bodies bear the evidence of their ancestors' sins. Here then are certain tropic elements of the crime genre: the motif of childhood harm as auger of both later transgressions and heroic resolution; the slippage between criminal, victim, and detective; the centrality of bodily clues in the solving of a murder. But disability is more than representational; it also circulates in the text, its meaning dependent on which part of the story we're in, which role Oedipus is currently playing. A symbol, then—for the inscrutability of divine injunction, for example, or in David T. Mitchell and Sharon L. Snyder's words, "humanity's incapacity to fathom the dictums of the gods" (*NP*, 62)—but also highly contextual, instructing us in ways of reading, foundational to the workings of story, facilitating not mystical insight but the acquisition of experiential knowledge. The ultimate misfit, as Garland-Thomson writes, demonstrating what happens "when the shape and function of [the body] comes in conflict with the shape and stuff of the built world" (594).

Disability is never just "itself" in the Oedipus tale, of course, as we might wish from more "realistic" narrative; it is strenuously overdetermined. It is also what Ato Quayson refers to as "articulation of disjuncture between thematic and narrative vectors" (41), where, in effect, plot seems to move one way and representation in another. My readings of the novels to follow are shaped by attention to how disability serves story and the unfolding of narrative as much as character and the portrayal of kinds. Consider, for example, how Golden Age mystery series defy the fact of time: Miss Marple was never really young, Hercule Poirot will never truly age. That suspension manifests in bodyminds that themselves resist the forward-motion of narrative arc; the *story* advances, but the corporeal/cognitive condition does not. This grants us an opportunity to experience disability as integrated into, rather than ancillary to (or disruptive of) an ongoing working life. The persistent anomaly might remind us of threat, the presence of danger, the incursions of criminality, but it simultaneously resists that alignment through its own ongoingness—the very fact that detectives carry on.

In a study of ethnicity in popular detective fiction (primarily Native American, Latino, and black detectives), Gina Macdonald and Andrew Macdonald ask, "does the ethnicity simply provide interesting local color or is it essential to the nature of the detective or to the social milieu in which s/he works?" (79), and cite the novels of Cherokee author Jean Hager, who "suggests that truth can be reached through different means" (72). The same question pertains neatly to stories with disabled detectives, where bodily difference does often seem designed simply to generate interest and curiosity, rather than deriving from any concerted effort to explore disabled experience or cripistemology. But a search for *different means* also characterizes the methods of the sleuths in question, as they maneuver themselves through the spaces of investigation. Different moves lead to perceptual alternatives, alternative ways of getting at truth—or, to put this otherwise, different truths altogether.

The Disabled Detective makes no claim to comprehensiveness. Any fan of crime and detective fiction knows that the genre is voluminous, and there are many books on the subject that undertake a more taxonomic project than my own. My goal here is not to catalog every instance of disabled detection, but to explore in depth select examples of a phenomenon that spans decades and many varieties of sleuthing. I have made choices and organized my material according to frequency and some degree of representative effect, and focus mostly on detective stories that follow the double plot of present investigation into past crime. Sensory and mobility impairments are by far the most common groups in print, while cognitive and psychiatric impairments dominate on television. The fact that disabilities of "mind" are so prevalent on TV strikes me as a feature of the age—we watch more than we read—but also of contemporary movements both toward and away from such conditions: that is, we live in an era predominated by greater activism about neurodiversity but also by fascination with neuroscience and the medicalization of psychiatric conditions (which is itself coincident with a romanticizing of mental illness). The chapter on detectives with impairments to hands and arms came somewhat late in this project, as I realized that they constituted a category unto themselves. Most of my selections are mid-twentieth century and later, where the persistence of deeply entrenched stereotyping and mythologizing about disability strikes me as most urgent to observe, but I also consider post–First World War and Second World War stories that depict impairment with obvious sensitivity to matters of public health and social justice. Some of the sleuths I study appear in twenty books or more; others are not well known at all.

My chapters are organized by condition: blindness, deafness, mobility impairment, injury to hand and arm, and psychiatric/cognitive disability. Print and TV are considered together in these chapters. Detectives with more than one impairment are grouped according to the more representationally dominant. Readers may object to the collocation of figures in Chapter 6, whose conditions range from amnesia to telepathy to schizophrenia to OCD, as the least coherent; but while I am alert to the distinctiveness of these conditions, I am also interested in the generalized representation of neurodiversity and impairment to thought, given the obvious correlation in the genre of crime between rationality, intellectual prowess, logic, and deduction. Disabilities are freighted with unique cultural symbolism, and we come to a reading of them with long-established ideas about what bodily conditions *mean*: the mystical insight of blindness, for example, or the equation of deafness with silent isolation, the presumption of asexual dependency in paraplegics, the frightening unpredictability of "madness," and so on. Throughout these chapters, I ask how, given that representational weight, detection happens. How do disabled sleuths "work"—do their jobs, and function in their narratives? This may be a question of how credibility is maintained or regained as a narrative maneuvers the anomalous detective into a position of authority, but more interestingly, and significantly, of how an atypical engagement with people, things, language, and space makes *knowing* happen. What sort of *cultural* work, then, is also performed by these tales? What sort of alternatives does the simultaneity of crime detection and disability offer us, at the start of the twenty-first century, for how to understand our very humanity? The answers to those questions are imbricated with the symbology of particular impairments.

It is something of a staple in detective stories to announce that anybody is capable of anything. Whether this is psychologically valid doesn't matter; the adage is meant to implicate us, as readers, listeners, and viewers, in the drama of crime—to heighten tension and anticipation. Can the culprit really be *anyone*? This is why we need our sleuths among us, to be one of us, to root out the terrible possibility of wrongdoing that is in us, that *is* us. Disabling the detective as the locus of that stabilizing may compound a sense of troubling unsteadiness in the surround, if only to then provide a greater satisfaction of solution. But excitingly, the disabled detective also utterly explodes the boundaries upon which these dynamics teeter (*could* be anyone, but is in fact *only* one; *not* us, comfortingly, after all). Disability is not a fixed identity category; it exists only in relation to what is deemed normal, which is itself a chimerical outgrowth of human fascination with, and also terror of, human variation. If the criminal is within and the disabled detective without, who are *we*? Sleuths of all stripes are notorious border-crossers and shape-shifters: they must be able to "go"—by whatever means—toward crime. Leading the way with their thinking, feeling bodies, their embodied minds, the plurality of their forms, their atypical modes of communicating, they take us into those spaces of the fearsome and strange and show us how else we can know. They are, after all, all of us.

Notes

1 Cf. https://beyondrivalry.wordpress.com/2009/07/02/crime-fiction-book-list-disabled-isnt-unable/. Others include http://librarybooklists.org/mybooklists/mysteriesable.htm; http://www.thrillingdetective.com/trivia/triv107.html; https://www.goodreads.com/list/show/109321.Blind_detectives; http://bestmysterybooks.com/handicapped-mystery.html.
2 The concept of "narrative prosthesis," now a standard concept in disability studies discourse, began with Mitchell and Synder's 2000 volume of that name.

3   This is said by Waldo Lydecker, the obese narrator and murderer of *Laura*. The novel also features a detective with a silver tibia bone (injured in a shoot-out) whom Lydecker derisively refers to as "'the limping Hawkshaw'" (165), though it is nowhere mentioned that Mark McPherson walks with a limp.

4   Franco Moretti writes that Doyle participated in assuring readers "that society is still a great *organism*: a unitary and knowable body" (145).

5   Price explains that "because mental and physical processes not only affect each other but also *give rise to each other*—that is, because they tend to act as one, even though they are conventionally understood as two—it makes more sense to refer to them together, in a single term" (269; my italics).

6   The latter occurs in an episode of ABC's *Castle*, called "The Wrong Stuff" (2015, 7.16).

7   For a thorough discussion of debates among disability theorists about the utility of body theory generally and Judith Butler specifically, cf. especially Siebers, *Disability Theory*, and Samuels, "Critical Divides."

8   Cf. also McClain and Cripps, "The BBC's Sherlock."

9   Cf. Rzepka, 123. In *A Study in Scarlet*, the bullet is in his shoulder; in *The Sign of Four*, it's in his leg.

10 *The Murder of Roger Ackroyd* (1926) and *The Endless Night* (1967).

11 Rushing writes, "It is rare in Christie that characters have anything like real depth" (59). Yet one has only to read *Appointment with Death* (1938) to dispute any claim that Christie *consistently* ignored the wider social and political world in her work, or that she had little interest in psychological complexity. This odd tale of child abuse is thoroughly inflected with ideas about mental "sadism," the war, women's rights, and the "'strange things buried down in the unconscious'" (35).

12 By way of contrast, consider Greta's teasing of Gabriel in James Joyce's "The Dead," where Gabriel's galoshes are derided as a sign of nervous and old-fashioned protection—not just against rain puddles, but against modernism itself. Christie is sometimes contrasted with Joyce—along with other British Modernists—to underscore her conservatism.

13 Frontispiece to *Agatha Christie* (1984).

14 He is "a little upstart of a foreigner" in *The Murder of Roger Ackroyd* (114), "an outsider" in *Cards on the Table* (159). In *Hallowe'en Party*, he becomes "a little more foreign" by speaking a phrase in French (111). And so on.

15 *Hallowe'en Party*, from 1969, is especially stuck on the idea of the "mentally disturbed" being released from psychiatric facilities and roaming unsupervised across the countryside, killing children.

2

Seer Detectives

From Clinton H. Stagg's private detective Thornley Colton, who debuted as the "Blind Reader of Hearts" in 1913, to Jane A. Adams's ex-policewoman Naomi Blake (2002–16), the figure of the blind detective is so established in the history of crime fiction as to constitute a legitimate subtype of the disabled-detective subgenre. But if, as investigator Mr. Carlyle declares in the first of Ernest Bramah's Max Carrados stories, good detecting is "nothing more than using one's eyes and putting two and two together" ("The Coin of Dionysis," 28), how does a blind detective accomplish the necessary observation that precedes deduction? Carrados provides a few answers. For one thing, "blindness invites confidence" because the blind are "out of the running—human rivalry ceases to exist" (20). This suggests that blindness may be beneficial to detecting only because people react to Carrados *as a blind man* and so out of condescension and subtle disrespect. The idea that disability mystifies interrelations—that a disabled person doesn't count, constitutes no "competition" for goods, women, and/or status—is a conventional one. The disabled figure lurks on the periphery of normal human bonding, but that marginal position may grant the blind detective a unique vantage point from which to garner otherwise hidden facts.

Though Carrados does assert that his blindness is not "an advantage," it nonetheless has "compensations": "New powers awakening; strange new perceptions; life in the fourth dimension" (19). Many blind sleuths are recuperated this way, by being granted such powers of "second sight" (that mystical insight attributed to blind seers since Tiresias) that they operate with a sixth sense in another reality. The blind man is radically different from his sighted compatriot; he exists *elsewhere*—across thresholds that root more emphatically material beings in this world. These detectives suggest that they are able to penetrate more swiftly to the core of a case both because they are protected from visible distractions and because they have access to levels of awareness and understanding that do not pertain to seeing individuals. Blindness carries this particular connotation of an unsullied, near-spiritual vision that opens onto supernatural realms of mental ability. If we were inclined to fret about a blind investigator navigating a room or supporting himself financially (as Carlyle implicitly does upon first realizing that Carrados is blind), such worries are assuaged by the promise of improbably augmented perceptual and intellectual capabilities.[1]

There is in fact no more potent metaphor for knowledge in the Western philosophical and cultural imagination—and so also in our daily idioms—than sight. "I see" means *understand, think of, imagine, consider, create*; "I smell" does not (though "sniffing out" clues and "smelling a rat" do capture the gritty underworld of wrongdoing and the bloodhounds of criminal chase). Keen understanding is measured by insight, not in-hearing (an expression like "I hear you" reflects interpersonal dynamic more than, though perhaps as a premise to, intellectual acuity, as I explore in Chapter 3). Conversations begin with *Look* when our attention is demanded, not *Touch*; we wonder how the future looks, not how it tastes. Shortsightedness refers less to physiological myopia than to ignorance or willful disregard of obvious truths. So thoroughly embedded in language is this epistemological link between seeing and knowing that, as many scholars have pointed out, few dictionary definitions of "blind" concern physical vision at all. David Bolt argues that "the use of visual terms to make epistemological points invokes the notion that seeing is synonymous with knowing" (18); blindness, conversely, is associated with "irrationality," lack of preparation, confusion, and an inability "to judge or act" along normative lines (20–21). Martin Jay writes similarly of "how ineluctable the modality of the visual" is to our linguistic as well as conceptual habits of signifying cognition, intelligence, and ethical strength (1).

So when Berthold Lowenfeld some forty years ago described blindness as an "injury, not only to the eyes, but to the human being as a whole" (qtd. in Bolt, 89–90), he neatly encapsulated a deeply entrenched cultural prejudice against visual impairment as existential lack—the absence of some crucial component of rational thought, the very basis of our humanity. To lack sight in this scenario is to be plunged into a terrifying blankness that is both dreaded as symbolic diminishment and assumed to be literal—despite the fact that, as Julia Miele Rodas puts it, the actual "range of blind experience ... is infinitely diverse" (119). This metaphorical darkness is what Bolt refers to as the "blindness-darkness synonymy" (21ff), a conflation that, in assuming that all visually impaired people see no light at all, in turn marks them with "epistemological inferiority" (99). D.A. Caeton goes further, writing that in an ocularcentric, ocularnormative society, "a life of blindness is necessarily devoid of autonomy, agency ... [B]lindness represents ... an absence not only of sight but also of independence, intellectual acumen, morality, and productivity" (36). As a direct result of such sighted assumptions, says Caeton, the blind person becomes "a totem of daily miracles," with the performance of "even the most quotidian activities" beheld as "extraordinary" (36).

Given the kind of easy uncriticalness that accompanies our vernacular use of visual metaphor, along with potent anxiety about blindness as an idle, ignorant, nearly depraved child-state, how do crime authors portray their visually impaired detectives? If blindness connotes a basic inability to hold down a job, how does a visually impaired sleuth actually solve crimes? And what narrative purpose is served by such an apparently contradictory figure—one whose superior powers of deduction and perception would presumably be all but annulled by the confusion and irrationality, the clumsy "groping," associated with blindness since the ignorant blind watchmen of the book of Isaiah?[2] One answer derives from the supernatural side of the blindness binary, of course, which Max Carrados represents: the assumption of a visionary sense that plays into powerful cultural fantasies about insight. The following brief exchange is typical of encounters between Carrados and sighted visitors, registering the marvel of the blind man who can nonetheless comport himself in "normal" ways and the magical capacities supposedly granted him:

> "Blind!" exclaimed the old fellow, sitting up in startled wonderment. "You mean it, sir? You walk all right and you look at me as if you saw me. You're kidding surely."
> "No," smiled Carrados. "It's quite right."
> "Then it's a funny business, sir—you what are blind expecting to find something that those with their eyes couldn't," ruminated Hutchins sagely.
> "There are things that you can't see with your eyes, Hutchins."
> ("The Knight's Cross Signal Problem," 71)

The classic sleuths—Dupin, Holmes, Poirot—flaunted their preternatural grasp of details and ability to make connections, to fashion the story that would combine wildly discrete parts in a causally logical way. A detective like Carrados, whose "sightless eyes" are repeatedly set before us, exaggerates that startle effect of solution in that Bramah's early-century readers, maneuvered into the position of Hutchins, might have doubted that a blind man could conclude moral truths from physical clues he could not see.

Blindness functions here as a kind of mystical guarantor. If the genius detective pleases in part because his uncanny powers of understanding are inimitable—because of that distinctive, wizard-like status that raises him above the grubby world of material criminality of which he is nonetheless inescapably a part—Carrados does the generic convention one better, thrusting a stereotypical trope like *blind beggar* toward its own opposite, into the rarified realm of high intellect and intuition. He performs not so much logical deduction as a magic trick, a breathtaking transformation in which a disabled body, blatantly on display, is nevertheless denied its quotidian reality, what it "really" means to have a visual impairment. And in that gasp of awe that Carrados can do something the reader can't, that even the normative bodies surrounding him in the text cannot—in the realization that figuring it out *works*—everything that is unseen, the lurking evils and deceptions of modern life, are securely corralled.

Something else is at stake in the fascination that sighted crime writers have had for the blind sleuth, deriving from what Bolt describes as the particular pleasure of an asymmetrical gaze. The very definition of voyeuristic gratification is staring at what cannot, does not, stare back. Blindness becomes a spectacle only according to the expectations of sightedness, where vision presumes mastery and cognizance, and blindness seems the epitome of embarrassing display—bodies lurching down blind alleys, veering into blind spots. "The unseen stare," writes Bolt, "involves those of us who do not have visual impairments doing something to those of us who do" (96), in an exercise of power that is "rewarding precisely because of [its] covertness" (102). Crime fiction installs this kind of panoptical surveillance at its core. John Scaggs names "a concern with vision and perception" as "central to [the] hard-boiled fiction" (88) of the 1950s and '60s (though even earlier the benign and all-seeing Miss Marple reminded her villagers of the ubiquity of the law). Police procedurals in particular, Scaggs writes, "become a sort of textual Panopticon" (89), where the group collective of police squads within plots and the multiple texts of a series both act as the *mise-en-abîme* of disciplinary order. The detective who must absorb the gaze of sighted others will both amplify and explode these specular dynamics. Such a detective may be subject to the surreptitious glances or bold stares of others, but authority becomes even more formidable in that his or her gaze literally cannot be seen—because there is no gaze there, or "gaze" is being uncannily performed. This type of reversal might appeal to sighted readers for its presumed unlikeliness, but it also entrenches the sovereignty of law: to upend the symbolic meaning of Pinkerton's ever-wakeful penetrating private eye, to blind the clue-hunting sleuth even as he or she continues to intuit and discover, is to suggest a kind of deeply invasive surveillance that cannot be monitored, countered, or fathomed.[3]

For sighted readers, again, this "objectifying asymmetry" (106) deepens in relation to the text, amplifying what may be pleasurable about crime fiction in the first place—its assurance of order. A reader "watching" sighted characters watching the blind detective may experience an intensified thrill, wielding a kind of vicarious command over the character who represents social regularity and control. Death, as Page Dubois has argued, "is managed, made comprehensible through the agency of the detective, who labors ... to find the contaminated or polluted actor and to remove him from society" (110). By such a definition, the blind detective is an incomprehensible contradiction, corporeally damaged but endowed with numinous faculties of insight that sustain the work of expunging criminals, a kind of fabulous hybrid: seeing everything, though blind; moving everywhere, though blind—always with the guarantee of a sharp and sprawling consciousness.

A still more complex understanding of the conundrum of the visually impaired detective involves the technologies (if also clichés) of blindness—animals, canes, other people—as these factor in a unique interplay between disability, the navigation of space, and the epistemology of crime. It is true that blind detectives are almost always endowed with astonishing intuitive capacities; they are also often depicted as unusually graceful. The one quality seems to deny the body altogether, the other to wishfully repair its damage—its complex unsightliness. Both qualities participate in a clichéd romanticizing of impairment. And yet the blind tecs are insistently, *ordinarily* embodied, too, in ways that connect directly to their modes of navigating, and so knowing, their surroundings. Much more is involved here than steering effortlessly through a crowded restaurant with cane or companion, or remembering the number of steps between elevator and hotel room—though this kind of detail tends to get noted. As crime-space becomes *blind* space, detectives extend their boundaries, not only (or at all) through supernatural perception but because blindness entails composite embodiment—the intimacy and extension into space of service dogs, canes, assistants. The genre's conventional insistence on singular, spectacular intelligences is complicated by such imbrications, where knowing is located not in the magic of an instant but in subtle, communicative relationships between embodied selves and environments.

Blindness, then, associated as it is with interiority and intuition, becomes in crime narration a kind of willful exaggeration of Deleuzean territoriality, a *place* more than an individualized condition—in which clues and cleverness, scenes and suspicions, internal and external experience merge and divide and coalesce again in the development of a truthful conclusion. Or, to put this differently, not a place at all but a series of moves and touches, thoughts and sounds; not simply lack and its compensations but *possibility*, for ways of knowing that might defy, because they do not depend on, the maintenance of secure boundaries. The threat of crime, the pressure to thwart and solve, positions the detective at the locus of situations that are at once actual—the *here* of what happened—and virtual—the terrifying anywhere of what happens next. Detection, like crime itself, is in turn a form of border-crossing. Blind detection maps space in alternative quadrants, establishing its contours in non-visual ways, redefining it altogether, in fact, according to other-sensory—by which I do not inevitably mean *extra*-sensory—perception. Blind detection avenges our fear of the dark precisely because it warns us that seeing is not the only way to believe.

Nowhere is a fantasied association between blindness and penetrating mastery over criminal activity made more obvious than in the eight stories and short novel that comprise the mystery oeuvre of Clinton H. Stagg, the young writer who, before his death in a car accident in 1916 at the age of twenty-six, inaugurated the blind detective trope with his character Thornley Colton, "The Problemist." So-called because he prefers to tackle only the most puzzling of criminal cases that "'baffle other men'" ("The Keyboard of Silence," 10),

Colton is a wealthy uptown Manhattanite who dines out every night and does his sleuthing as an amateur and a gentleman. He is indisputably the object of his author's fascination—a man somehow charmed by the impairment that utterly defines him—for as much as the stories also try to account "naturally" for behavior that leaves sighted characters dazed and staggered. At the same time, Colton also offers a first hint of what will be crucial to my discussion of later detectives, whatever their impairments: the confounding of norms and an interest in thinking through the body.

In his genteel milieu of wealth and status, Colton has cachet. He tackles "clean" crimes—jewel theft, bank robbery, opium addiction, espionage. He is first introduced, on the first page of the first story, from afar, so that we can stare "openly, unashamed" (9), along with other characters, at

> the man who stood in the doorway, calmly surveying them. The smoke-glass, tortoise-shell library spectacles, which made of his eyes two great circles of dull brown, brought out the whiteness of the face strikingly. The nose, with its delicately sensitive nostrils, was thin and straight; the lips, now curved in a smile, … seemed out of place on that pale, masterful face, with its lean, cleft chin. The snow-white hair of silky fineness that curled away from the part to show the pink scalp underneath contrasted sharply with the sober black of the faultless dinner-coat that fell in just the proper folds from the broad shoulders. (9)

The details of this *blazon* are closely reiterated in every story. What do they coalesce to reinforce, if not the simple point that "the blind man," as he is called on nearly every page of a 460-page collection, is not the slovenly stereotype readers might expect?[4] That sly aside—"calmly surveying them"—implying sightedness, introduces the uncanniness of Colton's physical presence: he is openly stared at *because* he is clearly blind (he *can* be stared at because he is blind) and yet he mimics sightedness in the aspect of his face and the ease with which he moves through space with his slim ebony stick. That unsettling simultaneity is then emphasized in the various color contrasts of Colton's appearance—white hair on pink scalp over black jacket, dark glasses against pale skin—which, beyond insisting on the problemist's privileged status as a white man of means, also render him somehow wraithlike, a ghostly, ethereal presence whose fluid movement through a crowded room quite literally brings it to a standstill. Such are the basic motifs: the spectral quality of blindness, the discomfiting impression of sightedness, the effortless motion. *How does he do it?* But also, beyond those clichés, control of the relays of environment as Colton maneuvers through physical space and commands the interpersonal dynamics within it.

To say that Colton is objectified as a person with visual impairment is both obvious and not precisely right. The almost comical repetition of the phrase "the blind man" (five times on one page alone in "The Thousand Facets of Fire" [154]) is what Bolt refers to as "nominal displacement," whereby sighted authors reduce visually impaired characters to this one distinguishing feature, "the strategic setting aside of names in favor of labels" (36). Why is Colton, then, as the *hero* of these stories, so frequently referred to this way? If the label "blind man" has an overtly trivializing effect, it also places readers in a specular position where we can never forget that one way in which Colton is different, so that everything we read about him doing is presented as a function of visual impairment. Our attention is trained not on a detective working a case but on a blind person bestowed with compensations for that disability even as he functionally dominates the narrative by organizing the details of cases. Wonderment is the hinge here. Colton is not like anyone around him. He inspires fear, pity, and resentment, but in his unraveling of puzzles—he figures things out in a matter of seconds—also amazement and awe. Into that layered captivation, Stagg's modernist readers are invited to cast their "fears of a loss of individual authority and control," to quote Peter Messent (79). The blind problemist is a condensation of anxiety and relief.

Stagg also makes the point in every story that blindness is Colton's advantage as a problem-solver. This is in part transactional, in a banal sort of way; Colton's other senses are everywhere described as made more precise by the absence of sight. He has "hypersensitive fingertips" that locate objects "unerringly" ("The Thousand Facets of Fire," 144). He has "supersensitive ears" that follow "each footfall unerringly" ("Unto the Third Generation," 50). His "'sense of smell … is more than doubly acute'" ("The Gilded Glove," 184). He has a "perfectly trained brain" and "unerring instinct" (15). But exaggerated as such statements seem—"unerring" tells us that ineptitude and mundane mediocrity may be more fearsome than crime, and variations on the sputtering question "'How—did—you—know—that?'" ("Flying Death," 115) recur throughout these stories—they also indicate a redistribution of perception across Colton's body. What is on one level mere compensatory logic suggests, on another, an intriguing remapping of bodily cognition; every instance of *sensing* is an important moment of figuring out. The fact that Colton's exceptional rational skill is also attributed to his blindness is similarly twofold—formulaic (the myth of mystical blind insight), but interestingly phenomenological, too: Colton thinks well because he engages the world through a whole range of sense perceptions. As he says in "The Ringling Goblets," "'even a man with eyes instinctively closes them when he is trying to figure out some particularly intricate problem'" (219).

At work here may be an early twentieth-century "disenchantment with the eye and its supposed objectivity," as Maren Tova Linett writes, that some scholars have linked to the "inward turn" of modernism with its preference for "inner experience" and the artistic dimensions of consciousness ("Blindness and Intimacy," 30). The "traditional axis of knowledge" (31), Linett suggests, is disrupted in stories that foreground the other senses as instrumental in forming intimate connections. This idea of proximity to others is important. Even Thornley Colton, however isolated his staggeringly subtle analyses seem to make him, does not operate alone. In fact, what might look like exaggerated inwardness—the workings of Colton's "brain" are absolutely unfathomable to anyone else even as (or especially as) they gaze upon him—can also be understood as a process of outward movement that is necessarily engaged and social, as in the emphasis on the problemist's "'*mind-reading* stunt[s]'" ("Third Generation," 48), the "*telepathic* thrill" that comes from being close to him (11; my italics). When the international spy of "The Gilded Glove" cries out that "'minds that are closed to all the world are an open book'" to Colton (172), she articulates two important qualities of the sleuth's blindness: that it is *intersubjectively* meaningful and that it has a cartographical nature. She suggests that Colton can *travel*, and in leaping distances, blindness involves him thoroughly with others.

One might protest that all of this betrays mere ocularcentric prejudice; "beneath the superhuman" assertions of all that a blind character can do, as Bolt has argued (73), lurk all kinds of distressing "subhuman assumptions" about what she or he *cannot* do. The norm throughout the Colton oeuvre is surely sightedness, as indicated by the fact that Colton doesn't just hear or smell more accurately than others: he also *visualizes* better than sighted companions:

> Something of grave portent had given its significance to the man who could not see, while he with five perfect senses, had seen nothing. ("The Keyboard of Silence," 19)

> Two detectives who had not seen until a blind man had shown them. ("Keyboard," 42)

> In less than five minutes the sightless problemist had proved a fact that twenty pairs of eyes had failed to see. ("The Flying Death," 123)

> Swiftly, unerringly, the blind man had found the murderer whose very being they had not suspected a short time before. To the men who had followed every step of the problemist, who had seen things that he could not see, the finding seemed magic ... wonder, tinged with awe toward the man who had built [sic] a wonderful structure of truth from the pieces he and his hundred men has either discarded or had not seen. ("The Flying Death," 128)

> In ten minutes the man who was sightless had shown him details that neither his keen eyes nor the eyes of his hundred men had seen, and Colton had made of those details startling, vivid possibilities. ("The Flying Death," 119)

But literal seeing is also critiqued in these excerpts as unaesthetic and unknowing, almost extravagantly inadequate. "The blind man's unerring instinct for truth," finally ("The Flying Death," 123), is located not in the eye but elsewhere in his body, which is in turn revealed as creative and full of possibility. Blindness may be abstracted and romanticized as source of wonder, but it is also construed in more material terms, as structural, resourceful, inventive. Blindness doesn't simply intuit. Or rather, the way the blind detective arrives at knowing truth is a process of "build[ing]" it.

The Colton stories might thus be said to waver between gothic supernaturalism and an argument for an alternative epistemology. This would explain why an old myth of nocturnalism—the association of blindness with night, dreams, and darkness—threatens depictions of Colton's advantage in moving about with the lights off, where the latter is naturalistic and provocative, the former reductive and contrived. In "The Gilded Glove," for example, Colton exploits sudden darkness to overturn a heavy table on three Russian spies with guns. In the confusion that ensues, he subdues one man with poison, topples another with feline agility, and runs down a hallway with "every nerve, every faculty alert to warn him of danger before a man with eyes would ever suspect its presence" (202). The contrast between the thugs' "bewildered brains" and Colton's ability to move "without conscious effort" (202), his bat-like navigation of darkness, is surely embellished along ableist lines of prejudice. At the same time, the idea that a person with visual impairment might be less disoriented if the lights are suddenly switched off represents what Rosemarie Garland-Thomson refers to as the kind of "subjugated knowledge" that emerges when we reconsider how impairment and environment interact ("Misfits," 597). It is right to be suspicious of Stagg's renderings of his blind hero as an animalized creature of the night. But the kind of light/dark inversion that turns armed criminals into "'helpless'" men (205) and makes a "'normal self'" of the wraithlike Colton also reterritorializes the space of blind detection. Or to put this differently, blindness redraws space itself, makes it *mean* differently—enlarges it, even (counter-intuitively, given an ocularnormative orientation), and *only* through those redefined encounters of body and terrain does Colton solve a mystery. There is "reality in darkness," as D. H. Lawrence once wrote (qtd. in Linett, 39). To condemn Colton's comfort with life out of light as mere ableist fantasizing is to trivialize all that can be found out there.

Space in the Deleuzean sense is not a matter of distances. It is instead a way of thinking about how the myriad intensities of our embodied lives determine the edges of what we name as particular types of location, an awareness that we never enter into predetermined spaces but instead define those spaces by what happens within and around them. The type of space that emerges in Stagg's Thornley Colton series is measured by far more than architectural footprint, even if the sleuth does have to dodge wayward legs and familiarize himself with the layouts of crime scenes. The stories' geography may be predominantly visual, but it is also an intersubjective one that Colton navigates with a driver who can be called at any time of day or night and the slight touch of Sidney's sleeve against his own. The tone of the Colton stories promotes the radically inward, unknowable recesses of blind deduction, but to attend *only* to the ways in which the character's impairment differentiates him is to miss the intersubjective outwardness constituted, or implied, by his acts of "reading" scenes and minds. Colton's blindness is a mode of ranging over the stuff of the world, useful in the service of knowing. What is registered as supernatural in these stories can also be understood as the interpenetration of spatial realms, as consciousness interiorizes the external material world and casts itself across the topography of spaces that are defined in sensory ways the sighted simply ignore.

A generation after Colton, another suave, debonair blind detective hit the streets, one who owes much of his characterization to his predecessor: Baynard Kendrick's Duncan Maclain. The Maclain novels have been celebrated for their commitment to representing visual impairment in the most realistic of terms. Like his detective hero, Kendrick was a decorated veteran of the First World War, but the character of Maclain is more activist than autobiographical. Kendrick became interested in the experience of blinded veterans when a visit to a former friend at a London charity hospital introduced him to a serviceman who, as Susan McHugh tells us, "accurately detailed Kendrick's … military record simply by 'brailling' his uniform" (40). According to McHugh, the novelist Kendrick, both "astounded" by that encounter and "frustrated" with the boyhood friend's "miserable obsession" with the "utterly impossible feats" of Max Carrados, later attempted "to create not the first blind detective, but rather the first realistic one" (40). Kendrick would eventually work as an instructor for blinded veterans during the Second World War, and, interested in matters of mobility, investigate guide-dog training programs. The first fictional Seeing Eye German shepherd, Maclain's companion Schnuke, is Kendrick's creation.

Well before mid-century civil rights and disability activism, Kendrick approached fiction as a particularly effective arena in which to raise social awareness about the challenges that people with visual impairments would confront, less from blindness than from the powerful stigmas attached to it. The Maclain series represents its detective's adventitious blindness (the character is blinded by gas at Messines in 1917) as a physical condition requiring adjustment but hardly pity; it neither diminishes the man nor denies him fulfilling work. Kendrick was meticulous about authenticity, and so careful never to depict Maclain performing the astounding stunts of detectives like Max Carrados and Thornley Colton. If Maclain can shoot accurately by sound, it is not because blindness has miraculously improved his hearing, but because he has diligently *trained* it: "a patient matter of six years' practice, for two long hours each day" (*Violets*, 26). When best friend Spud Savage suggests to Maclain that they open a private detective agency, the venture is plausible because Maclain had been a US Army Intelligence officer, not because blindness in itself makes him particularly perceptive.⁵ If blindness is an advantage to Maclain's detecting, it is only because, in Maclain's own words, "'I've had to train my other senses to be sensitive to inconsistencies'" (*Violets*, 56).

Given Kendrick's specific interest in matters of mobility, it makes sense that the Maclain books focus on the spatial dynamics of crime-solving from the perspective of physical motion, especially Maclain's working relationship with Schnuke. Maclain's movement through rooms, down hallways, up and down staircases gets particular emphasis, as do the hands that Kendrick frequently shows us helping Maclain to orient himself around furniture. Such details have obvious pedagogical designs on sighted readers, teaching the uninitiated something about how a person with a visual impairment makes his way around material objects; in his Manhattan penthouse, for example, Maclain "move[s] with ease … confident that each piece of furniture was in its accustomed place, firmly fixed to the floor" (*Violets*, 23). Elsewhere, beyond that known pattern, a finely tuned choreography with Schnuke facilitates navigation, as when she "[leads] him unerringly to a chair" ("The Silent Whistle," 21). Schnuke is more than just a functional guide; she is an important character, her behavior deliberately revealing, and she has a role to play in the subtler spatial dimensions of Maclain's interpersonal communication. Upon entering a room of possible suspects, for instance, "Schnuke moved forward, eyeing the Tredwill family with canine dignity. Helena stood up, and the dog unerringly directed the Captain past the barrier of a library table to Helena's proffered chair" (123).

More than bodily maneuvering is at stake here, as the words "dignity" and "unerringly" suggest. Schnuke is an extension of the man's corporeal identity, mediating moments like this when the vectors of multiple, asymmetrical gazes might threaten to overwhelm Maclain's stature as an individual worthy of some deference given his military record and connection to government officials. Instead, "under Schnuke's guidance"—a phrase that recurs throughout the series—Maclain commands both the physical and the intersubjective spaces of the room; he becomes an object of respect and admiration. Whether it is Schnuke "skillfully" (*Violets*, 208) guiding Maclain through doors or Maclain's impressive memorization of steps in unfamiliar locations, then, the detective's body-in-space actively resists what one character in *Violets* assumes of "blind men," that they move "clumsily, and were generally shoddy. Duncan Maclain, quick and at ease, fitted the picture not at all" (144). Behind such descriptions we can again discern Kendrick's political intentions, as well as an investment in demarcating the outlines of both embodiment and architecture along alternate channels of meaning. Maclain's very ontology is articulated through Schnuke in interspecies hybridity, and his body—or more precisely, the interaction of body, movement, and spatial planes—brings space into a very particular form. We only know where we are in these stories as Maclain and Schnuke together constitute the perimeters of their locations.

Such features of Maclain's characterization read like carefully deployed refutations of common if simply ignorant prejudices about blindness. But Kendrick also represents his hero in terms of a puzzling duality: not just a competent man and exceptionally skilled investigator, Maclain is both mysteriously unusual and unnaturally mechanical, as if the author could not quite avoid the impulse to invoke familiar compensations. Despite the naturalistic emphasis on training and effort, for instance, there *is* something wondrous about Duncan Maclain—in kinetics, emotion, detection. References to Maclain's "wonderful brain" and "consciousness" (*Violets*, 217, 289) seem beholden to familiar metaphors—ones linking blindness to inscrutable interiorized realms of understanding and detection to a private, mysterious process of "forg[ing] a chain of events" (292) to which other characters in the text are not made fully privy. "'You live by your brain,'" Spud tells him (*Blind Man's Bluff*, 182), a brain whose "functioning" is described as "uncompromising" (45). "'Damn it, sir,'" a more ordinary detective protests to him, "'I'll thank you to quit reading my mind'" (106). His detecting is described by other characters as "'miraculous'" (54), almost a kind of "'witchcraft'" (57), "'infallible'" (114). "There were moments," says the narrator of "The Silent Whistle," "when powers slightly greater than those possessed by ordinary mortals seemed bestowed on Duncan Maclain." His "prescience" is "abnormal" (55).

Maclain's physicality is also portrayed as preternaturally elegant. In *The Odor of Violets*, he "[stands] up, flow[s] to his feet, with a motion so commanding that it dominate[s] the room" (159), and later leaves "his bed with the smoothness of a materializing apparition" (293). Learning the layout of a room, he touches a chair "with a movement almost too swift to follow" (143); he does jigsaw puzzles with "the uncanny prescience of fingers which could see" (166). In *Blind Man's Bluff*, his "marvelous fingers moved swifter" than sighted eyes can follow (47), and others look upon his movements with guide dog Schnuke with "mesmerized fascination" (67).

Against these expressions of sinuous motion, Maclain is described in mechanical terms: as "some impersonal machine" (*Violets*, 146), "'an unemotional machine'" (275), "no more a man, but a killer out to destroy the God of War's machine" (294). He is "an infernal machine" in *Blind Man's Bluff* (210), "a perfect human machine" (36) whose fingers can move with "machine-like rapidity" ("Silent Whistle," 56). We are repeatedly reminded of how hard Maclain has worked to refine his skills. Perhaps this is what motivates Kendrick to underscore Maclain's "perfect efficiency" (*Bluff*, 35), to say that Maclain is "deadly efficient as an automaton" ("Whistle," 9)—because there is always a chance that he will be "underestimated because he [is] blind" (*Violets*, 211), that "people who don't know [him] are more than apt to underrate [him]" (105). Kendrick was of course determined to teach his readers that it is through practice that a blind person might complete a puzzle, not magic, through intelligent listening and not supernaturalism that he might detect someone lurking around a corner. But training that turns Maclain into a robotic assassin has little to do with ordinary visual impairment—or with everyday investigating.[6]

Given Kendrick's instructional intentions, what are we to make of this dichotomy between mechanical proficiency and the marvelous, neither of which is realistic? How can Maclain be unemotional, and yet "feel everything," as Spud says of him (*Bluff*, 180)? Much of his success as a detective derives from an incongruity between how Maclain appears and what people assume, the bemused or flustered reactions they have to his authority. Many of Maclain's "unfortunate antagonists" ("Silent Whistle," 9) become so precisely because they do not expect a blind man to control his movements, to have precision aim, even simply to act with dignity and poise. This recurring emphasis on Maclain's body-in-space reminds us that what is *anomalous* becomes *disabled* not because of an exclusive and individual problem but through the interface of social and structural relationships—in the mismatch between *this* person and *that* environment. And this explains the oscillation, I think, between the ethereal and the mechanical, the effortlessness of Maclain's movement and the hours of labor that subtend his variously remarkable performances. To become legible, in a Foucauldian sense—to *fit in*—the anomalous body is subjected to what Margrit

Shildrik writes as the "managerial, normativizing, regularizing, biopoweristic forms" of law (109). Maclain's delicacy, his fluid movement around corners both metaphorical and real, suggests a literal escape from those regulatory mechanisms, a capacity to elude and to transgress—he is not quite earthbound, not quite subject to the rules of surveillance whereby we police ourselves (and each other) into obedient quiescence. A nearly impossibly graceful bodily self, Maclain can also imaginatively be in someone else, can *be* someone else through the shape-shifting locomotion, the *feelingness*, of blindness. And at the same time, there is an instrumentality to him wielded not by humanity—corrupt as that might seem in wartime—but by the cosmic forces of justice.

So when Maclain cries out to the world, "'You think you've wrecked me with blindness—but I still have a brain. Your weapons of death and terror are helpless against it'" (171), he locates his current condition in the context of chaos wrought by civilized nations, and this is why his "wonderful brain, shrouded in darkness, might give him what his eyes forever lacked—the power to see" (*Violets*, 217). Maclain becomes a weapon to combat the weaponry of crime, whatever the scale; he absorbs emotion because not to is to risk crime's arrogant numbness. That he thinks with luminous revelation—"an internal clarity of vision bright as the light of a magnesium flare" (289)—strikes me as having less to do with visual impairment than with an oblique kind of rage against the grasping cruelties of human vice. By the end of *The Odor of Violets*, Maclain's genius blazes with such radiance that he ceases to be a man at all, in fact, and takes on an almost entirely allegorical presence, the manifestation of "the implacable blindness of Justice" (294):

> The granite of resolution and the marble of anger had driven out every lovable quality in Duncan Maclain. As he stepped into the hall he was as impersonal as a piece of metal come under a powerful magnet's sway, and forced by the immutable laws of physics to answer its imperious command. He had no eyes, but he could shoot with the devastating accuracy of lightning at the most infinitesimal sound. (294)

This is more than righteous anger against a gang of saboteurs bent on destroying the utilities infrastructure of the United States in the early years of the Second World War. It is instead a rousing depiction of Goodness that depends for its impact on Maclain's status as a man injured in war and a thoughtful, *humane* fighter of crime—only from that foundation can he earn his status here as a comic-strip superhero. Ruthlessly moral, Maclain swells to infinity, as if the bodily limits of one blind man were far too narrow to contain the expansive sweep of history that his own blindness, a function of prosaic, all-too-common military conflict, actually represents. He becomes a force of nature, stealthy and omniscient. He is a man, somehow literally, of steel.

I have been suggesting that blind detection brings matters of nearness and juxtaposition to the fore in relational terms as well as in physical and geographical spaces. In this context, consider the depiction of British ex-policewoman Naomi Blake, whose visual impairment is primarily factual rather than metaphorical.[7] Blake has a guide dog named Napoleon, and when people take her arm or ask if she wants the sound of a TV turned up in a hospital room, such details seem integral to a scene more than they call attention in a mystified way to the blind person's capacity to function. There are references to darkness and absence of light in the Blake books, but not to clairvoyant powers. In fact Naomi Blake is not the primary solver of crime in her own series—murders happen around her, somehow involving people she knows, and cases are worked by ordinary police.

It is that very proximity, though, coupled with visual impairment, that makes blindness *interesting* in these novels; it explains why Naomi is no longer a cop. Blindness is to the Naomi Blake series what gardening is to the amateur sleuths in the BBC's *Rosemary and Thyme* or mystery writing to crime-solving authors in the shows *Castle* or *Murder, She Wrote*—that is, a device that grants sleuths special access to criminal investigation while freeing them from the kind of establishment regulations that might be assumed of a police force. In this sense, blindness removes Blake physically and structurally from the machinery of power that the novels (inherently police procedurals) simultaneously endorse. It shunts her to the side, displacing her even from secure attachment to a sense of home; in later books, when Naomi and her husband Alec, also a former detective, travel around England in search of somewhere to settle down, the placelessness that blindness has effected in her career expands to encompass her life.

More significantly, though, blindness makes Blake's involvement in cases perceptual and emotional rather than operational: what she contributes to any particular story has more to do with how she feels about a crime than what she does to bring about its resolution. In effect, Blake *absorbs* the impact of the murders that happen around her rather than combatting or dominating them. The fact that books in this series are nonetheless identified as "Naomi Blake Mysteries" signals something curious about who—or what sort of activity—controls the narrative. Such categorization cues readers to assume that Blake is the series detective and so at its formal as well as ethical center. Blindness has the immediate effect of therefore accounting for her ambiguous status as an affective but also passive heroine. Jane A. Adams might have invented through other means an ex-cop somehow still connected to the incidence and solving of crimes, but such a character, I would argue, would lack the peculiar inflection of an inwardly oriented disability. If blindness serves in crime drama as a condensed locus of a policing surveillance, it is also, these novels imply, a source of heightened *reaction* to crime. Just as Duncan Maclain feels everything, so too does blind Naomi Blake.

Blindness thus becomes in these stories both a way to register the emotional valences of crime and the circulation of that affective reaction through the spaces of community: crime doesn't just happen somewhere; it happens *to* people, who must decide what to do next. In conventional narratives, the detective is a lone operator (think of characters like Hammett's Continental Op or Sam Spade), even if he has a collegial relationship to law enforcement. Blind detectives tend to exaggerate that defining isolationism in part because visual impairment is so emphatically linked to terror of the unknown, to a presumption of defenselessness, but also to defy it through their relationships with companion animals, personal assistants, and investigating partners. As *detectives*, in fact, they are especially well-positioned to counter a basic assumption that visually impaired people are vulnerable. Mike Longstreet, for example—the eponymous insurance investigator of an early 1970s television show—thrusts the stereotypical inwardness associated with visual impairment back into urban, social environments with an obviously gendered aggression. Blinded in an explosion, Longstreet proves his mettle in scenes of overt physicality, in street fights that evoke a venerable tradition of old-fashioned Western brawls. But there is something about him that also resists the formulaic equation of white, autonomous masculinity triumphing over the diminishment of disability.

Susan McHugh has critiqued the Vietnam context of the show's early episodes, in which the investigator learns Jeet Kune Do from guest-star Bruce Lee, a partnership that recuperates, as McHugh puts it, the "spectacle of wounded white manhood": "Longstreet's friendship with this Asian character is premised on the disabled white man's newfound vulnerability." According to McHugh, the relationship is "motivated by the blind detective's increasingly self-conscious sense of defensiveness, rather than … political alliances against interlocking oppressions" (57). Without refuting the problematic coupling of exoticized Eastern mind–body holism and the mystical abilities of the blind, I would nonetheless suggest that the martial arts component becomes more intriguing than it might initially seem when we consider that Li Tsung, Bruce Lee's character, trains Longstreet in a fighting style defined by explosive attack and the ability to adapt to the conditions of combat. The kind of violence that occurs in *Longstreet* (as between the sleuth and a criminal longshoreman in the first episode) is not exactly *necessitated* by the hero's impairment, though it does play on assumptions of blindness as an estranging bodily condition that disarms opponents because they expect nothing from him. What interests me here is the notion of adaptability—the premise that blindness becomes an opportunity for dynamic adjustments of self and space that entail learning how to learn, in ways other than visual. When Longstreet says that he is "an expert on limbo and states of suspension," then, he doesn't just invoke the indeterminate dream-state, the unreal obliviousness, associated with blindness. In precisely the opposite way, he also implies that he exists in a realm unencumbered by strict impediments of boundary, and is therefore better able to penetrate the defensive barriers of criminal activity. Longstreet—the very name seems significant—doesn't stay put.

The series *Longstreet* is in many ways unsentimental and naturalistic. In the pilot episode, in the wake of the explosion that blinds him and kills his wife, Longstreet learns Braille, takes up a cane, and starts working with a guide dog named Pax. His use of technology evokes James Bond more than fumbling childishness. He has a small cadre of assistants, including a woman, but seems neither cosseted by them nor threatened by his reliance on them. Peter Messent argues in a different context that "some of the dominant ideas on which the detective novel form is based have to do with vision, supervision, and control" (101)—that is, can "social order" be regained through the ministrations of a PI or police force. "Blindness, randomness, and riot," in Messent's formulation, become convenient markers of the "violence and general mayhem" that represent failure of that system, worlds out of whack. By this logic, the blindness that happens to Longstreet signifies "not making sense" (101). It is no accident that the opening scene of the pilot features Longstreet and his wife cruising the streets of New Orleans. Urban crime is about public spaces; Longstreet's blindness proves the hazards of the world out-there and symbolically reacts to an increasingly divisive and unmanageable social arena. But it isn't *only* that. The technologies of blindness just mentioned, Longstreet's relationship with his dog Pax, his friendships with Li Tsung and Nikki Bell—each of whom is also displaced from the norm—constitute forms of extended, hybrid, and intersubjective embodied experience whereby the sleuth relearns and reshapes his environment. Far from retreating from the public space in fear or anger, Longstreet becomes a man *of* the streets—literally, by name—and his advantage in moving into such space is that no one expects him to, that he is already understood to occupy his own mysterious, eccentric plane of existence. It isn't that blind subjectivity lacks cohesion, though it might seem to, to Longstreet's opponents. It's that it travels outside the lines. And that is precisely its advantage.

From Max Carrados and Thornley Colton to Naomi Black and Mike Longstreet, blindness is thus associated with a fluctuating spatial plane that expands and contracts according to the requirements of knowledge, an inward/outward flow whereby the detective gains important access (to information, minds, domains) with both sensorial and interpersonal intensity. The occult quality of those engagements notwithstanding (sometimes more pronounced than others), what seems significant in the context of detection is the uncoupling of epistemology from physical vision and the extension of "mind" across both bodies and objects.

In his Mo Bowdre novels, Jake Page situates these transgressively peripatetic characteristics in the context of cultural awareness. Bowdre—a self-proclaimed and highly ironic redneck—is a sculptor of massive stone and metal pieces. His backstory is that he "grew up like any bumpkin," graduated college "sixth in his class," dropped out of medical school after a year and a half (*Stolen Gods*, 1993; 8), "*bummed around*" for a few years (9, italics in original), and was then blinded in a mining accident. He enters the first book of the series as "T. Moore Bowdre, the fabled blind sculptor" (7), living with his half-Hopi, half-Anglo girlfriend Connie Barnes. The educational story is rarely referenced again after the first pages of the first book, but it seems to provide Bowdre with habits of mind significant to his sleuthing activities. He is a renegade of sorts, disinterested in a life circumscribed by conventionality, as well as intelligent, curious, and motivated to root out and fix what's going wrong in the system: he'd had thoughts of becoming a surgeon. The plots of the Bowdre novels feature the smuggling of sacred Indian art and artifacts, incursions by Anglo commercial culture into tribal lands, clashes of ancient custom against the promises both false and legitimate of modern life. Bowdre's status as the blind sculptor, the redneck rubbing shoulders with wealthy art dealers, the white man living with the Hopi woman, the amateur sleuth called upon for help by law enforcement—these multiple instances of liminality are what make Bowdre an "unusual" but effective unraveler of crimes so entangled with precarious issues of belief, long-held ideas about embodiment, and the relationship between bodies and landscapes both terrestrial and otherwise.[8]

It seems highly convenient to have a blind man on the case when crime involves such acts as the theft of Hopi religious icons too potent even to be looked at. The Hopi themselves are reputed to be intensely private (photography and even sketching of religious ceremonies, for example, are not permitted); blindness is what allows Bowdre to penetrate more fully than he might otherwise, what grants him access to cultural rituals and beliefs that neither the sighted white man (Collins, the FBI agent) nor the Hispanic policeman (Ramirez) can "see." Visual impairment seems narratively advantageous in this sense, bound up with a familiar presumption of emotional sensitivity, and so linked with the dual movement I have been tracing throughout this chapter. For if blindness is part of what propels Bowdre into sacred spaces (closer to the seat of traditional rituals or objects), it is also what pulls him into emotional realms of deep intimacy. When Connie, for example, wonders how it is that she "love[s] this white man so," "this blind white man," her answer to herself is that "he sees so well"—"he *sees me*" (*SG*, 101; my italics). The conflation of blindness, metaphorical vision, and empathetic, even empathic understanding is obvious, but then so is a point that Linett makes about earlier fictional representations in which blindness "gives rise to a genuine contact" between people, "foster[ing] human attachment" (39). The fact that Bowdre "fits" in certain spaces *because he is blind* might call our attention to the absurdity of sighted—as well as white or Anglo—outrage at not being "allowed" to look; that he knows things as a blind person might ask us to consider the alternative modalities of that knowing, rather than denigrating knowledge per se as inherently suspect because "uncanny." Outward and across thresholds, inward toward intimacy and understanding—always, in effect, one and the same—this is the basic fulcrum of the novels' narrative arcs.

Bowdre occupies a good deal of space in terms of physical "bulk" (67)—his own and that of his artistic work—as well as the distances he covers. He is not a man to go unnoticed by the sighted characters around him. He is "immense" (6), well over six feet tall, with large hands, beefy arms, a big belly—even his teeth are big. He wears a black cowboy hat, vests and jeans, and "dark" (14), "opaque glasses" (3), but does not use a cane or a companion dog. When we meet him at the start of the first book, he is lecturing a reporter on touch as a "better guide to the three-dimensional world than any of the other senses, including vision." This is hardly surprising coming from the creator of massive bronzes and marbles—why *wouldn't* a sculptor's hands feel like "the most reliable guide to reality" (5)?—but it also emphasizes Bowdre's bodily contact with the physical world, that tactile knowing.

Bowdre's motion *through* space is also mentioned far more often than anyone else's, and his interiorized geography is distinctly different. He is sometimes "steered" (34) or guided, but just as frequently isn't: "'I can find my way'" (15), he says; "'I can find my way out now'" (35). He has a "mental map" (48), "mental vision" (49), a "mind's eye where it [is] not always dark" (49), a "much vaster, more complex, map of the physical world" in his mind (223). And his manner of walking is carefully rendered to highlight both coordination and attitude: he "set[s] forth in a direct line" (66), "back erect, big forearms swinging with an odd precision, like a dancer's" (223). Bowdre *strides*, "erect and purposeful, with measured steps" (*Deadly Canyon*, 1994; 112), strides "purposefully across the green to use [a] pay phone" (139). He "walk[s] in measured strides with his dark glasses facing resolutely forward" (140). Alongside Connie, "Mo match[es] her step for step, giving the appearance not of a blind man but simply of a man wearing sunglasses indoors" (112). Ramirez watches Bowdre "sniff the air, and set off to the east, shoulders back, facing blankly and defiantly ahead" (*SG*, 35). "The blind man, erect with shoulders pulled back, turned and headed for the courtyard door" (15).

These repeated references to Bowdre's stature—to being purposeful and resolute, to walking unassisted, to his mimicry of sightedness—evoke other visually impaired detectives who also do their sleuthing with gracefully controlled bodies. Bowdre may be eccentric where Colton and Maclain are debonair, physically imposing rather than seductive, "'[a] weirdo'" who "'invent[s] himself every day'" (*SG*, 67) in the multicultural milieu of Santa Fe, but the effect is the same: he is not to be pitied, and he is far from alienated or inert. What Bill Ott calls the "superb metaphor" (33) of blindness, marking Bowdre as "the wounded sleuth," "cripple[d]" in his relationship to "the 'adobe theme park'" of his landscape (34), thus seems exactly wrong. Blindness is an easy target for a critic like Ott, who asserts that disability "isolates" Bowdre not only from other "private 'eyes'" but from "*the entire sighted world in general*" (33; my italics). The egregious bias of such a statement need not be belabored; I would merely point out that Ott's notion of a pathologically estranging blindness is easily countered by the kinds of spatial dynamics I have been describing, whereby Bowdre is dramatically in charge of the physical environment, which is always, in these tales, also a social one.

The "mythic richness" of "that blindness thing" (33), in Ott's words—*mythic* presumably because it is linked to Bowdre's artistic sensibility and to Hopi storytelling—misses something else about Bowdre's crime-solving tactics. Turning inward, after all, is hardly problematic in itself, particularly when that concentration results in art and story, both founded in "memory and imagination" (*DC*, 63). Bowdre treats mysteries as "'an idea, a mental image—a story'" (*SG*, 234); where other sleuths deliver oratorical reveals at the ends of their cases, Bowdre is more likely to spin a tale that requires the company of colleagues to generate meaning. "'See, these old guys,'" he tells his skeptical companions, "'they'd sit around the fire and wonder, and try to think up a plausible answer. They'd tell stories to each other'" (228). "A story," "[a] myth" that makes sense (233)—that makes sense *of* experience—this is indigenous ritual. Are Bowdre, Collins, and Ramirez then a kind of multicultural synod, an homage? A loose approximation, or worse—blunt appropriation? Perhaps the answer lies in Bowdre's effort to figure out how "three utterly unconnected crimes" are, in fact, connected (231)—in other words, connection itself, the sharing and community-building effected by his detecting. In the implication that crime-solving amounts to the kind of mythologizing that constitutes cultural knowledge, the traditional legends and lore whereby groups of people know themselves, Bowdre's "inwardness" is linked not to a lonely darkness but to the very foundations of fellowship and collective wisdom.

Connie, who provides Bowdre with his entrée to Hopi life, understands his process this way:

> He was beginning to weave a tale in his head, as methodically as her uncles had woven her white cotton wedding robe years ago ... concocting a story that began with an insight as flimsy and as unknowable to other people as something peculiar he had smelled or heard or touched. She knew it was no use asking him. He would explain in good time. He's like us Hopis that way, she thought. A storyteller, not to be rushed. (*DC*, 173)

"'Story time?'" she asks him. "'I'm flying blind here,' Mo [says]. 'Blinder than usual. Fragments'" (182), and then later, "'I'm thinking'" (185). The detail of the wedding dress is intriguing; it suggests again that what goes on "inside" Bowdre in these moments of silent cogitation is ultimately interrelational and embedded in community practice (one that itself crosses over boundaries of gender). If Connie is herself something of a caricature, a taciturn, "implacable" Hopi (*DC*, 161)—"an ancient mountain, beyond the scale of human follies, unreachable ... unfathomable as a lake of oil," and also "seeing for two, of course" (159)—she is also, like Bowdre, a liminal figure. These are stories invested in the straddling of identity lines, in the possibilities of not quite fitting the categories—and yet in Santa Fe, appealingly free from normative scripts (if not always *entirely* devoid of caricature), "just about the only place in the world where someone like [Bowdre] can be what [he] want[s] to be" (67), fitting right in.

Artistry matters to the Mo Bowdre series. Attuned to questions of creation and beauty, to the significance of objects of reverence to the spiritual workings of a community, Bowdre, wielder of a blow torch and welder of words, repeatedly calls our attention to material existence. Perhaps the least associated with darkness of all the blind sleuths I study here—he lives, after all, in the sunny southwest—Bowdre pulls us into an interwoven world defined by the things people touch, whether that is with hands, language, or belief. Daniel Jacobus, written by Gerald Elias, is the opposite sort of artist-sleuth: a crotchety, caustic, unshaven violinist with amazing aural acuity and a vicious disinterest in other people's feelings. Blindness, as a mechanism of spatial flux, seems to represent in the Jacobus books a kind of extravagant permission to hang out at the edge of wrongdoing without sacrificing an authoritarian gaze. Where visual impairment, sculpture, and sleuthing coalesce in the thick social interplay of Mo Bowdre's embodied existence, Jacobus's motion is far more dichotomized, defined by aggressive incursions into the world and equally pronounced recoilings into solitude.

The Jacobus series is set in "the seamier corners of the classical music world," as the Author's Note to *Death and Transfiguration* (2012) declares, and the mysteries that Jacobus helps to solve include stolen violins, murdered and vanishing violinists, the cutthroat antics of music competitions, and tyrannical conductors. Elias is himself a violinist, concertmaster, and academic, and the books do not shy from lengthy expositions on how bows are made or what happens to the tendons of the wrist if said bows are held improperly (despite the critical accolades the books have received, many readers experience them as grindingly professorial). The Prologue to *Devil's Trill* (2009) explains Jacobus's blindness as foveomacular dystrophy, a genetic mutation causing blood to leak into the eye, which comes on just as Jacobus is about to audition. Refusing immediate treatment, Jacobus plays on, unable to read the music; when subsequent treatment fails to correct the loss of sight, he retreats into a "self-imposed chrysalis" (viii) from which he emerges only months later to take up teaching. The premise of Jacobus's character is thus a literalized blind ambition, and his reluctant sleuthing has a distinctly redemptive air, as it is only "an abiding love of classical music" (viii) that pulls Jacobus out of the exile of his "life-shattering" affliction (vii).

The tension here is between beauty and damage, the purity of art and the disgust of the body, with mystery serving as catapult to force a reckoning with the hateful fact of impairment so that an unsullied musical domain can be restored. Pedantic detail is lavished on the instruments and intricacies of this world, while blindness—and blind sleuthing—are almost comically clichéd. In *Devil's Trill* alone, Jacobus "sit[s] in his personal darkness," "rummag[es] with fumbling fingers" for a cigarette, pities himself as "blind, friendless, and put out to pasture" (18). His is a "black, bleak solitude" (19), an "endless blackness" (154), a "desolate[e] … world of darkness" (211). His "years of solitude [have] made it almost impossible for him to endure more than small doses of human contact" (90). He is "disheveled" (66), "unkempt" (42, 67), unshaven, and uncombed (43). He spits (20). (He can also "[pick] up [a] cup without spilling a drop" [75]—extraordinary!). The flip side of pathetic "grop[ing]" (34) and bitterness are "hunches" based on "a logic that defied normal analysis" (117), "uncanny accuracy" (55), "momentary blaze[s] of intense mental lucidity" (155). Jacobus "'see[s] better than people with sight'" (49), and the power of his "[p]enetrating" eyes (164)—when he isn't wearing dark glasses—can make a person "actually stumbl[e] backward" (25). He "see[s] into" people like no one else (164).

How does blindness serve the failed musician in the context of ensuring justice? To put this another way, how does blindness aid in the attempt to reestablish a set of values that *music* represents—so clearly employed here as the measure of all that is potentially base but also noblest in human behavior? Jacobus's ears obviously make up for his "useless eyes" (*DT*, 113), as if the author quite literally turns off vision to force us to listen.[9] But Jacobus is a master violinist: he doesn't "need" blindness to hear the subtle difference between a real and a faked Stradivarius, or to discern that an imminent victim of murder is "short and feisty" by the way she plays her instrument (*D&T*, 27). The *novels* need blindness, however, as a measure of limit: the impulse that drives Jacobus to play through the complications of foveomacular dystrophy is either noble self-denial in the name of art or useless self-destruction, a hair's-breadth from murder and theft; art-space becomes crime-space throughout these stories, interpenetrating as blind eyes also coincide with masterful ears and fingers. Art verifies depravity (if people will kill for a violin, what next?), as blindness tests the question of why civility or decorum matter in the first place. Jacobus is reluctantly pulled from within that circularity to solve mysteries not just because of his knowledge of the milieu but because only the blind man can heal the environment that has already failed him.

There is something of the classic hard-boiled PI in Jacobus, Chandler's notion of a "complete man and a common man, yet an *unusual* man" ("Simple Art," 237), and a "*hard*" one (*Trouble*, viii; my italics). He flouts expectations about how he is supposed to behave because the tropes of both genre and disability guarantee that freedom—allowing him to bark outrageously at students and deliver doctrinaire speeches to criminals that his woundedness at the end of a bow seems to excuse. He is, even more overtly than a figure like Thornley Colton, a "single, token exotic" (Munt, 72). Jacobus does remind us that the margins can be a provocative place. Displaced from the center of things, "Jacobus, blind," "blind Jacobus" (*Death and the Maiden*, 2011; 5–6), with his "seemingly limitless ability to disturb people" (*DT*, 111), productively stirs up the muck. But he is ultimately static, a figure who, in hating where he is, goes nowhere. That he can wend his way "through a maze of desks ... as adroitly as if he could see" (74) is irrelevant to any meaningful recalibration of how, why, or whom he knows.

I emphasize the conceptual inertia of the character of Daniel Jacobus as a counterpoint to R.D. Zimmerman's early 1990s novels in which blind (and paraplegic) former psychologist Madeline Phillips uses hypnotic trance to escape material constraints altogether. Maddy, the "double-crip" (*Blood Trance*, 23), hypnotizes her brother Alex (who narrates the stories) to access, through his heightened sense-memories in that state, details of murders he has witnessed or is somehow connected to. In the series' first novel, *Death Trance* (1992), Maddy "age regresses" Alex so that he can uncover the murderer of his former girlfriend; in *Blood Trance* (1993), Alex is dispatched to Chicago to unravel a tangled web of familial rage and treachery involving two of Maddy's former patients and later hypnotized to recover the details of his adventures. The crimes are thus revealed through flashback, Alex's trance-induced narration occasionally interrupted by instructions or encouragement from Maddy. What makes the scenario especially farfetched is that, though we understand that Maddy is listening to Alex speak, the novels collapse that distinction so that she seems to experience his memories along with him as if they share a single trance. In effect, she is able to get inside him—to infiltrate his psychic space.[10]

This premise trades heavily on common stigmas about disabled people as isolated, tragically broken, and desperate for reparation; nearly every detail of Maddy's story recapitulates a stereotype. Madeline Phillips becomes blind as a young woman from retinitis pigmentosa; in her thirties, her spinal cord is severed by "a huge, diesel-powered Chicago Transit Authority bus right in the Loop, right in broad daylight, right on a supposedly safe curb," with an inebriated and thrice-warned driver at the helm (*Death Trance*, 13). Maddy then sues both the bus company and the city of Chicago for a tidy sum—$8.5 million—which she in turn "more than quintuple[s]" (13) on the stock market. The money is significant (as is the setting of the accident, to which I will return); such fabulously unlikely material "winning" is what recuperates this "blind paraplegic girl" (13)—whose professional work and personal life, we are made to understand, are as definitively ruptured in the accident as her back. Maddy was one kind of detective as a psychologist; blindness and paralysis turn her into another. But the economy of the novels explicitly denies her professional identity continuity across the threshold of disability. Maddy is rich, but not because she works, and it is specifically and only through settlement money that she "champion[s] over" the "terrible tragedy" (13) that befalls her. Money allows her to restore a twenty-five-room Victorian house on a lush, pine-scented private island in Lake Michigan, hire a husband-and-wife pair of Jamaican servants, and sequester herself completely from a sinister urban environment of drunks and murderers she cannot control. "This was her world," brother Alex explains, "one she'd created so that it would never offer any surprises. … This was what she'd bought with all that money. … Like a big prison" (17). Disability is itself, in this metaphor, a crime.

My interest here is not primarily with the actual crimes of Zimmerman's novels, which are conventional ones. Corrupt cops, unethical psychiatrists, incestuous pregnancies, cultish sexual abuse—these have a lurid cast, but the stories are not unfamiliar. What makes Maddy Phillips a sleuth to study is also not that, as a former therapist, she listens well and can attend to the latent significances of imagery and association as Alex recounts his actions. It is not even that she is an effective hypnotist. What mark her as the locus of resolution in the books are her disabilities. The unique mode of detection here requires impairment for its logic. Because paralysis roots Maddy to home, Alex is "hired to search for and go after things she couldn't," "to be her outer-world probe" (*Blood Trance*, 22–23); because Alex is a ready subject for hypnosis ("'one of the best'" Maddy has ever known [39]), he is also her conduit into experiences she could not otherwise share. It is blindness that connects these different realms, blindness that opens the door—a recurring metaphor in these novels—to the otherworldly of Alex's repressed memories and thus to meaning, knowledge, order.

Corporeality in crime fiction, Stephen Knight argues, graphically realizes our suspicion that the body is merely "a fragile physical reification of the idea that human subjectivity is itself no more than a fragmentable construct" (209).

Making Maddy a psychologist allows Zimmerman to invest his character with mysterious prowess under the guise of scientific knowledge, but it is blindness that inflects the practice of hypnosis with fantastical, Sybilistic power. Only in impairment does Maddy become an allegorical intermediary between modes of knowing and being that can annul such fears of vulnerability. This is why Maddy wears "sunglasses over her failed eyes" (*DT*, 43) even indoors and at night, why she is repeatedly described by her brother in terms of "black magic" and "witchcraft" (*DT*, 43): she is "the great seer" (*DT*, 11, 254; *BT*, 36) who "enchant[s]" her brother (14), a "goddess" (*DT*, 182), a "sorceress" leading him into hypnosis (*DT*, 43, 48, 111), "gurulike" and "godly" (*BT*, 38), a "paraplegic Zen master" (*DT*, 194) whose compassion for and intuition about other people are surely "heightened … by her lack of sight" (*DT*, 23). Perception, as Sally R. Munt puts it, is "intrinsic to investigation," and in the urban dystopias of midcentury and later postmodern crime fiction, perception "is at best unstable, at worst morally flawed" (103). Zimmerman's trance novels exemplify the flawed mechanism of perceptual bias even as they seem to long—through the condensed trope of blindness and hypnosis—for unfettered access to insight.

Despite seeming to understand that his sister unnecessarily deprives herself of a fuller life, for example, the "disability-in-description"[11] of Alex's narrative keeps Maddy's impairments before us in the most unabashedly stereotypical of terms. First-person narration from a nondisabled character ensures that the physical impairments in question will be conveyed with very little countering evidence from the disabled person herself. Aside from brief dialogue, everything we learn of Maddy derives from Alex's interpretations of his sister's existence—her actions, her motives, her desires—which constrains our understanding of it thoroughly. At a simple level, for example, the novels call on readers' sympathy for Maddy by having Alex repeatedly refer not only to her beauty but to its being wasted: she is an "elegantly casual," "very beautiful" figure with a "long trim waist" and "long neck" (*BT*, 23), an Audrey Hepburn in sunglasses day and night with "so much grace" (*DT*, 14) that—"*if she were both a seeing and walking person*"—she would have "suitors galore" (*BT*, 24; my italics). The glasses, the worst of the props, call attention less to blindness than blankness, a disconcerting flatness where readers, looking along with the narrator Alex, might crave recognition and the security of a steady regard: it is because her eyes "rolled this way and that" that Maddy wears the glasses—they are thus for us, not her (*BT*, 22). At the same time, Alex's looking has a distinctly erotic cast; his descriptions of his sister read like Renaissance paeans to the cool and unattainable lady; to seal the point, Maddy touches his face "as if [they] were lovers" (*DT*, 12), and Alex asks her if they "like this too much" (*BT*, 38)—"this" referring only ambiguously to actual hypnosis.

Here then is Bolt's notion of an asymmetrical gaze at a woman rendered both fragile and sexual by "the tragedies of her ... life" (*BT*, 27). Alex's looking repeatedly frames Maddy in a range of tableaus that spotlight her as disabled: Maddy in the doorway of her balcony overlooking the lake that divides her from Chicago, Maddy eating lunch with delicate and over-precise gestures, Maddy's wheelchair about to bump a wall. Such positions, in the context of Alex's prison metaphor quoted above, remind us that disability symbolizes a radical diminution of a person's viability in the world—a foreshortening of perspective—even as hypnotic detection enables a widening of visual knowing across both bodily and relational boundaries. By moving blind, paraplegic Maddy to an isolated house on a remote island, exaggerating and elongating space across the waters of Lake Michigan, the Zimmerman novels equate crime and disability as instances, or evidence, of a kind of spatial damage. In the flashback scenes of Alex's memories, people are in nearly perpetual motion through the spaces of cities, parks, malls, houses, and yards, mapping architectural and geographic edges—the terrain of social organization: they stalk each other; they chase each other on foot and in cars; they spy through windows and creep around walls and doors; they run for their lives. Getting hit by a bus (which, it is implied, happens to Maddy only because she is visually impaired) is both proof and violation of the basic spatial demarcation by which social relations are controlled. The drunken bus driver who injures Maddy, in physically crossing a boundary between *pedestrian* and *vehicle*, and in turn disrupting the orderly function of her body, exposes a dangerous spatial unpredictability (his own drunken body is also out of control). Movement in this context is itself endangering, an emphatic reminder of why the regulation of space matters to orderly and hierarchical social functioning. Alex's physical "legwork" in Chicago puts him at risk; it is only when he returns to the stable geography of Maddy's island that his safety can be guaranteed.

In this way Zimmerman's trance novels carry on an American hard-boiled tradition of urban collapse where cities are dangerous milieus inhabited by imperfect and morally ambiguous citizens. Maddy's island, though, evokes an older, British strand of detective fiction in which murder and mayhem are the specialties of otherwise innocuous country villages and manor estates. In both *Death Trance* and *Blood Trance*, the murderer ends up on the island or in the house, where Maddy's excessive control of the environment is first violated but later serves as a useful cage. Maddy's house and island are colonized spaces. She can physically navigate them only because she has emptied them of any living beings other than servants and dogs (who are themselves grotesquely relegated to "appropriate" domains—servants' quarters, the woods), and reshaped them according to the requirements of her body. The implication is that disability necessitates a radical stabilizing of setting to allow the uncoordinated, ungainly body to move—a level of control that would be impossible in the rapid shape-shifting territoriality of a city. This is not mere "fitting," in Garland-Thomson's sense of crafting spaces that might sustain a range of body types and cognitive styles. It is instead a powerfully frightened suggestion that if the contours of bodies and backgrounds do not exactly match, we will inevitably fall victim to the depredations of lawlessness. This is why the hypnotist-sleuth is a disabled one, who occupies so unrealistically unchanging an environment and who solves crime from an equally improbable limitless mental space. For house and island are also described as extensions of Maddy's mind. Disability operates here like a collapsible cup, moving us steadily inward—from land to lake to island to house to Maddy to mind, ever-smaller areas of being and knowing, until at last "forensic hypnosis" (*BT*, 19) radically re-expands them again.

We might say that what happens to space on Maddy's island constitutes a third crime-narrative paradigm defined by way blindness intersects with detection. If the scene of actual crimes in these novels is Chicago (the American tradition), and the arena of investigation a rural and boundaried island (the British), the space of solution is trance—boundless psychical space, space with no outer limit, no horizon. It is as broad and extensive as Maddy can get Alex to go in terms of memory; it inflates nearly effortlessly. Maddy is an impossible coalescence. She is an injured party, but she also perpetrates the insult of the spectacle of her body (she may be beautiful but it is difficult to look at her). And so she is also the sleuth who must restore bodies and identities to their proper positions. In that simultaneity she becomes Alex's "Sorceress of the Trance" (*BT*, 45), a mystic, a "swami" (*BT*, 35). The trances

Alex and Maddy enter together are flights of fancy into the mind—not just mind-*reading*, which we have encountered before, but mind-*melding*, a total disruption of bodymind boundary that depends for its logic not so much on the fantasied acuity of blind perception but rather the ableist conviction that disability means a total loss of potential.

One wonders which came first in Zimmerman's imagination, hypnosis or disability. There is no obvious *narrative* reason why the novels couldn't have plotted the recovery of details of a crime through trances induced by a nondisabled psychologist in her time-regressed patients—or, conversely, why a disabled sleuth must also boast utterly unlikely powers of awareness. What Zimmerman adds to the plots by making Maddy as stationary and physically limited as possible is to heighten the import of her mental (read: "blind") capacity to "travel" hypnotically with her brother. Two movements are at work here. Laura Marcus describes the contradictory "two directions" of the crime fiction genre, "towards an order in which reason and law prevail and, in an opposing movement, towards enigma and the fantastical" (248). Maddy makes this dichotomous nature of the genre both literal and simultaneous, as her magical ability to take her brother into trances allows her to penetrate into the past, into her brother's memory, thereby unearthing the orderly facts of the cases they solve.

Impairment functions in Zimmerman's novels as an extended conceit, a set of scenes and locations, that concretize the crimes we dread and the restitution we hope for. Setting aside the caricature of the hermetic disabled person supported only by wealth and anger in a hyper-secure space she dominates (revealing fear and mistrust, not confidence and self-actualization), the fact that Maddy is quite literally an island invokes without a trace of irony a most terrified suspicion that no institution we depend on for safety and meaning—family, church, police department, therapist's office—can be relied upon. Only because Maddy occupies so circumscribed a location, only *because* she is disabled, can we plunge into trance to dredge up what's been repressed; only by linking ourselves to the mysterious metaphysical powers associated with the broken body do we discover the clues that lead to the criminal impulses we harbor at the core of self. And only in that expansive space of hypnosis, the self laid bare, can we diminish "symptoms" and restore order. Crime may sully by disregarding boundaries, but the broken borders of Maddy's body lead us into a limitless but also highly protected space of guided memory, where everything can be known, secrets revealed and sins punished. Maddy is vulnerable, pitiful, damaged, but also gorgeous, sexual, rich. That dichotomy is what allows us to join up with her, a body that forces us to confront the basic fiction of social and bodily control. Only in that disembodied and unencumbered space, these novels imply, are we freed from a "pitifully small, self-conscious world" (*DT*, 119), from the distortions of being "blind" to the truth.

In a genre historically predicated on the possibility of figuring it out, on knowing all, the absence of that one sense-perception held up as the equivalent of epistemological mastery would seem the ultimate contradiction-in-terms. Blind detectives defy normative modes of gathering information, and in this sense represent a subversive streak in the novels in which they star. From Thornley Colton on, blind detectives seem to warn the sighted that they rely exclusively on vision to their peril. When blindness, by mythological definition the very antithesis of order and understanding, becomes the site of solution, one's faith in "the machinery by which social control is maintained and existing hierarchies policed" (Pepper, 211) must necessarily be questioned.

The fact that so many of these stories depict their sleuths in ways that both exaggerate and deny their blindness also reminds us of what Ellen Samuels refers to as the "obviousness" (131–32) of disability—the idea that disability is socially validated and accommodated only when it can be *visually* certified by a nondisabled agent of the law or of social services. The characters studied here are certainly obviously visually impaired—we cannot take our proverbial eyes off of their movements through physical space—and yet (as Alex repeatedly says of his sister Maddy) we can also "forget" about the reality of impairment precisely because those same motions so uncannily mimic those of sighted people. Authors seem fascinated by this simultaneity: blind people who behave as if they are not blind, even though the accouterments of blindness make difference unignorable.

The performance of normalcy is at once reassuring and strange, and it tells us that we cannot assume, as Pepper argues, "that crime fictions necessarily secure culturally dominant ways of perceiving the world," that they offer us "unproblematic control and closure" (211). If the stories that feature blind detectives too often seem to reiterate the primacy of the all-knowing and masterful eye—and, to be sure, we are frequently reminded of the primacy of sight as the guarantor of control, the ways things *ought* to be—that very guarantee has always already been undermined by impairment. When Max Carrados "[runs] his finger along a column heading" of a newspaper while looking at his visitor and then proclaims that printers' ink is as tangible to him as "treacle on a marble background" would be to a sighted person ("Knight's Cross," 47–48), his blindness is made marvelous as well as disguised. But Carrados is not seeing. He is touching. To the degree that blind sleuths so regularly do and do not appear to have the very disability that defines them, they prove a fundamental unsteadiness at the core of crime fiction—and of the normative motivations of the world it strives to understand.

Notes

1. For a putatively naturalistic account of "what the blind see," cf. Oliver Sacks, "The Mind's Eye," *The New Yorker* (July 28, 2003): 48–59.
2. Blindness, more than other disabilities included in this study, seems to lend itself to the historical novel of crime, such as blind Jewish physician Isaac of Gerona, by Caroline Roe (pseudonym of mystery writer and medievalist Medora Sale), or Bruce Alexander's series starring Sir John Fielding, the real-life blind half-brother of novelist Henry Fielding, who started the Bow Street Runners from his house on that street. Sir John was a magistrate of the Bow Street Police in eighteenth-century London. He became known as the Blind Beak of Bow Street.
3. Pinkerton's National Detective Agency, founded in 1850 by Allan Pinkerton as a detective and private security firm, accompanied its motto "We Never Sleep" with an image of an open eye. Its current logo is a graphic—and wide-open—eyeball.
4. Lest we assume, as does the unnamed narrator of Raymond Carver's story "Cathedral," that a "blind man" will inevitably be unkempt.
5. When Spud declares that Maclain "would become the master of them all, greater than any detective who could see" (26), though, his enthusiasm that a visually impaired sleuth is not simply different but *better* betrays an underlying set of assumptions about blind powers of insight and vision.
6. Books about acquired blindness feature occupational therapy far more than other impairments.

7   Much of what we read about Naomi is nonetheless obviously directed at a sighted audience who might need to know, for example, how she finds the chicken on her plate in relation to the vegetables (her boyfriend tells her to rotate her plate). Indeed, eating plays an improbably prominent part of stories not otherwise concerned with that sort of quotidian event, as if authors of blind detectives are themselves fascinated by how a person with visual impairment manages to feed herself without cutting a finger or making a mess.

8   Page (who died at the age of 80 in early 2016) wrote extensively about southwestern US Pueblo Indians, and his portrayal of native cultures in his crime fiction, set in and around New Mexico, demonstrates a wry knowingness about what it means to be an Anglo man living at the edges of a Hopi tribe. Readers have praised Page for the authenticity of his portrayals of the social, religious, artistic tensions of New Mexico, where native American, Spanish, Anglo, and Mexican cultures reside in a precarious balance, and for the wisdom of narrating the Bowdre series from a primarily white perspective so as to avoid the pitfall of authorial exploitation. What interests me about such reactions to Page's location vis-à-vis Hopi and other native cultures is that no one questions the reasonableness of a sighted author writing a visually impaired hero.

9   That Elias's website includes audio clips of him playing the music invoked in the novels reminds us that classical music aficionados may be especially interested in these plots.

10 Are there hints here of Wilkie Collins's *The Moonstone*? Cf. Knight, 45.

11 A version of what Hafferty and Foster call "disability-in-dialogue."

3

Deafness and the Penetrating Detective

Detection necessitates the crossing of boundaries. Facility with multiple forms of discourse is often cited as an advantage in solving crimes: a good sleuth must be able to enter into any community or class with some fluency in the vernacular of its denizens. The prevalence in early crime writing of a hero-detective who, as Julian Symons writes, "is a criminal, or pretends to be a criminal, or behaves like a criminal" (8)—or the penchant among fictional sleuths for disguise, perhaps a precursor to real-life contemporary undercover work—reminds us of this crucial intermingling. Consider one episode of ABC's *Castle* (2009–16) in which the wealthy eponymous crime writer and amateur sleuth outfits an entire NYPD precinct in 1970s garb, complete with scripts, in order to elicit information from an aging mobster who is psychologically stuck in 1978 due to trauma ("That 70s Show," 2014; 6.20). Illogical and over-the-top, to be sure, but popular among fans of the show precisely because it exaggerates what we love about so many detectives: their ability to slip easily in and out of characters, accents, and subcultures, the fact that they can so readily and convincingly masquerade. As Peter Messent writes of Hammett's renowned protagonist, "[Sam] Spade is a shape-shifter, adjusting his identity to the situation at hand" (140). Detectives in this way seem to live out a childhood fantasy of becoming something other than what one is—eluding the constraints of self—even as their investigative skills reassure us that a grown-up is in charge.

The shape-shifting aspect of crime stories dovetails with an aspect of deaf experience that Brenda Jo Brueggemann calls (following Homi K. Bhabba), "cultural translation" (16), where deafness traverses the borderland between hearing and not-hearing. This idea of translation has something to do with the fact that deafness is, in itself, unobservable, and also that at least some deaf people read lips. "Deaf people appear 'normal,' like one of 'us,'" as Christopher

Krentz writes; "deafness ... only emerges through behavior" (104). It is thus often written as a kind of invisibility cloak that allows the detective special forms of access in an aural world; unlike visually or mobility-impaired detectives, deaf detectives can seem to slip in and out of hearingness as other sleuths convincingly don and doff aliases, which allows them to penetrate hearing space without being observed as impaired. As I discussed in the previous chapter, the fantasied clairvoyance of blindness leads to effortless solution in unbounded mental space, trading on mystery's privileging of disembodied calculation even as it complicates the genre's presumption of orderly mental progress toward restitution of a stable environment, since it is not vision that gets the job done. Detectives with hearing loss trouble the status quo in another way, operating in arenas dominated by sound but always exposing such places as hostile to difference and their edges as constructed. Deleuzean space, created by being within it, becomes coterminous with Deaf space, determined in large part by the kind of language that is produced there, "organic and curvilinear and bathed in light" (Bauman and Murray, 250).[1]

Crime stories managed by deaf detectives complicate the very nature of *story*. From Ellery Queen's retired Shakespearean actor-turned-sleuth Drury Lane to Dr. Gil Grissom in the CBS crime drama *CSI: Crime Scene Investigation* (2000–07), it is language that catalyzes the unique relationship between embodiment and epistemology in the context of deafness. Kathryn Woodcock and Miguel Aguayo write that acquired deafness (as is the case for all of the sleuths I study here[2]) is "a virtual thesaurus for the word 'catastrophe': thunderbolt, shattering, calamitous, disastrous, traumatic, devastating" (34). Where the blindness binary redeems visual impairment through perceptual acumen, there is no such ready opposite for hearing impairment. What is the deaf equivalent, as Lennard J. Davis asks, of "insight" (*Enforcing*, 105), the prophetic sensitivity linked to blindness? Davis argues that whereas "the blindness/insight paradigm is a well-established part of the meaning system," deafness "has been more excluded precisely because it seems to be outside of meaning. Blind people are never considered outside of language, while deafness is conventionally seen as such" (105). So entwined is language with speech in Western philosophy, and in turn subjectivity with language, that to be without hearing is to lack "voice" as our most potent bodily metaphor for agency. ("There is nothing more personal than a voice," announces Jonathan

Rée at the start of his philosophical study of language and the senses [1]). The stigma of deafness has long been coded as a lack of "intellectual and moral cultivation," as Harriet Martineau declared in 1861 in *Household Education* (110; qtd. in Esmail)—or worse, according to Christopher Krentz, who demonstrates in *Writing Deafness* how often the condition is linked to sin, malevolence, and "the sign of Satan" (102).

Without the advantages of language, then—signed communication having been denigrated well into the twentieth century as primitive, subhuman, and disturbingly *foreign*—and in the alleged soundlessness of deafness (often exaggerated by the hearing just as blindness is falsely presumed to entail a total absence of light), what can be imagined for the deaf but "tragic" isolation and mental impoverishment? This is the oral/auralist bias that ascribes to literary deaf characters, to quote Maren Tova Linett, both "an agonized desire to communicate and a stark lack of access to knowledge" ("Deafness," 89). Both deafness *and* detection, therefore, foreground what Linett calls an "epistemological crisis" (97), raising the question of how deaf detectives manage the discrepancy between what they may be considered unable to do and what they are also expected to do: that is, to *know*, to arrive securely at meaning, and to embody the moral and ethical principles of the law. Again, unlike blindness, associated with instantaneous knowing and available to myths of intuitive wisdom that favor the professional identity of detective, deafness initiates a very specific conundrum. If it is true, to cite Linett once more, that literary deafness is often linked to an "inability to deduce the simplest causes from their effects" (94), then deaf detectives would seem categorically excluded from the rational processing, the reasoning and inference, that are the foundation of deciphering clues, the bread-and-butter of even the most garden-variety sleuth.

The series I consider in this chapter offer a complicated solution to the apparent puzzle of how detectives outside of language and thus meaning manage to assert themselves at the core of truth: they read lips. In stories whose bias and narrative structure are auditory, where character is established through dialogue and the deaf-sleuth is singled out in a cast of hearing cops, villains, lovers, and red herrings, the onus is on our hero or heroine to lip read and speak. Narratively, lip reading serves an obviously compensatory need to recuperate deaf detectives by installing them in spoken culture and so guaranteeing personhood. The emphatic oralism enacted by lip reading would seem to offset a long literary tradition in which deafness evokes loneliness, existential suffering, the anguish of soundlessness as itself a metaphor for the empty surfaces of modern life—as well as "idiocy, bestiality, imprisonment" (Krentz, 101). Oralism "is not merely the teaching of speech to the deaf," of course, as Linett explains; "it is, instead, a broader ideology that calls for deaf children to be taught to lipread and speak *exclusively*" (86-87; italics in original), tied to the notion that only through spoken language can people fully engage in social and imaginative life. ("It has been said that the blind lose contact with things," as Queenie Stearn puts it, "whereas the deaf lose contact with people.") Lip reading and the expectation of speech, problematic capitulations to otonormativity, mask the painful legacy of educational policies that aimed to eradicate signed communication and uniquely Deaf identity; being forced to speak has historically oppressed rather than liberated deaf people. Lip reading sleuths who can "mimic" hearing, then, who can "eavesdrop" across distances, are recuperated contradictions, secured in normative positions even as their bodies defy the kind of command a convincing detective must have—not just in dialogue with witnesses and suspects but over the uncertainties of meaning inherent in acts of crime.

Lip reading might thus be crime fiction's answer to the question of what counts as "insight" in the case of deafness. So journalist and amateur sleuth Connor Westphal (in a series by Penny Warner, 1997–2010), private-eye Annabelle Hardy (in two books by Hialeah Jackson, 1997–9), and Jack Livingston's PI Joe Binney (in four books, 1982–7)—all to be discussed below—are so skilled in reading lips that, in some instances, whole pages of dialogue elapse without any direct mention of what the deaf individual is doing to participate in oral conversation. They are "disguised," in other words, as hearing. Or take the example of Sue Thomas, who worked for the FBI from 1979 to 1983 in the surveillance unit, translating videos. The short-lived television series *Sue Thomas: F.B.Eye* (PAX, 2002–05), loosely based on Thomas's 1990 memoir *Silent Night*, emphasizes deafness as a key feature of Thomas's work and so capitalizes on the nearly occult mystique of lip reading. One scene from the pilot episode exemplifies the way in which the stigma of deafness is recuperated by this skill. Over a meal in a crowded restaurant, a new colleague asks, "You mean you can just look around the room and know what everybody's saying?" "Yeah," confirms the slim, blond, elegant Thomas (played by deaf actress Deanne Bray), as her male friend gazes at her in admiring awe. The obvious fact that not even the most practiced lip reader could possibly discern the words of *everyone* in such a setting—some half of the diners actually have their backs to her—misses the point of what makes Sue Thomas "F.B.Eye" a viable lead. Her lip reading is what Stearn would call "covert," which gives Thomas both a spatial and epistemological advantage over everyone else in the room. What matters is her assertion of instant, accurate, and also *secret* knowing.

Edna Edith Sayers remarks that "[c]rime novels are notorious" for "faultless," "supernatural," and "effortless" lip reading (305–06). But contrary to what such flawless performances suggest, lip reading is in fact relatively ineffective as a means of communication. "As an expert lip-reader I can tell you," writes Terry Galloway in her memoir *Mean Little deaf Queer*, "lip-reading is a true talent and hard as hell to learn. Most people never can" (79). Frederic W. Hafferty complains of fictional deaf detectives that real-life lip readers "make a lot of mistakes," "respond inappropriately," and learn how to "[get] people to repeat themselves without having to ask them to repeat themselves." Characters like Sue Thomas thus symbolize a hearing world's prejudice toward oral rather than signed conversation, English over American Sign Language (ASL), and perpetuate a misconception that deafness, like blindness, enhances other senses—as if lip reading were akin to Superman's X-ray vision. Indeed, lip reading, one website says of *Sue Thomas*, allows the sleuth to infiltrate into places no electronic listening device can go. She is no mere mortal FBI agent; she is the proverbial supercrip, her communicative capacities rendered at once magical and mechanically perfect.[3]

But the deaf sleuths I study here are endowed with more than mere lip-reading skill as part of their investigative resources. Where Sayers suggests that these "lip reading wonders" are "just one of those devices for which readers must willingly suspend disbelief" (306), little more than unrealistic if inevitable components of the "mechanics of storytelling" (307), I would argue that something more is at stake than the simple requirement of dialogue to forward a plot. For one thing, the very otherworldly quality that Sayers explains away serves a distinct fantasy of infiltration and subterfuge—a wish to get away with something, to go unnoticed in one's acts of "listening in," to know without being known. Lip-reading sleuths hide in plain sight, literalize an advantageous form of espionage. They are camouflaged without costume, intercessors between realms of language and identity. "Deaf characters stand at the limits of knowing," writes Krentz, "serving as mediative figures on the threshold of difference" (100). As a local sheriff remarks to deaf amateur sleuth Connor Westphal, "nothing is as it appears." If crime is always a matter of transgression—violating the boundaries of a jewelry box, a confidential file, a home, a body, the very foundations of social being—then a deaf sleuth both embodies that destabilizing liminality and corrects it through the security of a kind of bilingualism. More to the point, what Krentz suggests of deaf characters in general, that they "represent a certain threatening epistemological disorder" and "transgres[s] conventional boundaries and ways of thinking" (103), exactly captures the quality of detective work that is by definition (because it must *always* involve a duality of languages and modes of gathering information) carried out in the interstices of social, civic, linguistic locations, where lawfulness is always but a hair's-breadth from crime.

At the risk of collapsing too simplistically the myriad forms of novelized crime, from the coziest Golden Age house-murder plots to the most twisted of contemporary forensic thrillers, it is an obvious tenet of mystery that violence provokes incomprehension. There may be a motive at the base of every fictional wrongdoing (at least since authors became curious about the psychology of perpetration and not just the puzzle of crime), but it is precisely the obscurity of origin that creates an exciting tension between the forward-motion of plot and the retroactive movement of solution.[4] As represented by deaf sleuths, the process of arriving at a logical explanation for something inherently unfathomable entails mistranslation, guess-work, and filling in the blanks. Deafness concretizes an essential danger of misinterpretation, the fact that there is always the possibility of error and false assumption, of trusting as secure language and information that is intrinsically indistinct. The unraveling of mystery *alongside* issues of legibility sets in high relief the ways in which triumph over violence is both contingent and precarious. It is always only ever an approximation.

So the "enigmatic void" that is deafness, "forever beyond the reach of logocentric comprehension" (Krentz, 100), is in detective novels crowded by an abundance of verbal and communicative styles, misprision and understanding, distance and bodily proximity. Far from being cloaked in speechless silence, "hover[ing] indistinctly in the background" (Krentz, 106), the deaf sleuths studied here are a wholly social, interactive bunch who grumble about the obtuse assumptions of "hearers" and tackle their investigations with all the physical risk-taking and obstinate inquisitiveness of Holmes, Marple, and Poirot. The forms of communication that dominate, both lip reading and sign language, limn the contours of embodied spaces in which inquiry and analysis take place. Following a conversation without being discovered, as several of the detectives included here often do, privileges less the deaf person's ability to participate in spoken conversation than it does a kind of peripheral positioning that nonetheless requires a clear line of sight between sleuth and suspect. Lip reading in the context of one-on-one exchange requires that "you ... keep your eyes on the speaker," as Connor Westphal tells us in the first of her mysteries—a level of "eye contact [that] comes across as intense to many hearing people" (*Dead Body Language*, 1997; 41). There is, too, a great deal of touching throughout these texts—tapping on shoulders and arms to get someone's attention, people being physically turned toward one another to facilitate conversation. And then there is the visual and gestural nature of signed communication; when deaf detectives are shown signing, they emerge from a falsely dichotomized world of silence and vocalization into the dynamism of an embodied language.

In all of these, a geometry of arrangement makes the process of detection "kinesthetically real," as Ernst Daniël Thoutenhoofd has written of the "graphic," iconic, theatrical quality of deafness (273, 276). As deaf detectives negotiate crime-solving according to the contours and requirements of their bodies, everything changes: measurements of pace and distance, the spaces of interpersonal engagement, ways of processing information, the very nature of meaning—which is itself, as Shelley Tremain reminds us, "carnally informed" (87). Douglas Baynton argues that "hearing loss" ought to be understood as "deaf gain" and that "diverse sense experiences can lead to valuable alternative ways of understanding" (50).[5] Like Thoutenhoofd, Baynton emphasizes keen visual perception as fundamental to deaf experience, but deaf sleuths also signal smell and proprioception as elements of a phenomenological detection. They are fluent in body language, attentive to nuance, masters of idiom. They read, they border-cross, they perform. They *look* intensely; they close their eyes and absorb. They are distillers of knowing.

*

Drury Lane, appearing in four books published in 1932–3 under the name Barnaby Ross (a pseudonym for Ellery Queen, itself the pen-name of two Brooklyn cousins[6]), is a classically eccentric sleuth—a sixty-year-old cape-sporting, cane-carrying former Shakespearean actor who lives high above the Hudson River in a replicated Elizabethan estate, with moat, turrets, and a "hunchback" make-up artist sidekick. Lane is introduced by the authors in their "Open Letter to the Reader" as "the most extraordinary detective who ever lived" (*The Tragedy of X*, 1932). Having retired from the stage due to deafness—in the first book a "growing deafness in both ears" (front-matter), in the last "suddenly and tragically … stricken stone-deaf" (*Drury Lane's Last Case*, 1933; 17)—Lane comes to the attention of law enforcement when he solves a murder case entirely on the evidence of newspaper accounts.[7] *The Tragedy of X* opens with the district attorney and a New York detective approaching Lane for assistance on another complicated murder. What follows in the tetralogy are pyrotechnic feats of deduction that leave the lawmen with mouths agape, sputtering to catch up.

Like blind sleuths, Drury Lane does sometimes seem to grasp the significance of clues in an instant, to figure things out in "'a blinding flash of light'" (*X*, 255), and when Inspector Thumm exclaims that Lane's analytical skill "'isn't human!'" (239), we are in the realm of *unheimlich*, where Lane's intelligence estranges him from others and distance is marked bodily by deafness. But deafness in the Lane books opens onto a space that is not so much one of wondrous consciousness as it is an intensified and extending reasoning. It is more the "careful structure of his analysis," "his acuteness to grasp and utilize" (*The Tragedy of Z*, 1934; 240), "the loftiness of his thinking processes" (*Last Case*, author's note) that distinguishes Lane from the average run of policemen (the kind who are prone to thundering in rage and barking out commands like, "'Now cut out the weeps, Sister, and let's get down to business'" [*X*, 39]). Lane delivers his solutions in page after page of explanation that foreground that process rather than the fact of knowing. (It is useful to recall that intuition, the particular "gift" of blind detectives, is defined as an immediate and direct apprehension of knowledge *independent* of reasoning.) Deafness attaches symbolically to Lane's "'powers of concentration,'" which impairment "'has contrived to sharpen'" (*X*, 9). "'I have only to close my eyes,'" he says early on, "'and I am in a world without sound and therefore without physical disturbance'" (*X*, 9). Throughout the books, Lane is shown repeatedly closing and opening his eyes, as if that action alone were the difference between distraction and an extraordinary degree of absorption—a thorough-going suspension, it is implied, of external awareness, facilitating thought.[8]

Discursive dilation, in turn—especially retrospective summations of what *has* happened rather than what *is* taking place—exposes the subtlety of Lane's mental machinations more than it includes readers in the shared enterprise of solving a case. It also emphasizes Lane's continued ability to speak, as if to reassure hearing readers that whatever his "unfortunate affliction" (*X*, 9), Lane has not fully entered that inhuman realm of an alienating absence of language, what Davis calls "the nothingness of nonspeech" (123). Even Hercule Poirot, doyen of the theatrical reveal, would be outclassed by Drury Lane, who delivers a *thirty-page* "explanation" at the end of *The Tragedy of X*, one equally epic at the end of *The Tragedy of Y*, and so on in the subsequent books. ("'As usual,'" he "chuckle[s]" somewhat sheepishly at the start of his *Last Case* [38], "'I'm in the throes of a monologue.'") These monumental oratories, Lane's feats of talking, clearly demonstrate the point Brueggemann makes about "a [rhetorical] tradition that places ... all the authority on speakers" (17). Talking—and lots of it—repairs the insult that is the actor's career-ending infirmity and rescues him from the fate of a soundless obscurity.

Speech is thus coded throughout these novels as the guarantor of intelligence, the medium—in the sense of mode but also intermediary—of the sleuth's ratiocinative talent, which is linked to deafness via attentiveness: Lane's "unwinking concentration" (*X*, 69), "candid concentration" (90), "unswerving concentration" (215), "his habitual attitude of concentration, with closed eyes" (179). A "'little concentration'" (*X*, 233) is what gives Lane the edge, and it is explicitly tied to an idea that the advantage of not hearing is not being distracted. ("'Can't think at all with so many disturbing influences around me,'" he says [*Drury Lane's Last Case*, 77]). Lane's speechifying is predicated on the heightened focus that silence, as the metonym of deafness, signifies, and yet it also eradicates deafness, privileging spoken English and denying the terrifying and also dehumanizing effects of occupying a silent world. An imperviousness to life's mundane (or threatening) commotion is of course implicated in audist arrogance about the isolation of being "stone-deaf"—as Thumm's daughter Patience, narrator and Drurian protégé of *The Tragedy of Z*, reveals when she says of Lane that "only his facility in reading lips kept him in touch with his surroundings" (222), utterly discounting other ways of knowing and interacting.

This presumption that soundlessness positions Drury Lane outside the clamor of everyday human activity is countered—or perhaps *accompanied* is more exact—by focus not just on visual perceptiveness but also on the very quality of Lane's actual eyes, those anatomical "orbs" freighted with metaphysical significance.[9] And it is almost as if, because deafness seems to shroud Lane in silence, he is also assumed to *be* silent (a point demonstrated, I think, by the fact that he speaks "softly," "quietly," "mildly," and "gently" throughout the oeuvre, that he is "apparitional" [*X*, 79]), so that his panoptical vision can take the measure of a suspect or a crime scene somehow unobserved. Lane's eyes could not more obviously be deployed as the agents of his meticulous and comprehensive surveillance of objects in space as well as a conduit to understanding. They are "remarkably keen eyes" that notice things other people "overloo[k]" (*Z*, 193), "sharp eyes" that "observ[e]" what no one else can discern (*Last Case* 72). They are "sharp" and "bright" (*X*, 107, 61, 185); they "flas[h] with remarkable brilliancy" (178); they "glea[m] weirdly" (51), "fi[x] unblinkingly" (53), "stud[y a] man intently" (107), watch a companion's lips "keenly" (126), and "stud[y] the face of [a] host unobserved" (149). Lane "sit[s] quietly in a chair watching" (*X*, 68), or "[stands] quietly to one side, watching" (*Last Case*, 161). He is "able to visualize the component elements" of a crime "as clearly as if [he] had been present" (229). "'It is a matter of complete astonishment to me,'" he announces to a lawyer, "'that not one of the keen minds surveying this case has pierced the veil of nonessentials and seen the—to me, at least—perfectly photographic truth beneath'" (*X*, 136). He thinks in "pure pictures" (*Last Case*, 111). He has, simply stated, "'excellent eyesight'" (*Last Case*, 88).

It may be true that "the seeing eye ... has become the very sign and signal of detection," in Peter Messent's words (61), but rarely is so much emphasis placed on visuality as the sleuth's primary mode of navigating the spaces, both physical and psychological, of crime. Though we have no indication that Ellery Queen was dedicated to writing a realistically visual epistemology for his deaf detective, the kind of looking that typifies Lane's investigations, the intensity of his stare, would seem to evoke the "highly developed visual ways of being in the world" that H-Dirksen L. Bauman and Joseph J. Murray cite as "brought about by the unique sensory orientation of deaf individuals" (248). But Lane's deafness is late-onset, and the specular dynamics of his investigations go well beyond simple representation of someone who "perceive[s] the world primarily through vision" (Krentz, 53). I would argue that the sleuth's interpretive shrewdness cannot be uncoupled from sensory hyperbole: an overstated profundity of soundless concentration alongside eagle-eyed insinuation into the cracks and corners of motivation and clue. Deafness, if not always explicitly named, accounts for both the still and expectant postures in which Lane watches, their quality of hushed suspense, and the authoritative mapping of physical space that that watching enacts—both of which are, in turn, cast as the physical signs and conduits of Lane's "'peculiar talent for getting beneath the surface of things'" (X, 160).

There is something at work in this series about paying attention that goes beyond the obvious (that "'observation of minutiae is of vast important to the detective'" [Z, 17])—some anxiety about the chaotic hubbub of life, especially family relations, and the law's astounding ineptness for controlling criminal behavior, that Lane's silent theorizing and keen, intent staring, seeming to fix others in place just by virtue of his watching, works to stabilize. We are accustomed to detectives whose rational skills surge ahead of the lesser intellects that surround them, but Lane is particularly defined by knowing *in advance*. Where other mysteries generate momentum through a protagonist's developing awareness of truth, the urgency (if also the security) of the Lane series lies partly in the fact that the sleuth is an egregious hoarder of information, holding back what he knows—almost from the beginning—from the police ("'But why don't you tell us, man, for the love of Heaven?'" cries District Attorney Bruno in *The Tragedy of Y* [226]). The pleasure is not that we're sure he *will* know, but that he *already* knows, long before the denouement, and so we sense that Lane is simply biding his time, perhaps waiting for one final piece of evidence to fall into place ("'You know how he keeps his mouth shut till he's sure'" [Y, 217]). If Poirot is often positioned as an avuncular vis-à-vis the vulnerable or the lesser wits of his tales, Drury Lane has a more *professorial* effect. This may be his signature characteristic, that he "'know[s] nearly everything'" (Z, 207).

Nowhere is all of this more overt, and more gothic, than in *The Tragedy of Y*, where Lane is deployed to serve a kind of corrective function for panic about social and sexual excess. Written at a historical moment when anxieties about disease and contagion were being mapped onto "a pervasive fear of the urban masses, the growth of the cities, and the changing nature of familial relationships" (Brandt, 427), this story of the dissipated New York Hatter family (the "Mad Hatters" [16]) reflects concern about degeneracy and the weakening of American "blood." At the center of the drama is matriarch Emily, as a result of whose loose morality comes syphilis, which courses through the generations leaving wreckage in its wake. Emily's various descendants are hysterically described as "wild," "vicious," "reckless" and "strange," as "wild, willful … rampageous" and cruel, as "vicious," "lecherous," and "despicable" (14–15), as "weird, orgiastic, eccentric, [and] unpredictable" (12)—all of these "abnormalities" (141) "chained down in a lustful, unreasonable, vitriolic, lunatic environment" (12). This unlikely sociopathology has its apotheosis in Emily's oldest daughter Louisa, whose particular condition is "so unusual, so tragically, gigantically pathetic that the vagaries of the others paled into normality beside her," for Louisa "had come into the world hopelessly blind and dumb, and with an incipient deafness" that leads inevitably to "the final humiliation" of becoming totally deaf (15). Louisa is, to put it bluntly, a spectacle of abjection.

What is astonishing in this bizarre tale (it involves the suicide of York Hatter and subsequent murder of Emily) is its unapologetic narrative casting of Louisa as beyond recognition as a human being, despite the fact that she is also figured as a canny supplier of the clues with which Drury Lane unravels the mystery of her mother's death. She is said to be "stranded on a lonely planet of her own" (15), her existence mere "negation, a lack, a life sucked dry" (16). She is barely living at all; indeed "she might have been dead" (16)—she is "a human tomb" (141). She seems a classic grotesque, infirmities piled on, a macabre authorial experiment in education and learning—eyes, ears, larynx all irrevocably damaged. So what has Louisa to do with the plot? Lane calls her the "'storm center'" of the crime (146), but it is not just that Louisa was in the room when her mother was killed: it is that she calls into question the very meaning of *witness*, of how we understand evidentiary proof. There is something koan-like in this. What is the status of an event that is neither seen nor heard? Does crime even *happen* if it is neither seen nor heard, if those two master-status senses of knowing are disabled? And how trustworthy is a statement that cannot be uttered aloud? "'A murder with a live witness, by God,'" grumbles Inspector Thumm, "'and she has to be deaf-dumb-and-blind. Might's well have been dead last night for all the good her testimony will do'" (84). Emily's corpse speaks clearly enough for the brute reality of murder, but Louisa embodies a different kind ontological puzzlement. How do we understand a living witness who has already been written off as dead?

Though she is in fact fully capable of communicating through a Braille letter-board as well as in sign language, translated for the hearing by her nurse, and though, as Inspector Thumm confirms, "'they taught her lots of things'" (31), Louisa is referred to by everyone as "the deaf-dumb-and-blind woman" (21, 41, 46, 51 and throughout). She has the "sixth sense" and psychic intuitiveness, as well as the rigidly outstretched arms ("unbending as a steel bar" [89]) of blindness, the "mute absorption" (88) and animal vocalizations (a "mewing … so utterly alien to any normal human sound" [87]) of deafness. She is eager to convey to the others what happened on the night of the crime, but her manipulation of the letter blocks and her manual signing are rendered as utterly estranging: "those waving fingers were like the antennae of a bug, oscillating with intelligence, clamoring for enlightenment. Her head was jerking from side to side anxiously, quickly, heightening the insectivorous resemblance … It was the odd features that impressed them—the piscine eyes, the still, blank, almost lifeless features, the quivering fingers." When "her nostrils quivered, as if she were trying to scent" someone, the narrator declares flatly, "It was weird" (55). Her "working" senses are compensatorily "hypersensitive": "the nerves at the tips of her fingers, the taste-buds in her tongue, the olfactories in her nose [all] acutely developed'" (93). If only she were a talking *dog*, Lane muses, "'how simple it would be!'" (93).

Yet it is Lane, in all his shape-shifting mobility, who establishes connection. Two kinds of translational detection become operative in this scenario. First, it is as if clues are transliterated from one sensory lexicon to another, with Lane acting as intermediary between Louisa's perceptions and normalized apprehension of details. So the footprints in talcum powder beside the dead woman's bed become, once Louisa reveals that she swiped the killer's cheek with her fingers, an occasion for Lane to deduce height, stance, and gait—one person's touch translated to everyone else's visualization of the perpetrator's stature. Louisa's insistence that she noticed a strong scent of ice cream in the room, first dismissed by the able-bodied Thumm as evidence of sheer Hatter family "'nuttiness'" (95), takes Lane to the laboratory where he figures out the use of a vanilla-smelling poison, whose milky *visual* appearance will factor in a final punishment that Lane himself metes out. And second, no one but Lane pieces all of this together; though the nurse is described as a "medium" (85) (as if Louisa were literally communicating to the living from the astral plane), only Lane has the kind of body-bilingualism that draws him into physical contact with Louisa—grasping her hands, for example, by way of reassurance or encouragement—and allows him to take her sense-perceptions seriously.

The excess of bodily trouble in *The Tragedy of Y* crystallizes a eugenicist anxiety about what happens when the boundaries of body (particularly women's sexual activity) and of state are not securely guarded.[10] Neither the law nor the family commands authority in this text; the police are helpless without Drury Lane and there is no one at the helm of the Hatter household (Emily Hatter had two husbands; both are dead; she herself is killed by her thirteen-year-old grandson, who "'had in his veins the diseased blood of his father and grandmother'" [246]). But the plethora of linguistic modes—and Lane's enthusiastic efforts to take Louisa at her "word"—intimates an unexpected resolution: that the shame of the Hatter family isn't so much the sexual indiscretion of its matriarch as her children's intractable monolingualism, their inability to communicate outside of normative roles. If the tainted bodies of the Hatter offspring, their violent and excessive urges, manifest powerful fears about how swiftly a criminal class may be propagated, Lane's brand of detection suggests that the answer is not necessarily to patrol the gates more stringently. As an "outsider" whom the police "'let … have his own way'" (201), a border-crosser whose own experience of bodily change is construed as facilitating translation of one linguistic form to another, Lane models a fluid adaptation to unfamiliar modes of expression. He reminds those around him that other senses may be "'alive'" (228) and that deafness is hardly beyond language. Indeed, he avows that even the most apparently extreme language barrier is, as he instructs us, "'not insurmountable'" (227).

The relationship between Drury Lane and the multiply impaired Louisa Hatter does to an extent exemplify what Sayers has suggested more generally of deaf characters written before the 1970s, that they will "almost inevitably [be] one of two things: (1) a well-assimilated lipreading and speaking marvel ... or (2) an isolated 'dummy,' a scarcely human two-dimensional character who functions more as a circumstance in which the hearing characters find themselves or with which they must deal" (324). Such characters, Sayers argues, are simply vehicles for revealing something significant about hearing ones—tests, for example, of other characters' morality. Louisa is obviously a puzzle that readers may be sure the clever Lane will decipher, but the writing of her character is also complex; it is Louisa, even more than Lane, who insists that knowing is a whole-body affair, that to be without hearing is not to be deprived of language but rather to learn to feel language as a matter of the body's movements in physical space, the actions of her hands or the touch of Braille beneath her fingers. Getting to the bottom of the crimes that occur around her is less a matter of solving the riddle of disability than simply learning the multiple languages of the star witness.

At stake here is a basic structuralist conundrum about how the raw material of existence and experience gets divided and classified: where and what language is, which senses we privilege and why, whose story about what it all means will prevail—and it is this last, of course, that makes disability so significant within the crime-fiction template. A condition of the body like deafness, an already loaded problematic of knowledge and of social belonging, puts in high relief the requirements of psychological complexity that increasingly dominated the genre after the Second World War, as puzzle stories were replaced by crime novels in which "whodunit" gives way to questions of *why* and *what happens now?*, and straightforward plotting cedes priority to characterization and an interest in relationships. The deaf sleuth centralizes the difficulty of investigation when it entails not solitary ratiocination but interpersonal engagement and an ability to know emotion in addition to scientific fact or encyclopedic data—when the story of crime has as much to do with narrative bias as it does with factual truth. Because deafness provokes fundamental questions about language and knowing, the deaf sleuth reminds us that to fully understand a crime is also to interrogate the ways in which people communicate, as well as the discursive systems that foreclose (and so produce) defiance.

This may account for the hearing impairment of Dwight Steward's amateur sleuth Sampson Trehune in *The Acupuncture Murders* (1973),[11] where the hero's body becomes a literal site of resistance to the primacy of Western master narratives, including medicine, religion, and psychoanalytic theory (the first words of the novel proper are "'Fuck Freud!'" [1]). Binary oppositions abound in this novel, and at the center of it is a man whose every feature both endorses and complicates a reader's trust that existential and social chaos can be contained by expected dividing lines. Its central crime involves a fairly commonplace stew of corporate embezzlement, arson, and murder; its *interest* derives from its gruffly impatient hero, marked by difference, and philosophical arguments occasioned by the interplay between deafness and acupuncture (which Trehune undergoes in an attempt, somewhat half-hearted, to cure his condition). The book is crammed with facts and overly long lectures on these subjects, at the heart of which lie obvious debates about the authority of systems of knowledge and the degree to which we can count on our sense perceptions to insulate us from violence and greed.

Deaf at age eight from scarlet fever, Trehune is a contradiction. He is introduced to us in a frontispiece as a Cambridge graduate, a consultant to UNESCO and the Library of Congress, an antiquarian book appraiser, and the author of scholarly volumes on book preservation; he is also a fan of *Winnie the Pooh*. His mother is titled, and he belongs to prestigious, presumably white, gentlemen's clubs; he is also a member of the "Hispanic Foundation" and something identified as the "Utek Indian tribe" (though these ethnic designations are never again addressed). Both deafness and Trehune's erudition will matter to his solving of the crimes in this story, but the novel takes an inconsistent position on hearing impairment insofar as it represents a challenge to normative modes of being and knowing. The prefatory note introduces "the world of the deaf"—as if to insist on it as alien—with a brief lesson on the challenges of lip reading and the improvisational quality of sign, but we may be legitimately skeptical about the author's claim that "the [novel's] point of view" is that "of a deaf person" when he instructs us to read the verb *sign* "as the equivalent of 'said.'" It is exactly that kind of collapsing of one modality into another that Trehune's own self-possession, and the debates about medicine and national identity that unfurl here, would seem to resist. That the novel can't sustain that resistance, especially in a moment of direct address to readers assumed not to be deaf, frames the novel in terms of an intriguing failure. At what cost to Trehune, or to some goal of deeper understanding—call it an embodied multilingualism—do we arrive at closure?

There are two essential plotlines in the *The Acupuncture Murders*: embezzlement and the deaths that ensue, and a debate about alternative versus orthodox medical practice. As crime fiction, it is a somewhat plodding mystery about corruption and greed, full of sweeping cultural stereotypes and women whose swaying hips earn the appraising glances of men. Its *primary* investment seems to be in the clash between East and West—more subtly, in understanding how it is that the one is exoticized by the standardizing motives of the other. As the book begins, Trehune is preparing for treatment by a practitioner of acupuncture who is "the first Western physician to claim a positive cure for nerve deafness" (5). Since the setting for the first murder will be a clinic where acupuncture is demonstrated, the novel begins with a brief lesson on this "strange practice of curing illness by sticking the body with needles" (8). Reading along, Trehune is both amused by the notion "that the foundations of all Western medicine might be wrong" and sure that "tales of universal energy were hardly creditable" (8–9). There is supposedly "'disinterested science'" on one side and, on the other, a procedure on which "'one-fourth of the world's population positively thrives'" (24–25); there is also the arrogance of the one and the childishness of the other (what "grown man," Trehune asks himself, could seriously believe in the wonders of "*Ch'I*" [8]?). Chinese acupuncturists complain about being dismissed as "'witch doctors'" (77), while Trehune thinks back to the "monstrous experiment" (106) of American surgical convention and the procedures done to him in the name of correcting the defect of deafness ("'fenestration procedure,'" "'tympanoplasty,'" "surgery ... to activate the foot plate of the stapes" [26]). The impaired body mediates these poles, acting as the physical ground on which tensions of cultural primacy and ideological disagreement play out.

The novel everywhere emphasizes such collisions and criss-crossings, from East to West, expert to amateur, hearing to deaf, language to body, voice to hands and back again. The murders each involve acupuncture, but one is skilled while the other is a botched mimicry—a kind of imperfect translation that only Trehune, whose deafness makes him a "'very intelligent observe[r],'" able to "'notice things other people miss'" (35–36), can read. Acupuncture does not cure Trehune's deafness, but neither did the more standard procedures he underwent as a child. Trehune sometimes speaks, though his voice is "all wrong" (123) and others bristle at the "loud and eerie" sound of it (49). He and his hearing psychiatrist friend Abel sign liberally throughout the book, a form of communication that discomfits other hearing characters (as the prefatory note assures us, readers at least are "spare[d]" the annoyance of any "'translation'" through a comprehensive act of grammatical "normaliz[ation]"). More radically, Trehune "had long ago perfected a special way of being invisible," which is to disguise himself as a deaf beggar so as to "'snoop'"—an obsession that Abel declares as inevitable in a person who is "'cut off, isolated from normal human communication'" (60). "'You feel compelled to poke about,'" lectures Abel (with his "maddening Western thoroughness" [72–73]), implying that Trehune's amateur sleuthing has a pathological, compensatory etiology and is guaranteed to succeed precisely because of it.

At stake here is a question about how we read the marks of the body and the signs of the world around us, what we take as a legitimate clue for a mystery we're involved in unraveling, and how quick discursive systems are to domesticate anything that defies their terms and conditions.[12] In combining crime, disability, and a dispute about healthcare, *The Acupuncture Murders* makes quite overt its interrogation into the power of discourse, what it elicits or suppresses. Steward's novel suggests that the truth-claims of metanarrative, with its autarchic pressure, are inherently deceptive; we would do well to resist their totalizing allure, from psychotherapy to hard science. This is why the novel has Trehune speak the history of ableist oppression. "'I may be deaf,'" he signs to Abel, "'but I am not insane. I am not DUMB,'" interrupting that entrenched association between hearing impairment and cognitive liability (2). "'If I had been born in Athens,'" he later says, "'Aristotle would have labeled me mentally defective and dropped me in a river. Romans no better. Saint Augustine would damn me to hell because, he said, "knowledge of God comes only through hearing"'" (113).

Whether or not acupuncture is a "legitimate" (76) treatment functions in this novel as controversy over signed communication or prejudice against deaf sexuality also do: to interrogate the authority of a monological "explanation" (78), and to recognize "belief" as "contagious" (80). It is no accident that the first crime happens under the gaze of more or less doubting observers who cluster about a body upon which—or more properly, *into* which—the penetrating needles of acupuncture are being manipulated, seeking out pulse points and meridians the existence of which the novel acknowledges are in dispute. The very definition of human anatomy is at issue. Or that Trehune, momentarily impressed by a sensation of sound after his own session, says to Abel, "'I want to hear again'" (91), even though he has already cautioned himself, "be realistic. I am deaf—never change" (17). Such moments ask us to consider a basic Foucauldian insistence that bodily experience is governed by the daunting and pervasive teachings of the master institutions: medicine, religion, psychiatry, law. How manipulable *are* bodies, in fact?

That the two plotlines of the novel are only awkwardly integrated (the murders of the title taking a back seat to larger and more compelling questions about ideology and embodiment) is ultimately an instructive imbalance. It suggests that the very thing we seek in orderly solution—bodies that behave, that mask their porousness; knowledge securely grasped; authorities actually in control—will always be undone by the endurance of *other* possibilities for how to determine what's there and how to articulate what we think. To put this differently, the forward-driving motion of a crime being solved may be overwhelmed by, subsumed into, the inevitable friction and chaos of competing methodologies and beliefs. In rejecting the *obvious* solutions and culprits in the case, Trehune breaks it wide open. His conclusions seem "oracular" (172) only to those who aren't so willing as he is to take a risk, to "play a hunch" (103). The deaf "snooping" that his friend Abel diagnoses as pathological is more properly understood as a form of alternative thought.

"The deaf person might stand for the ideal reader," writes Davis (113), and indeed both Drury Lane and Sampson Trehune are attentive readers, proving that all bodies are legible as long as we are sensitive to the language of their details. As I suggest above, deafness serves the detective's need for fluency, even if—or because—it also points up some fundamental incomprehensibility at the core of social organization. That simultaneity is what drives the suspense of Ed McBain's *Let's Hear It for the Deaf Man* (1972), the twelfth book in McBain's 87th-precinct series, featuring detective Steve Carella. Crime novelist Julian Symons lauds McBain as "the most consistently skilful [sic] writer of police novels," and describes the lead this way: "McBain began with Steve Carella, a detective working for an unnamed big city police force, and equipped him with a wife named Teddy, who is beautiful but both deaf and dumb" (232). That "but" hardly needs mentioning; it is "equipped" that interests me here, as it signals something distinctly *useful* about the deaf wife that is not necessarily tied to the details of any given book's mystery.[13]

In *Deaf Man*, the detectives are racing to prevent the next crime to be committed by a man who telephones the precinct but "[takes] pains to announce that he [is] hard of hearing" (221). The discrepancy is meant to amplify something freakishly creepy about this killer—how can he be hearing impaired and also talk to Carella on the phone? Sensory impairment is the classic outward marker of evil, the bodily corollary of the "'maniacal mind'" of a "'diabolical *fiend*'" (95); it also literalizes the problems of communication that occur more generally in police procedurals: how law speaks to lawlessness, detective to criminal, right to wrong. This villain is not just crazy but *deaf*— that impairment seems almost the most terrifying thing about him. But Carella *can* talk to him, and that's in part because of Teddy. "Deaf mute" Teddy (25) sensitizes Carella in a way that, as Sayers would argue, tells us far more about the detective than about the woman, as in this sequence of paragraphs:

> He had, he realized, stopped considering the Deaf Man a deadly adversary, and he wondered how much this had to do with the fact that his wife, Teddy, was a deaf mute. Oddly, he never thought of her as such—except when the Deaf Man put in an appearance. There had never been anything resembling a lack of communication in his relationship with Teddy ... She was beautiful and passionate and responsive and smart as hell. She was also a deaf mute ...
> He had once hated the Deaf Man. He no longer did. (25–26)

Carella's fluency with sign language notwithstanding, Teddy functions here not as a three-dimensional character in her own right but as a humanizing device with which Carella is, indeed, "equipped." We're meant to understand something about *Carella* because of his love for his disabled wife (whose impairments, significantly, come into relief in *criminal* rather than *Deaf* company). He doesn't just learn a new "alphabet" (25) from the "deaf mute"; he is made a better man—a more compassionate one, more adept at communicating across dramatic lines of difference, somehow better able to understand the alien mind of the genius criminal. In short, Teddy's deafness makes Carella a better detective, endowed with heightened awareness and powers of comprehension: *her* bodily condition becomes *his* conduit to power in the terms that matter to his status as a white, able-bodied man vested with the authority of law.

The deafness of PI Joe Binney, in four books by Jack Livingston in the next decade (1982–87), similarly serves this specific task: to facilitate understanding between unlikely parties even as it manifests some unintelligible social trend that leads inexorably to violence. Livingston's penchant is for crime driven by avarice—where murder is just the inevitable outcome of a worse recklessness, of real estate transactions, banking scams, industrial espionage, insurance fraud, and show business. The US federal government receives particularly scathing critique for its nefarious overseas dealings, and the drug trade provides the requisite piquancy. The novels are a tame offshoot of hard-boiled fiction, full of pouty, voluptuous women (who, when they aren't in bed, are usually crying), improbably long rants on such brow-furrowing topics as prejudice against actors and the dangers of smoking, and booze, lots of it—polishing off three *pitchers* of martinis with a lady friend is nothing for Joe Binney. One can discern impatience with Reaganomics in the heavy-handed plotting of Livingston's novels, tempest-in-a-teapot crimes wrapped up in diatribes about the plight of ordinary workers and corporate "'fat'" (*Die Again, Macready*, 1984; 145). His is the New York City of the 1980s as well, when "Central Park [was] a racetrack of joggers and muggers in pursuit of joggers, and any children seen up there … [were] purse-snatchers" (87). The world is represented as rapacious and unfeeling. As someone says to Binney on the last page of *Die Again, Macready*, "'I saw … what you were like when you were dealing with the world out there. … That's a different kind of toughness. It's crazy, ugly, illogical, brutal, awful. I could never live like that'" (245).

Binney's hearing loss—caused by an underwater demolition accident during the Korean War, and therefore nothing if not virtuous—is constructed as evidence of the unpredictable threats of such a world, where money makes men ruthless and desperate and no one in charge can be trusted. But it is also a counterpoint. Unlike Lane and Trehune, Binney is a professional, a working man. From the "threadbare living" he eked out as "a recently deafened young man" (*Macready*, 44–45), doing bookkeeping "'so [he] wouldn't have to talk to anybody'" (63), to what he calls "'the detective dodge'" (63), the trajectory of Binney's working life is shaped by impairment, and his role in the mysteries he solves is in turn defined more by his job than by rarified curiosity. In this sense, deafness is explicitly connected to the novels' critique of easy and exploitative financial gain—drugs, money laundering, child porn, and the like. Better to be honest, gainfully employed, and honorably impaired, the texts suggest, than "full of detestable health and heartiness" but compromised by greed (*The Nightmare File*, 1986; 13).

Indeed, Livingston's concern seems to be the ways in which bodies are specifically imperiled by work. In *The Nightmare File*, for instance, a magazine writer forced by his employer's health plan to quit smoking becomes increasingly unhinged at the effort, fears losing his job altogether, and in the process of searching for a story to save himself, uncovers federally sponsored drug trafficking in Asia; he is killed by a trainer who has been blackmailing clients to falsify their medical records. In *Die Again, Macready*, a TV executive is driven to murder by fear that the titular actor, who has more artistic aspirations, will pull out of a show that stands to make millions. In *Hell Bent for Election* (1987), it's the publishing industry that comes under fire as a traveling textbook salesman carrying $150,000 worth of books dies while on the road in West Virginia. As the proverbial working stiff charged with unraveling these tangles of misconduct, Binney lacks the sophisticated erudition of Lane or Trehune, but the fact of his deafness lends a similar degree of translational skill to the process of detection. His body represents the intrusions of the establishment into the innermost locations of self—discursive power is literally inside of him in the form of war-induced injury—and Binney in turn mediates between individuals and that same implicated authority. His ability to figure out how *else* to do the job when it would be so much easier if he could hear suggests a kind of adroit pliability—the very "proclivity for adaptation" that Bauman and Murray cite as a hallmark of Deaf-gain (247)—that might stave off the juggernaut of institutionalized interest.

The story of acquired deafness is specifically about negotiating a problem of language, of discursive space, and in this sense, the Binney series is an intriguing legatee of hard-boiled fiction. As Scott R. Christianson writes of Chandler's Philip Marlowe, "All [he] can do is wait for the next case—and attempt to convey his experiences through language" (143). The "linguistic efforts of the hardboiled narrator," Christianson argues—"tough talk, wisecracks, hardboiled similes, and dialogue"—constitute a kind of meta-narrative, as the detective attempts to articulate the "lonely" position from which he "[tries] to make sense of it all" (142). In effect trying to explain the experience of trying to explain what defies understanding: such circularity is a paradoxical effect of the "discontinuity" that Christianson locates in the hard-boiled tradition's origin in modernism. Classic PI crime stories end where they begin, in futility and repetition. Joe Binney is the inheritor of this tradition; his cynical takes on technology, say, or corrupt international trade offer a kind of update on the disaffected urban settings of Chandler and Hammett. Deafness—with its presumed silence and isolation, the imprecision of understanding between deaf and hearing individuals, the "downward story trajectory" of deaf experience (Sayers, 347)—could easily seem a corporealized version of the "disgruntled alienation" that is represented in the signature "language elements" of earlier PI novels (Christianson, 142). For the deaf sleuth in a hearing world, every interaction becomes an exaggerated effort to make sense of mystery, not just the body on the ground but the moving lips of others that alternately withhold or divulge.

It's as if Livingston has softened the hard-boiling, taken away the peculiar linguistic moves of a Spade or Marlowe, but then heightened the linguistic effect readers might expect of an urban PI by deafening him, making him work that much harder to converse in a world where men are driven by inculcation in capitalism to the limits of civilized behavior. At the edges of that world is someone who can't "hear" its explosions, its gunshots, its cries of pain—someone whose body displays its danger and the struggle required to make oneself understood. This is why, I think, Binney's deafness is everywhere before us and yet not a truly defining feature of his identity; our attention is called again and again to deafness even as the narrative erases it. "While the lone operator of hard-boiled fiction characteristically interrogates the social order," John Scaggs writes, "he or she can barely make a dent in its structures" (97). And so deafness has little to do with amplifying either fear or genius in these books, as we might expect; it is written as almost imperceptible to others until it becomes interesting (a feature of an "'intelligent, sensitive man'" who "'reads Karl Popper'" [*Nightmare*, 223]) or useful, as when Binney goes into his "deaf dummy act" (242). It can be advantageous: if a situation requires silence, Binney attends to "tappings" (*Nightmare*, 253), and he can "'listen' for vibrations" with his fingertips (*Macready*, 11); in the absence of light, he'll "sniff" (*Nightmare*, 249). But it changes nothing.

Or does it? The capacity to turn a normative sense impression into something else he can "read" involves communicating across what Bauman calls the "intersemiotic gap" of deafness ("Poetics," 323). Binney's admission that "'there are some people [he] can't read at all'" underscores what he *can* do: interpret the movements, the gestures, the delineations of embodied meaning in a way that another PI might not. Each time Binney tells someone, "'I can't understand you when you're running around ... Stand still where I can see you,'" "'I have to see you when you talk'" (*Macready*, 62, 4), he is commanding the spatial dynamics of idea-exchange. His disarming mode of communicating (as he says in *A Piece of the Silence* [1986], "it is hard to impress a guy who's reading your lips" [4]), his use of other people to help him on the phone, and his very divergence from the norm—these loosen the fixedness of existential despair and suggest an antidote to the rigid social structures the novels critique. Joe Binney is a thorough-going American male,[14] but there's something too of ludic resistance, the possibility of transformation, in his position as deaf PI.

This is why *Die Again, Macready* centers on acting as playful reinvention rather than inauthenticity. Macready is an actor whose mouth was damaged by shrapnel and who also spent time convalescing in a military hospital. Binney and Macready bond over this mutual process of adjusting to bodily change, of "reconstruct[ing]" themselves (83)—one "'learn[ing] a new way of hearing'" and the other "'a new way to talk'" (64)—and they are both, in their respective capacities, performers. Expending so much effort learning to talk around the damage of his mouth trains Macready for the stage, and he takes the name of an eighteenth-century actor to mark a kind of rebirth. It is hard to believe that readers in any era would acquiesce to Macready's assertion that "the rest of the world" thinks of the stage actor as "a freak ... a sex-maniac, a drunk, a pervert, a congenital liar, a coward, and a sort of world-class cheat who doesn't really work for a living" (61). Whence Livingston's beliefs on the matter, I cannot say—but his sleuth shares his antipathy for close-minded bigotry. "Nobody was supposed to live like Macready," Binney says. "People were supposed to be *normal*, schoolbook normal. Macready was an insult to the idea of normality" (72). Buried at the start of the second novel, this near-aside encapsulates how we are encouraged to regard Binney's own impairment—as a viable alternative to the status quo.

*

Looking: it is a key factor in dismantling "Western hearing 'metaphysics,'" in Bauman's words (317). Bauman picks up where Derrida failed to go, past deconstruction's ultimately audist philosophical neglect of deafness to the idea that deafness, and the spatial, embodied language of Sign, realize the non-phonetic, "visual-spatial dimension" (318) that is the very basis of grammatology. Deafness, Bauman writes, "signifies the consummate moment of disruption" (317), turning phonocentrism on its head and denying the primacy of "hearing-oneself-speak" as the guarantor of presence. What would happen, Bauman asks, if we pursued a Deaf philosophy to alternative modalities of being that do not rely on notions of "voice" and that interrupt entirely the foundational role of speaking in Western ontology? If we refuse to take on faith the dictum that Jonathan Rée invokes in stating unequivocally that "language itself exists in the form of sounds, and therefore *automatically* calls sounds to mind" (44; my italics), what might become of storytelling, and the subjectivities it is said to form? What might be a poetics of self, if self exists in a language that is embodied, four-dimensional, and inherently inter-dynamic? Sign, Bauman suggests, has the potential to resist the linear, logocentric bias of our conceptions of literature and identity. He also writes that "Deaf persons have been exiled from the phonocentric body-politic" (319). How does the signing sleuth uphold the "law," maintain notions of "civility," convincingly appeal to the collective to tell the truth?

The last two sleuths to be considered in this chapter are Deaf women who both lip read and sign, and their signing importantly modulates the way they are positioned—by which I mean both physically in space and epistemologically in ideation—but not to the same effect. Signing, whether it is simply mentioned or transliterated by an author for a hearing reader, tends to interrupt the forward flow of narrative. If it is simply remarked upon as a form of communication to which readers are deliberately not made privy, it instigates a kind of sideways movement; information is being circulated *there*, but not *here*—or to put this exactly oppositely, the margin displaces the center, and readers are no longer participating with the detective in the process of solution. When signing is described (in sometimes awkward parentheticals), it creates a kind of inter-text where multiple levels, shapes, and kinds of meaning are produced simultaneously, proliferating possibilities rather than narrowing to a single, explicable cause. Because Sign always happens between people, moreover, it carves out a private interdynamic area that includes the reader only at the discretion of the narrator.

Detective fiction is defined as much by how we read it as by how it is written, the forward motion of mystery generated less by our interest in what *will* happen than by the pleasurable experience of coming to understand what has *already* happened. As George N. Dove points out, we could "simply tur[n] to the last chapter" of a detective novel "to see how things turn out," but to do so would sacrifice "the real aesthetic experience of the story" (33), the tension of knowing we are on the brink of knowing. Crime fiction may be fundamentally linear in both form and content, then, but it also contains within itself the refusal of its own directionality; it is always tugging backward as it proceeds, and in any case, we want to know but we don't: the genre is defined by its own deferral.[15] To set detection alongside Sign, I would argue, is to heighten the effect of the yet-to-be-known, or the multidimensional quality of detection, in itself defined by vision, time, space, and the body. Crime-solving tugs in all directions, as any murder-board will attest. So does Sign.

It must be emphasized that the use of ASL in the texts to be studied here is highly limited, signed between the sleuth and one other person, usually a hearing/signing individual. This has the effect of isolating the signing pair in an otherwise aural environment rather than establishing Deaf community. And as Bauman also remarks, gender will inevitably mediate the spatial dynamics of deafness. Many scholars have pointed out the intensely visual interplay of both lip reading and signing, which require seeing and being seen. To what extent does a *male* gaze construct the *female* "body/text" of lips, hands, facial expressions (Bauman, 320)? To return momentarily to TV's *Sue Thomas: F.B.Eye*, I would argue that the show's emphasis on Thomas as a highly skilled lip reader ensures that she is looked at, allowing the camera to frame Thomas (or the actress Deanna Bray) in frequent close-ups. The effect is to disarm and eroticize Thomas, her attentive looking at others not very different, after all, from what women have historically been encouraged to do from the sidelines of action. Lip reading is Thomas's "gift"—without it, she would not be an FBI agent—but it is constructed in the show as a relatively passive talent: Thomas is not *doing* something to solve crimes so much as she *receives* information that she passes along to her (mostly male) team.

The same might be said of security-firm owner Annabelle Hardy in two books by Polly Whitney (writing under the name Hialeah Jackson) in the late 1990s, even though Hardy also signs with her partner Dave. Like Detective Carella's wife Teddy, Annabelle is "deaf but...," as in this blurb for *The Alligator's Farewell* (1998) from Goodreads:

> Before Annabelle Hardy took over her father's Miami detective agency, she was beautiful, married, and teaching at Yale. She's still beautiful—but now she's deaf, widowed, and learning the lessons of the streets from ... Dave the Monkeyman.[16]

It is as if deafness might detract from beauty, meant to elicit a sympathetic response from readers *no less than* the one we might have for the loss of a husband. In fact, Hardy is a John Donne-quoting English PhD who had planned to write a book on the law and sexual difference, details that obviously announce Hardy's learnedness as well as her feminism. Lest this impaired intellectual inspire only pity, however, we are assured that she is "still serenely lovely" in widowhood (33), with her "abundant almost-black hair falling over her shoulders," her "trim, tall body" and "shapely calf" (32–33); her superpower is quelling volatile male suspects with a single beaming smile or touch, surrounded by the confectionary pastel colors of south Florida. This is the stuff of romance, so it comes as little surprise that Hardy is repeatedly taken in hand by the men who would seduce her so that she can read their lips: "He put his hands on her shoulders, turning her gently to face him" (88); "Berlin put his hands on her shoulders, turning her gently to face him" (256).

Hardy is successful *and* rather than "but" deaf, but Dave does far more of the actual work of making connections than she does (she is just "*so pretty*" [192], "'the loveliest woman on the planet'" [215]); deafness in turn is regarded, even by Dave, as an alien world, a "silent cosmos" he "would never perfectly understand," one he is "on his own" to comprehend (as if neither he nor the author ever bothered to ask a deaf person) (236–37). Deafness represents something about Hardy's bravery in the face of trauma and loss, and it adds an exotic dimension to her physical allure (Hardy is also "thoroughly at home" [237] under water, like Joe Binney, as if deafness naturally primes a person for an aquatic existence!). She is, finally, a good example of what Woodcock and Aguayo call "specimens of good adjustment ... who conceal their disability so well that no one becomes conscious of it until after they have attained their success" (35).

What does happen, then, when Hardy signs with Dave the details of a case? For one thing, it discomforts onlookers: "'You and Dave ... go into this intense little world when you sign,'" someone tells her. "'I felt like the handicapped one, on the outside'" (88). It has a more threatening edge, too: "'I'm sorry I can't participate in that delightful sign language with you, although I quite enjoy watching it,'" someone else says, dismissively; "'he's translating what I say *exactly*, isn't he?'" (47). That worry about the accuracy of language is unique to this context. Can we be sure that signs and sentences coincide? What happens in the gap between the words on the page—or the words a character presumably hears—and the image of hands, bodies, in motion? Can meaning be guaranteed, or does it elude us into that gap, one that is, ultimately, less about the slippage between English and ASL than it is a constituent feature of communication as such? The classic mystery denouement grants the detective center stage and narrative direction over a captive audience; in Jackson's novel, the signal to the reader that Dave and Hardy are signing keeps opening onto a less-controlled space-between, where meaning is inherently ephemeral, and always in the process of being shaped.

It is Connor Westphal, star of seven books by Penny Warner (1997–2003), who comes closest to something like an authentic Deaf identity, signing with willing if not always proficient townsfolk and reading lips with acknowledged imperfection. Warner is the author of four discrete mystery series (each with a particular theme). With degrees in child development and special education, she writes with an educational bent; her background includes teaching sign language and preschool to deaf children, and the Westphal books have a distinct insider angle that the other works studied in this chapter do not. (The character is a graduate of Gallaudet University, for example, and well-versed in the controversy over cochlear implants.) Along with requisite information about the technological aids of deafness, from TTY phones to a bed-shaking alarm, there are subtler details—the chapters of each book are indicated with drawings of the signs for numbers, for example. There's also a great deal of actual rather than invisibly translated Sign—which is to say, Warner attempts to give readers a sense of the unique grammar and style of ASL by doing more than merely mentioning its use. One can imagine Deaf readers being amused by the heroine's wry descriptions of what it's like to deal with the blundering or overly solicitous behavior of "hearies" (*DBL*, 8), as much as hearing readers might welcome being informed by the books' depiction of Deaf experience. To the degree that all that pedagogy can make for a somewhat clunky read, distracting from the mystery at hand, Westphal is nonetheless an appealing narrator, cousin to Sue Grafton's highly popular PI Kinsey Millhone, down to the daily account of unglamorous outfits and her remarkable gusto for coffee and breakfast sandwiches.

Westphal is a former *San Francisco Chronicle* reporter who, upon inheriting a family newspaper called the *Eureka!* from her grandparents, ditches the big city and moves to the tiny town of Flat Skunk in California's Gold Country (a kind of Wild West version of Miss Marple's St. Mary Mead), where the slow pace of news gives her plenty of time for some diligent amateur sleuthing and reporting gives her an excuse to pry. "So what was all this to me? I was curious, naturally," she admits in the first book of the series. "I am, after all, a newspaper reporter. ... Hell, let's face it. I loved a mystery" (*DBL*, 61). And in the second: "Trying to solve a mystery is like trying to write a good story for the paper" (*Sign of Foul Play,* 1998; 113). This connection is stressed throughout the series (perhaps defensively—a reader might wonder why in fact Westphal is a reporter and *not* a PI or police detective). The job is important, I think, because it is implicated in her deafness: being a reporter allows her to exploit the marginality and shape-shifting that is associated with being deaf, and also confirms Westphal's relationship to language. Westphal explains that she went deaf at age four from meningitis but was raised by hearing parents who, as she says, "tried to raise me hearing, placing me in oral schools and forbidding me to sign. [I] had to be subversive to learn what I considered my native language" (*Silence Is Golden,* 2003; 34). To anyone cognizant of the argument that oralism is equivalent to colonialism, using education to regulate bodies and imposing an alien language, friendly Connor Westphal will sound downright revolutionary.

What interests me about Westphal as a sleuth is how explicitly deafness is linked to ideas of translation and transition. The books frequently establish analogy as a way of capturing what is both unique and akin in the nature of things, in nearly every detail thematizing an atmosphere of concurrent though not always congruent meanings. Consider the very town our protagonist has adopted as her own: "caught between two cultures, the past and the present. Somewhat like myself, being deaf in a hearing world" (*DBL*, 25). As a former mining town, Flat Skunk is a palimpsest of sorts, determined by tension between the pull of a romantic history and the lure of tourism and reinvention; as a town settled by Cornish immigrants, it also symbolizes displacement, exploration, and acclimation. "I feel at home here," Westphal says (*DBL*, 12), and her habits of detecting are strongly correlated to the kinds of bonds and familiarity that can be forged in a small town—and that allow her to transgress boundaries. She asks questions because she cares and is trusted, if also subtly dismissed: "It wouldn't be difficult to think up reasons for talking with people who might have had a motive … And most folks would probably overlook me if I snooped around a little. That's the way it is being deaf. Because we're sometimes silent, we're often invisible" (*DBL*, 129). That kind of liminality is staged to complicate other sureties. Analogy—reporter to detective, writing to solving, English to Sign—makes meaning lateral rather than hierarchical, opening the way to new ideas.

Key to this enterprise is the fact that communication has spatial choreography and proliferates more than it solidifies meaning. This is why some conversations unfold in an awkward but complex simultaneity, as in these moments (Miah is Westphal's part-time officemate):

> "Did you hear?" Miah signed fluently, which at this moment consisted of pointing to his ear and raising his eyebrows. …
> "What?" I struck my palm with an index finger.
> "Gold found!" Miah continued, using ASL syntax. …
> "Really?" I signed, pushing my index finger from my chin. (*Silence is Golden*, 19)

> I couldn't keep myself from staring at them. Of course, deaf people who sign are used to being stared at.
> "Do you want to do some gold panning first or ride the ponies?" the man signed. In American Sign Language he'd said, "First, gold panning, or pony-ride?" His eyebrows asked the question. (*SIG*, 33)

> "What are you working on? Something important?" Literally, *work you, what? Important?*
> ……
> Miah sat back. "What do you mean?" *What mean you?*
> "Didn't you even hear the sirens?" *Hear siren, you?* (*Dead Man's Hand*, 2007; 23)

As I suggest above, the interplay between English and Sign creates meaning in the interstices of symbols, temporalities, and gestures. Even brief moments such as these halt forward motion, call attention away from English and toward the intentional, assured bodies of the signers. In fact, communication takes a multiplicity of forms throughout the series, including TTY transcription, Sign, nonphonetic body language, email, lip reading, Sign-English translation, a signal-alert dog, spoken and written English. Such linguistic capacity exemplifies the "plenitude" that Bauman and Murray locate in deaf cognitive diversity (247), and because each of these modalities entails interaction with someone else, Westphal necessarily urges her community toward similar plasticity. As Carol Padden has written, a "differently abled body does not merely attempt to communicate, but ... compels new forms of engagement and interaction," "push[ing]" others into "expanding their abilities to interpret" (45).

Describing the phenomenology of witnessing a signed poem, Bauman defines the "volatile volume of poetic space" as a space-between, where poetry gets "incarnate[ed]" and "the borders between viewer and text, subject and object, inside and outside" are made "porous" (326). Respecting the significant differences between the kind of "text-as-event" Bauman is referring to and what happens on the page of written, linear English momentarily stalled by references to sign language, I would nonetheless argue for something of a resistant metaphysics in Warner's insistence on including Sign in her production of dialogue. Her subversive sleuth might speak and write, but she does not simply acquiesce to the primacy of a disembodied Word. She produces knowledge differently, distilling it along alternate lines of perception. Maureen T. Reddy argues that feminist crime writers "cal[l] into question that which is taken for granted in other crime novels"—power and judgment, the superiority of reason, "the nature of authority itself" (176–77)—and use the basic elements of a crime story to interrogate patriarchal privilege. The Connor Westphal series similarly complicates the *ableist* presumptions of order, truth, and justice by staging the discovery of "what happened" as achievable only by the Deaf woman reporter—not a male representative of law—and only through the abundance of communicative means that deafness makes possible.

It is no coincidence, finally, that so many deaf amateur sleuths have some professional connection to literature. Sophisticated fluency with language is asserted again and again in these texts, from the voluminous antiquarian reader Drury Lane to journalist Connor Westphal, former academic and John Donne scholar Annabelle Hardy, and rare book appraiser Sampson Trehune. Even PI Joe Binney reads philosophy. If deafness symbolizes "stupidity" and "stubbornness" in an audist world, as Woodcock and Aguayo put it (35)—where spoken language is championed as the onset of adulthood, and "dumb" will always denote "unintelligent" along with "mute"—then the writing of a deaf writer/reader raises important questions about what knowledge is and how it is acquired by the body.

In one way, the fact that hearing writers foreground their deaf sleuths' own writing and reading suggests that deafness, with its connotations of animal darkness and pathological infantilism, can only be survived by the transcendent application of Logos, which is just another word for law. But none of these sleuths is so monological as that. Even the most conventional among them subverts expectations of how and what to read, where and when to insert themselves bodily into the spaces of discourse and connection, what constitutes language in the first place. The role they play in reinstating normative structures in the wake of criminal chaos demands entirely unfamiliar ways of looking, moving, and understanding the dimensions of space. They make other people uncomfortable; they ask us to communicate otherwise or leave us out of the conversation altogether. They elude the strict boundaries of milieu—they break the fourth wall, swim underwater, eavesdrop in plain sight. They stare. They cogitate. Only then, yes, do they know.

Notes

1 Throughout this chapter, I will follow convention in using "deaf" to indicate a physical condition and "Deaf" a cultural identity.
2 The fact that so many detectives acquire deafness, whether through illness or accident, rather than being born deaf, suggests a perceived need on the part of hearing authors to retain some connection for their protagonists to the linguistic world of hearing (just as mobility and hand impairments are invariably acquired on the job, as I discuss in later chapters).
3 What the television series obscures but the memoir *Silent Night* details is that the real Sue Thomas's ability to read lips is the result of her parents' refusal to accept

their daughter's hearing loss or to foster Deaf identity. Thomas goes "stone-cold deaf" (8) before the age of two from idiopathic nerve damage. Her parents, who "[hold] out hope" that medical intervention might "turn [her] ears back on" (11), eventually "vow to each other" that they will raise Sue to be "as much a part of the hearing world as possible. They didn't want [her] to remain forever outside of their world looking in" (13). What follows is several years of intensive training in vocalizing and lip reading, until Thomas "debut[s] as a public speaker" at five years old (27). Thomas makes the hardship of this training very clear, writing that the "years of learning to speak were just too painful and the memories too raw" (28–29). This segment of the memoir ends, however, with Thomas describing her teacher as a "saint" and citing the "dogged and selfless determination," the "unwavering commitment that enabled [Thomas to] become a part of the hearing world" (29). When she claims that her talent for lip reading and speaking "enabled dreams to be fulfilled" (29), the dominance of oralism, and its pressure on children with hearing impairment to conform, could hardly be made more explicit.

4 I am speaking of classic detective plots here, which most of the texts examined in this chapter follow. In what some call the *whodunit*, two incompatible stories coexist, as Tsvetan Todorov lays out in *The Poetics of Prose*: the first story, "that of the crime, is in fact the story of an absence" that "cannot be immediately present in the book." The second story, that of investigation, "has no importance in itself," since it "serves only as a mediator between the reader and the story of the crime. ... We are concerned then," Todorov continues, "with two stories of which one is absent but real, the other present but insignificant" (46). My contention about disabled detectives, however, is precisely that the "present" story of solution is far from insignificant in that the epistemological modes made possible by difference from the norm demand our attention—and serve to swerve the very process of discovery in unexpected directions.

5 Cf. also H-Dirksen L. Bauman and Joseph J. Murray, "Deaf Studies."

6 "Ellery Queen" was a pseudonym used by two American cousins from Brooklyn: Daniel Nathan, also known as Frederic Dannay, and Emanuel Benjamin Lepofsky, also known as Manfred Bennington Lee.

7 This is an obvious nod to Poe's "The Mystery of Marie Roget" (1842), Doyle's *A Study in Scarlet* (1887), and E. C. Bentley's *Trent's Last Case* (1913).

8 On the "myth of fortunate blindness," cf. Schor.

9 For more on the symbolics of actual eyeballs, cf. Bolt.

10 It is thus also about the family as a microcosm of failed social arrangement; when the surviving Hatters break down under a kind of house arrest as the

case unfolds, we might suspect Ellery Queen of staging an inquiry about urban crowding and the conundrum of heredity over environment.

11   An apparent one-hit wonder. My researches into Dwight Steward have been unproductive. The book was published by Harper & Row and has the prestigious imprimatur of Joan Kahn on the copyright page; Kahn was a noted editor of mysteries.

12   And yet the novel is also thoroughly steeped in corporeal stereotypes. Henri Voisin, the acupuncturist, "like many of his Gallic compatriots," uses his hands when he speaks and wears a "typically European" cut of suit (14); Voisin also "'hates Jews'" (45). A physician named Hector Delgado has "characteristically Latin" gestures (41). Belinda Shaw, the Assistant County Prosecutor, "use[s] her mouth well" when she speaks, "her tongue darting out from her white teeth and crimson lips as if she were delicately devouring an ice-cream cone" (35). Claire Fletcher is "'one of the most influential journalists in the women's-magazine field'" (23). There's a typical "Southern aristocrat" (88) and a "widowed earth mother" (93). Aging is presented as the "'saddest'" of all the "'afflictions which rack the human body'" (139). Crime fiction is generally guilty of this kind of sweeping generalization, but it's surprising in a text that works so hard to drive a wedge into lazy habits of essentialism.

13   Teddy's beauty is not insignificant. Sayers writes of her that "what makes her so enchanting has everything to do with the fact that she neither hears nor speaks—her miming drives Detective Steve Carella wild" (330). Cf. Scaggs, 94, on her name and on being characterized as a "toy."

14   Sayers remarks that both Joe Binney and Sampson Trehune are rare "deaf sex objects," men who "display superior intelligence and fearlessness in the face of danger that prove irresistible to women" (330). Consider the unapologetic *blazon* Binney delivers as he gazes upon the "snowy, dazzling white" skin, the "perfectly circular" breasts, the "utterly perfect joinery" of slim thighs of Celia Listing, the dead man's niece, who is parading naked around her uncle's apartment, mixing drinks (94–95).

15   Rushing goes further in arguing that there is in fact "*no hermeneutic component to the detective novel. The reader simply waits for the effortless dissipation of the problem, albeit misrecognizing his own waiting as some other activity*" (161; italics in original).

16   http://www.goodreads.com/book/show/617487.The_Alligator_s_Farewell. The author of the blurb gets the business wrong: it is a private security firm, not a detective agency.

4

The Crip Sleuths

In Patricia Carlon's 1969 *The Whispering Wall*, a woman recovering from stroke overhears a murder being plotted; paralyzed and unable to speak, she manages to communicate danger via eye blinking and Scrabble tiles. Private investigator Fred Carver, in novels by John Lutz (1986–96), has been shot in the leg and now walks with a cane. PI Jeff Jackson (in the Martha's Vineyard series by Philip Craig, 1989–2010), like Carver also a former policeman, has a bullet lodged against his spine, as does Norwegian detective Hanne Wilhelmson in Anne Holt's *1222* (2007; first English translation, 2012). Marshall Browne's Italian inspector Anders loses more than his nerve after shutting down an anarchist terrorist group; he also loses a leg, which makes his subsequent crime-solving activities all the more crucial to the restoration of his identity as a champion of justice. Jeffrey Deaver's forensic specialist Lincoln Rhyme (1997–2016), a quadriplegic with cervical vertebrae damage, pursues serial killers from his Manhattan apartment with the aid of a junior colleague and an impressive array of expensive technology. Ex-military intelligence PI Cormoran Strike, in four books by Robert Galbraith (penname of J. K. Rowling, 2013–18), has lost his lower leg in Afghanistan; Dr. John Watson (Martin Freeman), in the BBC's newest *Sherlock* (2010–), was also wounded in Afghanistan, though his limp disappears after the first series; French detective Julien Baptiste (Tchéky Karyo), in the first season of "The Missing," has his leg smashed by a car door (STARZ, 2014).

Many of these injuries occur on the job, and the impairments that result—the missing limb, the paralysis from a supererogatory bullet—confer a specific legitimacy upon the sleuths, denoting heroism, often dedication to a cause greater than oneself. Solving crimes and unraveling mysteries for veterans of war and other political conflicts can take on an ideological meaningfulness that may be missing in other crime novels, and ex-cops wounded by gunshot similarly carry their scars with a particular pride that attaches to the moralized violence of good and evil. These are characters whose broken bodies are both badges of and spurs to courageous action; assuring readers that they can "take it," they become sentimental emblems of survivable atrocities. As someone says of PI Carver, he is "'one tough sonuvabitch'" (*Hot*, 66).

But search for a word like *sedentary* in a thesaurus and a litany of moralized "synonyms" appears: lazy, slothful, idle, indolent, sluggish. Mobility impairments may be taken as the quintessentially socially legible disability, as encoded by the graphic of the wheelchair: an instantly recognizable symbol connoting neediness, incapacity, and special accommodation. To be "confined" to a wheelchair (as is still commonly said) is to lose metaphysical worth—*stature*—to say nothing of being bedridden. The very word "crip," now deployed both proudly and ironically across the disability community to protest ableist oppression, derives from the derogatory "cripple" as the most salient instance of bodily monstrosity and the grotesque. Crippled *means* defective, according to our dictionaries as much as our vernacular— inferior, weakened, corrupt—and limited locomotion may be said to strike at the core of legitimate adulthood as defined by standing on one's own two feet. This is precisely the conceit of Alfred Hitchcock's thriller *Rear Window* (1954), of course, in which L.B. "Jeff" Jeffries (Jimmy Stewart) famously suffers the indignity of a wheelchair, and the fussy ministrations of paramour Lisa (Grace Kelly), as another man across the courtyard throws off the yoke of unhappy marriage by murdering his wife. As Robert A. Rushing puts it, the "oppressiveness of [Jeff's] immobility" (38) is simply the manifestation of a "more dreadful, more permanent confinement"—both of which, disability and domesticity, threaten "man as the mobile sex" (39). Jeff's wheelchair is not simply a convenient adjustment to his severely broken leg; it is professional compromise, sexual frustration, and emphatically coded as feminized stasis.

How, then, do limping, wheelchair-using, bed-reclining detectives go about the business of solving crime? How do we reconcile the contradiction of sleuths whose functional body parts and movements are "pumped up to superhuman levels," as Andrew Jakubowicz and Helen Meekosha put it, even as those same bodies evoke ineffectuality, malignancy, even the "violent slashings and dismemberments" of crime fiction *victims* (Messent, 80–81)? Do they, in a psychoanalytic sense, represent a condensation of fear and its own assuagement? The "disembodied ratiocination" of detection, in Sally R. Munt's phrasing (93), inherent in the genre,[1] attains a kind of hyper-explicitness in stories where the body does not easily transport (or not at all) its thinking detective into crime space. If the so-called armchair sleuth solves puzzles purely by report, often from the safety of his or her own living room and with the help of others who do the physical fieldwork, stories of disability of movement, making that trope literal, *insist* on the detective's perceptual virtuosity.[2] They also extend a cultural imperative to redress physical damage through mental accomplishment: the smarter the sleuth, the less apparent need he or she has for the prosaic encumbrance of a body; and the worse off the body, the greater the pressure to excel in intellectually creative ways. Anne Holt has written that "female detectives, without the physical strength of their male counterparts, have to be more resourceful, intelligent and tactical to solve the case"; when she disables her character Hanne Wilhelmsen (in the eighth book of her series), the intent seems to be to make the discrepancy between body and mind all the more obvious, and so to exaggerate Wilhelmsen's psychological advantages over criminals.[3] Jeffery Deaver has been similarly quoted as saying that he wanted to create a purely cerebral character in Lincoln Rhyme, whose mind is "independent" of a "destroyed" body.[4] He crafts a detective who can, in effect, do nothing *but* think, one whose effectiveness as a forensic detective seems to derive exclusively from his ability to draw brilliant conclusions from extremely subtle clues. The image of a vital, intelligent man "strapped to a bed," a phrase that appears in several online reviews of Deaver's *The Bone Collector*, seems designed to provoke horror at the terrible incongruity, the shackling of investigative skill in an unwieldy, uncooperative physique—thus ensuring that we will marvel at, and feel relieved by, the detective's ultimate and intellectual triumph over his adversary.

In one way, then, mobility-impaired sleuths overstate a Cartesian duality that demands mastery of wayward bodies through awe-inspiring performances of inspiration and idea; they are also extreme displays of an equally extreme fear of helplessness, since those wounded bodies remind us so viscerally of the breakdown of law and order, manifest the disarray of wrongdoing, materialize anarchy. Limping, scarred, asymmetrical, bedridden bodies may work as visibly inscribed tales of bravery, injury alerting us to the detective's heartening determination to persevere (a putatively metaphysical endeavor), but the permanence of the conditions at issue in these stories also guarantees a discomfiting awareness of conflict and chaos, compromises the presumed hierarchies of mind over body, law over crime. The spectacle of bodies damaged by violence might justify detectives' own defense of the structures of law, but those same bodies, their inescapable physicality, prove by their existence just how tenuous a barricade against crime the law and police actually constitute. Representations of disability function along these conventional, metaphorical lines as a sign of vulnerability to danger—criminality infiltrates, gets close up to our bodies, cannot be forestalled even by law enforcers, even when the vulnerable bodies are their own. As Rhyme thinks of it, the events that injure and paralyze detectives are usually ones that divide "the Before," from "how ... life had changed After" (*The Vanished Man*, 2003; 161): such obvious hindrances to the detective's motion as presumably to interrupt the possibility of crime-solving altogether. The detective who prevails over violent incursion holds out at least the possibility that individual *consciousness*, provided with ample information, might conquer, or temporarily hold at bay, an ominous world against which we may feel, in all our bodily fragility, powerless to do battle.

What I will explore here is the fact that Rhyme's quadriplegia, as much as his powerful brain, is continually put before us—as is Anders's wooden leg, or Carver's cane and limp, impossible to separate from the people they are as detectives and integral to their particular epistemological habits. Mobility impairment cannot be overlooked (as blindness and deafness sometimes can). The big body, withered body, clumsy body, unmoving body, the body rooted in house/chair/bed—these are emphatically *noticed*. Visual impairment is often portrayed as an advantage to detection because low expectations of the blind tec means he or she can move quietly and unexpectedly in the dark; the lip-reading deaf detective has a similar stealth capability. Mobility-impaired detectives have a different sort of tactical edge as a result of canes and prosthetic limbs; as Hanne Wilhelmsen thinks of her wheelchair, "It defines me as something completely different from all the rest, and it is not uncommon for people to assume that I am stupid. Or deaf. People talk over my head, quite literally, and I simply lean back and close my eyes, it's as if I don't exist" (23)—a tendency that allows her to observe and listen for clues relatively ignored. Writing about Lincoln Rhyme, Jakubowicz and Meekosha point out that the disabled detective both reinforces the binary of an "all-knowing, all-cerebral/mindful" investigator who triumphs over his or her damaged body and "confounds the stereotype" of disabled people as objects rather than subjects of their own lives. Such contradictoriness suggests a *subversive* edge to the crip detective, whose presence in the story maps out a way of living through, rather than collapsing into, bodily harm. (It will be important to the discussions that follow to remember that detectives do not always abide by their creators' stated intentions.)

In this sense the mobility-impaired sleuth turns upside down the paradigm formulated by Walter Benjamin in which "the original social content of the detective story was the obliteration of the individual's traces in the big-city crowd." Benjamin argues of a story like Poe's "The Man of the Crowd" (1840) that urban anonymity obscures the distinction between the "pursuer" and the *flâneur*, "an unknown man who arranges his walk through London in such a way that he always remains in the middle of the crowd" (qtd. in Marcus, 247). Consider too a previous "Defence" of detective stories by G. K. Chesterton, author of the early twentieth-century Father Brown series, who writes that "no one can have failed to notice that in these stories the hero or the investigator crosses London with something of the loneliness and liberty of a prince" (4)—where "crossing" the city is obviously imagined as ambulatory and unassisted. The relationship between "writing and walking" that Laura Marcus cites as "central" to authors of anti-detective novels like Thomas Pynchon and Paul Auster consolidates, even in the context of postmodern resistance to crime fiction's inherently conservative, "consolatory" nature (Marcus, 260), an equally conservative equivalence between intellectualism and normative mobility. The detective who does *not* blend in, then, whose movement through space is distinct and remarkable, is by definition a "misfit"—I borrow this usage from Rosemarie Garland-Thomson—indecorous, inconvenient, *wrong*.

Detectives like Carver, Rhyme, Anders, and Wilhelmsen conduct themselves physically with at least some (sometimes great) difficulty, and their solutions are similarly cast as earned rather than intuited. They manifest *strain*, in fact. (The struggle involved in learning to blink one eyelid on command brings Sarah Oatland, in *The Whispering Wall*, to tears.) It is precisely this quality of specifically physical effort that interests me. I want to suggest that, despite the evident stereotypes at work in these tales, there is more going on than a contrived pile-up of hardship designed to highlight a detective's analytical decoding of mystery. When spaces become awkward, maddening, pain-inducing; when movement is curtailed, constrained, even denied; when an impaired body confronts the topography of an ableist environment or relies on someone else for both spatial and investigative assistance, detection becomes strikingly embodied, phenomenological, and partnered. If blind detectives represent dispersed knowing, deaf detectives a multilingual embodied knowing, the mobility-impaired detectives give us relentless deciphering, the clever paradox of "standing up" to crime and danger from the sitting and lying down of impairment. Solving crime is, after all, hard work, and in this effortful context, not despite the evident burden of damaged corporeality but rather *because* of that physical reality, the crip detective becomes a uniquely corporeal figure of figuring, offering alternative modes of understanding our bodies as they relate to what things *mean*.

The "basic assumption of the [classic] detective story," Brian McHale once wrote, is the "adequacy of reason" (15), but Andrew Pepper has countered that contemporary crime novelists "neither resolve their narratives in neat, contrived ways, nor give their protagonists the kinds of secure, whole identities that enable them to transcend the materiality of their lives" (212). The crip detectives are resolutely material: flesh that must be washed, bones that ache; composites of unwieldy limbs; sites of frustration but also unanticipated connection. They boast no otherwordly properties. Their limping is far from sinuous; they do not rise from chairs with balletic grace. They move through space clumsily or not at all; they jerk, they lurch, using canes and bulky wheelchairs; they lie, obdurate and unmoving, in bed. They have scars, they itch. A runny nose on a quadriplegic demands mention. No manner of mystical concentration animates paralyzed legs. And in these various forms and locations, the crip sleuths reconceive both spatial and relational dynamics in rhizomatic patterns. We are accustomed in societies dominated by patriarchal ableism to associate legitimate subjectivity with upright, active, and *controlled* embodiment that we go to great lengths (surgical, pharmaceutical, dietary, athletic) to ensure—thereby denying but never fully suppressing the physical "disorder" that Sharon L. Snyder calls "foundational to life" (280). Throughout the books I examine below, bodies disobey that imperative to move in expected fashion. When detectives, charged with corralling the disruptive, violate bodily and mobility norms, it is not just the clean boundaries of right and wrong that might come under question. What *is* normal, if the defenders of legality are themselves different, their motions jagged, their relationships mediated by corporeal need, their sense of space radically atypical? What is a staircase, for example, for a man with a cane? What is a living room, if it is where bowels are voided? What is a home where gory photographs of murder victims are displayed on the walls to facilitate the work of the paralyzed sleuth? What is a house, if the detective never actually leaves it—does it become an extension of the body, a complex analogue for the prison to which the criminal will be sent? Where do we locate crime, how do we boundary it, if we cannot run toward it in capture or flee it with swift and sure steps, and who is the detective whose relation to the spaces and action of crime-solution seems so unmanaged—or rather, overly so? The body that doesn't "make sense," that occupies spaces in these surprising ways, that may demand of others an unexpected or uncomfortable awareness of need and of vulnerability—one that is all the while invested with urgent responsibilities of defense and often involved in dramatic races against time to *figure it out* before another murder takes place—such a body raises a thoroughly cripistemological question about how, where, and with whose help we navigate the spatial, relational dimensions of experience.

Consider the fact that every instance of PI Fred Carver's movement is described as limping. Carver is gritty, sexual, and smart; his injury is a fact of his history and of experience that *could* factor naturalistically rather than symbolically into the decisions Carver makes. Yet he limps to the refrigerator, he limps to his car, he limps down or up a staircase, he limps toward or away from a criminal. The word is used so repeatedly throughout the Carver series that it is impossible not to notice or to wonder why the author forces the issue so thoroughly. In one way, the limp threatens to compromise Carver's stature as an able-bodied male in charge not only of his own motion but also of the danger from which he is meant to protect us. The person who tells Carver that "after [he] was shot, [he] had to prove [he] was more'n just a cripple people could write off" (*Hot*, 1992; 25) voices a bias that the disabled detective must do more, be stronger, work more fiercely than ever, because he is battling his own body as much as the perps he pursues. In another way, Carver's limp announces the PI's toughness; it must be remarked upon because it is what distinguishes Carver from everyone else, what gives his every action—from the most mundane chore to his romantic encounters to his pursuit of criminals—that extra layer of challenge, reminding us of what Carver has endured, of the pain and perseverance that define him as a figure in whom we can justifiably invest our trust.

But Carver's injured leg is something else again, an element of an embodied epistemology whereby bodily movement, including exertion, is inseparable from work, knowledge, identity, because it is what establishes us as the people we are, our private and our professional selves. It is true that Lutz, like other authors I discuss below, can't seem to take his eyes off his own character's impairment for the way it marks him as a certain kind of private eye. In this sense, and as we shall discover with other crip detectives, Carver's limp is an "artifice," in the terms David T. Mitchell and Sharon L. Snyder lay out in *Narrative Prosthesis*: a form of deviance that "binds" him to "a programmatic (even deterministic) identity" (50). But the detective himself has other ideas about what his impaired leg means to his job. Like all the sleuths represented here, Carver solves crimes in and with his body, and it is precisely because he limps everywhere he goes that he challenges rather than insists on the subordination of corporeality to cognition. Impairments of the type I explore in this chapter may exceptionalize characters within stories, but their permanence means something else for the narratives in which they exist. Crip detectives may solve crimes, but they do not solve their bodies. Disability endures in these texts. It becomes a new norm.

Nero Wolfe, Rex Stout's corpulent, orchid-loving, women-fearing, agoraphobic private investigator, does not strictly belong in a discussion of detectives whose mobility issues derive from gunshots and paralysis (indeed, he belongs, and has already appeared, in Sander Gilman's chapter on the fat detective in *Fat Boys*). I include Wolfe here because I read his exploits, with their emphasis on his bodily state and the relationship between that body and Wolfe's investigative method, as a precursor to those of later sleuths who also do their jobs in atypically stationary ways. Obesity, too—or rather, the stigma that attaches to being perceived as fat—has been increasingly subjected to the same social and discursive analyses that retrieve disability from the exclusive domain of medicine and critique ideals of embodiment as embedded in the fiction of ableism. Fatness, in the manner of other forms of physical difference understood as individualized problems, at once physiological and subject to moralized condemnations about behavior, is what Kathleen LeBesco refers to as "a *political* situation" (1): we can rethink the *obvious* correlation of "fat as bad" as a "social construction" (28), just as we understand disability to be constructed as, rather than *naturally*, a worse state of being than health and able-bodiedness. The representation of body size, then, aligns Nero Wolfe's relative stasis with that of later detectives paralyzed by injury or stroke.

Starring in thirty-nine novels and thirty-three short stories between 1934 and 1975, Wolfe does not leave his West 35th St. brownstone except in the direst of situations. ("I rarely leave my house," he says in *Before I Die* [1947]. "I would be an idiot to leave this chair, made to fit me.") Suspects, information, clues, material evidence, NYPD homicide detectives, even a district attorney—these are routinely brought *to* Wolfe, typically seated behind the desk of his office, by a cadre of paid assistants. Crimes get solved in that interior, often after a great deal of both talking and silent contemplation on Wolfe's part: he sits with eyes mostly closed while others chatter nervously or threaten him or deflect accusation in his presence, and then he plays the role of the grand revelator, the explicator. But while many fans of the series home in on Wolfe's seclusion as his signature oddity, it is his relative motionlessness that intrigues me here.

By his own account in *Fourth of July Picnic* (1957), Wolfe was born in Montenegro and spent fourteen years traveling the world. By the time he is established as a private detective in New York, that kind of inquisitive wanderlust is long in Wolfe's past and he is installed as a barely moving fixture in his brownstone. Though Archie Goodwin, Wolfe's "confidential assistant" and the narrator of each of Wolfe's tales, does not explicitly link his boss's inactivity to his physical size, the details pertaining to both seem revealing, as in *Silent Speaker* (1946), a novel at the start of the series, where Archie describes the detective in terms of "bulk" (15, 87) and "beam" (99) and where Wolfe has "made to order" chairs "with a guaranty for up to five hundred pounds" (8). It takes "eight yards of yellow silk" to make him a pair of pajamas (123); he is a "'large object'" that must be "'wedge[d]'" into a car (98). One police inspector addresses Wolfe as "'my fat friend'" (59), another taunts him with the promise, "'I'll help you lose some weight'" (101).[5] Unsurprisingly, the exertion of physical movement is also implied—Wolfe "brace[s] his palms" on his desk to stand up (77) and "heave[s]" (15) and "maneuver[s] himself into motion" (88). It is "unprecedented for him to move vertically except with the elevator" installed in his house (123). And Wolfe has a curious aversion to his own profession. He is, according to Archie, "'the greatest living private detective when he feels like working, which isn't often'" (9), an assessment Wolfe confirms: "'I don't like to work'" (13).

But in contrast to this coupling of size and both inertia and effort (a potential client says at the start of *Might as Well Be Dead* [1956] that he's been told Wolfe is "'too fat and lazy'" to take a case [139]), Wolfe's movements are often intriguingly small—even as his genius (read, *large*) "brain" requires regular "exercising," as he says more than once in *If Death Ever Slept* (1957). Though we are *told* that Wolfe moves from office to dining room to orchid room to bedroom on the three floors of his brownstone, we do not *witness* ambulation through that space; what we "see" is Wolfe "wiggl[ing] a finger" (*Silent Speaker*, 83, 107, 133) and "[bringing] his fingertips together" (87), just "perceptibly" shrugging his shoulders (106), upturning his palms, lifting an eyebrow. His "average on head-shaking was around an eighth of an inch to the right and the same distance to the left" (86). He "move[s] his eyes" over an assembled crowd (59). His eyes are but "half open" (37); he appears "sound asleep" (49). Archie links such kinetic minimalism to that abhorrence of expending any more energy than is absolutely necessary, but this collection of gestures also reads, curiously, like those of quadriplegic detective Lincoln Rhyme, to whom I turn below—just as Wolfe's stated preference for having people "at eye level" (*Might as Well Be Dead*, 178) invokes any number of texts by and about wheelchair users who complain about nondisabled insensitivity to matters of height.[6] Rhyme, like Wolfe, also gets a lot of work done with just his eyes, neck, and finger; and he is similarly bored when his mind is not sufficiently stimulated.

What, then, is the effect, not of Wolfe's various bodily eccentricities—since all the classic detectives have what Archie calls "kinks" (683) in *A Family Affair*, the last book of the series (1975)—but rather the concentration of Wolfe's physical motion to these few body parts? We cannot rightly deem Wolfe a supercrip, since he does not inspire the kind of condescending admiration for *anything* a disabled person does that is simply a screen for pity and fear. Is he, nevertheless, the kind of stereotype that Jakubowicz and Meekosha argue of Lincoln Rhyme: "brain at work"? To be sure, Wolfe's skill as a detective has little to do with chasing down suspects on the wild streets of Manhattan. As Archie says more than once throughout the oeuvre, Wolfe dominates the mock-inquests he stages in his household because he is smart. He listens, thinks, asks questions, "'reads faces'" (*The Silent Speaker*, 57). He has a renowned talent for "'manag[ing] to get something that no one else gets,'" as one police inspector grudgingly admits (99). An FBI agent acknowledges that Wolfe's interviewing techniques are "superior" (71). And as I mention above, Wolfe talks, prodigiously: in one moment "making an oration" (61), in another, "still doing a monologue" (62).

But there is more at stake here than a dichotomy of excess, between the skilled mind and the denigrated body—constantly before us in its difference, remarked upon by others, the "colossal corpus" in their midst (*Might as Well Be Dead*, 143), a peevish "hippopotamus" (208). J. Kenneth Van Dover has suggested that Wolfe's refusal to leave home or "violate his routines in order to facilitate an investigation" derives from an "extravagant" preoccupation with regularity and safety: "Instead of spreading the principles of order and justice throughout his society, Wolfe imposes them dogmatically and absolutely within the walls of his house ... and he invites those who are troubled by an incomprehensible and threatening environment to enter the controlled economy of the house and to discover there the source of disorder in their own lives." From this perspective, Wolfe's bodily stillness becomes part of a reassuring, even soothing, domestic space quite opposed to those workplaces and apartments, the cars and stoops, where murder routinely occurs. This is not to say that Wolfe opens his brownstone as a refuge to others or that crime is in any way denied within its walls.[7] In fact, discussion of crime, pondering crime, untangling crime is essentially *all* that happens at W. 35th St. But in this regulated environment, bodies are allowed to behave in unregulated, non-normative ways. Sexualized, *busy* maleness—of the sort that gumshoe Archie embodies—happens beyond Wolfe's walls; inside is the languid tending of flowers, meals eaten slowly at Wolfe's preferred times, the meaningfulness of subtle gesture rather than muscular force. The issue may be less that Wolfe is all brain and static body than that the quiet of his body models a way of learning about what goes on "out there" that is intensively communicative and interpersonal, and which is also a highly particular, atypically masculine mode of occupying space.

The message of the Wolfe collection is to great extent quite conventional, if also problematic in obvious ways: as long as you're smart, wealthy, white, and male, you can behave as oddly as your fancy strikes you—buying and selling rare flowers, refusing to shake hands, outfitting your bedroom in black and yellow silk. But I want to argue for the importance of the detective's reliance on a community of loyal others and the intimacy he encourages, primarily between his physical needs and Archie's. Wolfe could not do his job—not in the way he prefers—without that cast of operatives around him. Archie, as the live-in confidential assistant, has the greatest proximity to Wolfe in their bodily routines: they take meals; they move around and in view of each other in the office they share; they exchange paperwork, letters and checks to be signed. Wolfe says openly to a client worried about speaking in front of Archie that the assistant is his ears, making the notion of confidentiality specifically corporeal—what disability scholars refer to as intercorporeality. More, far from suggesting that Wolfe needs the younger, more athletic man to somehow complete him or to compensate for Wolfe's own physical limitations, the stories present Wolfe and Archie as both dramatically different and affectionately companionable bodies-in-space who work with a finely tuned and unquestioned corporeal synergy to solve the cases that come to them.

It goes without saying that Wolfe's physical condition, if not entirely explained (he is a gourmand, but that is not the same as quantifying how much he eats), is nonetheless not involuntary: he makes choices that other detectives included here cannot. After losing some weight in *Not Quite Dead Enough* (1942) in solidarity with wartime rations, for instance, Wolfe is so distinctly not "himself" that he promptly gains it back again. Still, he has bequeathed certain characteristics to much more recent investigators impaired by accident—a generic inheritance that offers a provocative way to frame the quality of conditions like paralysis. Gilman contends that throughout the twentieth century the fat detective, counterpart to the "lean and hungry" thin philosopher, came to be associated with "the emotional, elemental, intuitive, and empathetic ... a form of judgment, oftentimes more compelling than 'pure' rationality" (189). Though I have focused here more on Wolfe's movement style than his size, I am interested in this concept of an embodied thinking in its connection to the investigative habits of detectives with more permanent forms of physical inactivity. The question I want to explore isn't whether

Wolfe's crime-solving legatees are also empathetic and intuitive, necessarily, but whether they get the job done in similarly communal fashion, and whether that quality of interdependence cuts through more predictable metaphors of "pure rationality" imprisoned in dead, useless bodies.

Patricia Carlon's *The Whispering Wall* was the Australian author's twelfth crime novel, but the first to introduce her to US audiences when it was reissued by Soho Press in 1996.[8] Only when Carlon died in 2002, at the age of 75, did relatives reveal that she had been deaf since childhood; no one, including her publishers, had been aware of that biographical detail. Fans in Australia were quick to latch onto deafness as explanatory context for Carlon's plots, which feature girls and women in isolated, perilous positions: one trapped in a kitchen, another in a vault, another blind, still another recovering from severe stroke. It is the latter circumstance that lends *The Whispering Wall* its unnerving quality, as the heroine Sarah, fully alert but unable to move or speak, overhears through the thin walls of her house a murder being planned. The suspense of the novel derives entirely from the question of how Sarah will communicate to others—since it seems obvious from the start that she *will*—the danger mounting in their midst.

Such a scenario epitomizes the spotlighting of mental powers over the prosaic fact of corporeality, but in Sarah's case the issue isn't figuring out the crime—since the crime, and its perpetrators, are known from the start—but rather how to take advantage of the embodied relationships within which the sleuth exists. The compelling aspect of *The Whispering Wall* is its emphasis on bodies as fundamental to communication with others and the demonstration of how thoroughly relational experience is: if Sarah needs some part of her body to make contact, she also can't do so without someone to make contact *to*. Intriguingly, given the fact that here, as in other Carlon novels, the heroine seems excessively vulnerable and alone, the author seems interested in the dynamics of society as much as the functionality of communication. The resolution of the conspiracy depends in large part on the willingness of others to interact with Sarah open-mindedly—not only to believe that she is still "in there," as the cliché about paralysis goes, but also to read her subtle body language.

Sixty-year-old Sarah Oatland has had a severe stroke, and is being cared for in her home by a nurse, Bragg. Complications begin when Sarah's avaricious niece Gwenyth decides to rent out two downstairs flats, one to a single woman with a young daughter named Rose, the other to a married couple, Mr. and Mrs. Phipps, who plan to murder Valma Phipps's stepfather for inheritance money. Sarah spends her time in her bedroom, being bathed, fed, moved, and spoken to by Bragg, and thinking. We know from the first words of the text that Sarah is very much aware of her circumstances, that she resents being referred to as a "mere lifeless fish on a slab" (3), "motionless human dough" (27), and also that imagination, "about all that was left to her," is her "shield against pain and weariness and despair" (18). The setting capitalizes on obvious elements of fright—it is a household dominated by vulnerable and/or untrustworthy women and one singularly sinister man—but it also quickly subverts our expectations by making the least likely subject of anyone's respect or admiration the heroine of the book. Despite how interiorized she seems, Sarah is the surprising hub of the novel's action. Bragg is highly attuned to her physical aspect, discerning at a glance whether or not Sarah has had a good night's sleep. The child Rose is the first to realize that Sarah is listening. The niece grudgingly acknowledges that her motionless aunt still owns the house she wishes she could sell. Even the would-be murderer Phipps is trained on the "corpse" upstairs—he uses the word repeatedly in reference to Sarah, three times on one page alone (22)—for the role she might play in his scheme.

Interestingly, the novel opens with Sarah remembering a book about another stroke "victim" who "recover[s] in the end," "[comes] back to movement and living" (3). Two things strike me about this detail as a premise for *The Whispering Wall*, given that Sarah does not "recover" this way by this novel's end. One is the equation between aliveness and mobility, the other the primacy of reading as a source of hope. If Sarah derives a form of ableist solace in the promise of full recovery in the form of movement of her limbs, a reader of Carlon's novel might feel differently reassured by this story of a woman who interrupts a murderous plot with the blinking of one eyelid. And this is more than a gimmick, in Carlon's handling of it, so concerned is *The Whispering Wall* to intervene in the attitude that renders a severely impaired woman less viable than "'a vegetable'" (5). Just pages in, Sarah complains (inwardly, of course) about the implicit equation between rational humanity and speed. To be alive isn't just to move; it is to move *quickly*. "If you'd only wait, give me time to relax, to force my lids up and down," Sarah thinks, hearing Bragg tell someone that they have tried to get Sarah to communicate by wiggling a finger or winking an eye—"but you go too fast" (12). Once we realize, with Sarah, that a murder is being hatched, the urgency of the generic race-against-time trope ratchets upward—but with a difference. Sarah *can* hear and comprehend, and it is able-bodied impatience that hinders her capacity to let others know as much. She must figure out how to get those around her to slow down and pay attention—in effect, to operate on *her* terms rather than theirs—precisely as the unsafe situation in the house gains momentum.

It is perhaps the least plausible aspect of the plot that the murderous Phipps takes so much into account the woman unable to speak or move upstairs when he is planning to bump off his stepfather-in-law, Roderick Palmer, in a separate flat downstairs. Before anyone but readers knows that Sarah is fully cognizant of what is going on around her, Phipps guesses as much, putting Sarah in as much danger as Palmer. This is obviously a device to amplify fear—as Sarah thinks to herself, "I couldn't even stop them killing me, if they find out I know" (80)—but the intensive focus on Sarah as the pivotal member of the household also demonstrates how fully *present* she is, however "lifeless" (134) she might appear. Well before she begins to make herself known by blinking, Sarah is being taken seriously—deadly so. That is the paradox that Carlon stages to give the lie to mobility as well as conventional modes of dialogue as defining features of personhood. As Bragg whispers, once the interactive quality of Sarah's blinking becomes evident, "'Oh yes, I never talked to you just for nothing, Mrs. Oatland'" (115). Assuming the continuity of Sarah's selfhood from the start, Bragg was always *conversing*, not simply monologuing.

Indeed, the key throughout *The Whispering Wall* is precisely *exchange*. Rose, yearning for attention, does not simply talk *at* Sarah; the two have important bodily interactions, as when Sarah responds to Rose's "anxious little face" with "two answering winks," intended "to reassure," and is "rewarded by a beaming smile, and a lifting of the anxious frown" (81). It is Palmer, the potential victim, now Sarah's bedside companion, who devises a "game" to entertain her and encourage dialogue (132)—a form of facilitated communication, first with a written alphabet and later with Scrabble tiles, that leads eventually to the words "murder" and "mystery." This is painstaking interchange, requiring patience and commitment on the part of Sarah's interlocutors, and a good deal of surmising, spoken out loud, to which Sarah is invited to consent or not. The fact that suspicious happenings in the house are described or discussed in front of Sarah, who is then asked for her reaction, indicates how central she becomes to the thwarting of Phipps's evil machinations. Like Nero Wolfe, who also but far more vocally commands a room and draws people and information to him, Sarah Oatland is the center of physical and cognitive action. "'You seem to know more of what's going on in this house,'" Palmer says, "'than the rest of us put together'" (159).

Carlon's novel is not without its hints of normative bias. Palmer's remark that Sarah might "'even study French grammar'" (120) does smack of the overly upbeat encouragement of a nondisabled person dispelling his own fear at the spectacle of mortality. The effort required to make herself known, the frustration of not being able to move at will, do fill Sarah with "fury" (131). Perhaps it is the accumulation of rage and exhaustion that produces, at just the right moment, one guttural scream, "a strange, horrible noise" (198), "that dreadful unvoiced cry" (199), that draws Rose to investigate what is going on upstairs. And perhaps, too, this is why Carlon grants Sarah the glimmer of a happy ending—because the specter of a paralyzed, solitary woman, even one capable of preventing murder, is finally too grim to endure untempered by hope. So, at the last, Sarah "lay there, quite content, not even regretting her lost voice. It had come when it was needed and it would come again, she was sure, and others things, too—the first faint stirrings of life through limbs and spine and body" (200). The final words of the novel are Roderick Palmer's, letting niece Gwenyth know that he has fallen in love with her (still) immobile aunt. So the disabled woman is retrieved from the very brink of illegitimacy by a narrative of progress, toward conventional romance and health, and the proper order of things is restored: crime squashed, the house returned to domestic stability.

Yet *The Whispering Wall* is a closed-house mystery with a twist. The conundrum for the "sleuth" in question here isn't just that she can't access crime-space in order to gather clues, for she occupies the very space where crime is about to happen, and can't escape it. Space is thus violently endangered—the very definition of criminal transgression of boundaries—and the protection of that space requires exceptional alertness on the part of Sarah's friends as she struggles to make known the threat of murder. It takes Bragg's concern, Rose's intrepid courage, and the opportune arrival of a family doctor, to save Sarah and Palmer as they lie, one paralyzed and awake, the other drugged and asleep, in a room being filled with gas. The stakes are high for our heroine, but also for the author, who may be urging her readers to pay more careful attention to a person who *seems* "inert" and unresponsive (like a deaf girl?); such a person might be actually and actively foiling a murder plot. The fact is that lives *are* at stake—or to put this differently, how we conceive of what it means to be alive at all. Bodies cannot be ignored or neglected. The mystery that gets solved by someone like Sarah Oatland has far less to do with her uncooperative body than with nondisabled habits of communication.[9] What really animates her in the end is not that she regains mobility but rather that others recognize her "desires and wishes" (116)— what they are, that she has them—and initiate conversation as a result.

Some twenty years after Sarah Oatland solves a crime by blinking—to slightly overstate the case—another detective operates largely from bed to nab Manhattan's creepiest serial killers. To borrow from several of his own titles, Jeffery Deaver is a collector of violated bodies. From *The Bone Collector* (1997) to *The Skin Collector* (2014) and beyond, Deaver's Lincoln Rhyme novels feature not only an assortment of tortured, mutilated, and otherwise anatomized victims but also the quadriplegic forensic analyst hero and his protégé (later fiancé) Amelia Sachs, an NYPD detective who is "plagued" (*BC*, 9) and "tormented" (*The Coffin Dancer*, 1998; 116) by chronic arthritis. In a prefatory note to readers at the start of a 2014 reprinting of *The Bone Collector*, Deaver explains that he set out to outdo Sherlock Holmes with a detective who "solve[s] crimes not with guns, martial arts, and quips, but with his mind." Quadriplegia—Rhyme's neck is broken by an oak beam during an investigation of murder at a subway construction site—"leaves [Rhyme] with only his rational thinking as a weapon." By way of explaining Rhyme's popularity, Deaver writes that "he represents all of us, in a way. Aren't we really our minds and hearts and spirits before we're our bodies? Those are what let us rise to meet the challenges we face every day, whatever limitations dog us."

Such an account of Rhyme's genesis makes the metaphorical function of disability in these novels patently obvious. To demonstrate his conviction in a disembodied and immaterial selfhood, Deaver simply paralyzes the body; to emphasize the sleuth's superior powers of intellect, he negates corporeality as a meaningful component in the formation of thought (the science fiction trope of alien super-brains suspended in glass jars is but a caricature of Deaver's essential plotline). If readers were inclined to receive Rhyme as a testament to disability rights and the possibility of meaningful experience after traumatic injury, the author's own statements—that it takes an enduring and uplifted spirit to prevail over catastrophic bodily damage—smack of the worst sort of ableist cliché. The neat separation of body from self also works to explain the determination that Sachs displays when arthritis pain threatens to interrupt her mental focus at a crime scene. She too is a crime-solving mind whose corporeal damage can be "overcome"—that shibboleth of the rhetorical triumph paradigm—by willpower.

If impairment is to be used to heighten our appreciation of a detective's triumph over deadly crime, so too will the effort of that enterprise inevitably be exaggerated. As *The Bone Collector* opens, Rhyme is planning assisted suicide, a desire presented as both a comprehensible reaction to calamitous injury and proof of Rhyme's ruggedly attractive individuality—this is a man who takes matters into his own hands, even when his left ring finger is the only body part below the neck that he can move, and such a man is one we want on our side in the battle against crime. When Rhyme asks Sachs at the start of the series to survey the crime scene that proves a serial killer is at work, she is herself on the brink of requesting a medical transfer out of Patrol because of the severity of her arthritis. Both bodies are under duress, somehow unsuited to the rigors of the profession, its demanding strain on joints, skeleton, muscles that cramp and tremble—which makes the fact of their labors, and their success, all the more impressive.

Or consider Rhyme's explanation in *The Bone Collector* of his ability to breathe on his own. "'Let me tell you about challenges,'" he says to Sachs as she tries to convince him not to take his own life:

> "I was on a ventilator for a year. See the tracheostomy scar on my neck? Well, through positive-pressure breathing exercises—and the greatest willpower I could muster—I managed to get off the machine. In fact I've got lungs like nobody's business. They're as strong as yours. In a C4 quad that's one for the books, Sachs. It consumed my life for eight months. Do you understand what I'm saying? Eight months just to handle a basic animal function. I'm not talking about painting the Sistine Chapel or playing the violin. I'm talking about fucking *breathing*." (373)

Breathing is, under "normal" circumstances, autonomic, largely unconscious; the effort of "wean[ing] himself off the ventilator" (43) is heroic, adult, and deliberate, requiring concentration and a sense of the future. Would Sachs be attracted to Rhyme if he could *not* breathe on his own?[10] Could he solve crimes if he could not speak? (Sarah Oatland does.) Talking—in some sense the epitome of specifically *human* consciousness—guarantees Rhyme as a viable hero, but so does the impressive display of his willpower. Because Rhyme could not will his limbs to move, it seems especially important to cast his breathing in terms of domination over some part of his body; he is "as much a hunter as the falcons on his window ledge" (*CD*, 531), damaged goods and deadly bird of prey, wrestling his body into some form of obedience to his masterful resolve. Given the extent of his physical damage, Rhyme is a unique, special case, set apart from the average run of paralytics, "one for the books." He is "Lincoln Rhyme, the crip with the killer lungs" (*BC*, 58).

By the third book of the series, *The Vanished Man*, Rhyme is spending "at least an hour most days exercising … to keep his muscles in shape for the day when a cure was possible" (161)—exercises he "pursu[es] *fanatically*" (379; my italics). This book goes so far as to name Christopher Reeve, the actor whose reaction to his spinal cord injury in a riding accident provoked outrage from activists for whom Reeve typifies both ableist horror at the specter of severe impairment and the insidious prevalence of triumphalist narratives about cure.[11] Rhyme's faith in the powers of science to correct his impairment, even slightly, signals the medical model, which situates disability as individualized bodily failure rather than a matter of social organization. It is true that Rhyme resents the embarrassed response "most people" have to the sight of a quadriplegic (*CD*, 64), that he wearies of the long list of indignities experienced in "the life of the disabled" (*The Steel Kiss*, 2016; 304). Still, it is in keeping with the logic of the medical model that Rhyme's body is presented in terms of diminishment—a "destroyed" encumbrance to his identity whereby he is "betrayed," reduced to "merely a portion of a human being" (*CD*, 286, 64, 65)—and that by the time of *Steel Kiss*, both Rhyme and Sachs have undergone surgeries to lessen discomfort and/or improve range of motion: more mobility is always better than less. To drive the ableist point home, at the end of *Steel Kiss*, Rhyme (visiting Sachs's mother in the hospital) enjoys a self-congratulatory thrill at "moving breezily down the hall" in a wheelchair, feeling himself to be "more fortunate" than the bedridden patients he passes (481).

This is the basic conservative arc of the series. Lincoln Rhyme's impairments are severe and unignorable, but he is not just withered legs beneath a blanket or beside a box of adult diapers; he has the stamina, grit, and courage to contest the dual "problems" of both his body and crime. This is why we are told that if Rhyme is not "muscular," he nonetheless has "a body of a young man" (*CD*, 208–09), that "once you overlooked his damaged body you saw what a handsome man he was" (232). This is also why Amelia Sachs is not simply a smart detective who falls in love with a quadriplegic; she is a "tall, redheaded former fashion model" (*VM*, 4) who prevails through surgery and has a reputation for going where "not a lot of people would've gone," down into the "dark 'n' cold" of bloody crime scenes (*SK*, 16–17). Such details reward readers' trust that as long as we persevere through pain, never capitulating to narratives of weakness, doctors will figure out how to recuperate our fragile embodiment, even reward our naïve faith in love stories.

Yet disability gives the lie to the confines of these familiar narrative shapes. Whatever metaphysical point Deaver thought to achieve in the symbolic exclusion of Rhyme's physicality from his sleuthing is undone by that very body, because the forms of interaction and communication that Rhyme's condition necessitates will always subvert conventional binaries. For who is Lincoln Rhyme: all mental "essence," as one suspect believes (*CD*, 424); or one of the over-compensating "serious crips, real crips, *macho* crips" who disdain modesty and measure self-worth in outputs of urine (*BC*, 42); or a far more complex being who is catheterized "with K-Y jelly four times a day" (*BC*, 41) and writes textbooks on criminal forensic science? Though Rhyme's character tends to teeter uneasily between the first two of these stereotypes—demonstrating, I think, Deaver's own inconsistency about the nature of disabled experience—the sleuthing methods that develop between Rhyme, Sachs, and the rest of their team *as a result* of Rhyme's injuries play out a very different narrative about embodiment and work.

Prior to his accident, Lincoln Rhyme was revered as the city's preeminent analyst of forensic data; he literally wrote the book. This specialty allows Rhyme to continue to consult with the police force post-injury, since he can review information from his town house as readily as he could from a precinct.

In fact, given the wealth that is everywhere implied, Rhyme simply recreates a sophisticated computer lab, worthy of a "space shuttle" (*BC*, 35), at home, where cops, attorneys, witnesses, and suspects gather under Rhyme's authority (hints of Nero Wolfe are obvious). It is this practice of coming together in a space that defies exact definition—it is referred to, quaintly, as a parlor, yet it is also "a forensic lab that would be the envy of many a small- or even medium-sized police department" (*SK*, 38)—that exemplifies the crip-detective style I'm investigating here. Paralysis is the hinge between the imaginative attunement of Rhyme's crime-solving partnership with Sachs and the blurring of spatial boundaries that tends to link detectives and criminals in their transgression of thresholds. In urban settings particularly, perpetrators and cops alike are on the move. The distinguishing feature of how Rhyme and Sachs solve crime is an intense, intimate, physical connection that extends Rhyme's body into spaces he could not otherwise easily access and brings details of the unfolding crime narrative back into that ambiguously interiorized domain of his "den."

In *The Vanished Man*, we learn that "before his accident Lincoln Rhyme ... had run most scenes alone and he insisted that Amelia Sachs do the same" (23). Thus Sachs travels to grimy boiler rooms and airplane hangars and fiery church cellars, places Rhyme can't get to even in his hi-tech chair, attached to Rhyme through a headset, to learn to "walk a grid" (113): meticulous square-foot pacing of a crime scene, gathering forensics, eyes like laser beams trained on the minutest of details—dust oddly swept, a single strand of hair, a stray scrap of paper. But she isn't *exactly* walking the grid "alone," given the sensory contact with Rhyme. Quite apart from the romantic relationship that develops between them, their working dynamic is powerfully intimate, their voices transmitted to each other's ears, Rhyme visualizing back at his townhouse what Sachs sees, Sachs performing Rhyme's spoken instructions as she paces the scene.

When we remember that Rhyme and Sachs begin working together because he convinces her to rescind her request for a medical transfer, the predication of their partnership on that willful tenacity about *doing it anyway* may seem paramount. But I would emphasize another dimension to the relationship, where vulnerable corporeality signifies the opportunity for collaboration and a kind of interactive thought-processing rather than simple adversity to be mastered. Leroy L. Panek writes that "the single most enduring theme of the police novel has been the solace provided to the individual by belonging" (170). Rhyme and Sachs become the detectives they are in this series *because* Rhyme's limited mobility invites those around him to amend their expectations about what it means to work a case. In the sense that Rhyme's paralysis makes the group effort inherent in any police procedural more noticeable, disability initiates a correction of sorts, to the lone-wolf trope of hard-boiled detection where the sleuth's emotional damage makes him an unreliable romantic partner or parent but an invincible force of truth and justice. Just how meaningful the "parlor" and all that happens there is to the solving of crime becomes explicit in *The Steel Kiss*, which opens with Rhyme having temporarily retired from his consulting position with the police force to teach. Sachs, now promoted to Major Cases and musing on these various changes, "misse[s] the stimulation of the give-and-take, the head-butting, the creativity that flourished from the gestalt." "The information was the same," she thinks of running scenes without Rhyme, "but the process of loading it into your brain was diminished" (55). "Cases [aren't] progressing" (56) because, beyond "Rhyme's parlor" (57), a space whose every detail is determined by the extent of one person's impairment, the whole team falters. The very act of *thinking* is compromised outside of that embodied dynamic.

It is too easy, finally, to read Rhyme as the suffering genius shackled by a useless body that deprives him of his masculinity and his agency, Sachs as the leggy beauty subordinated to Rhyme's tutelage and expertise, as Jakubowicz and Meekosha suggest, writing that Sachs "is the body … through which Rhyme will redeem himself again." From this perspective, Rhyme is a brilliant criminalist in his disabled state only because he has a functioning, supplemental body at his disposal; it says nothing about the ways in which Rhyme is himself emphatically embodied and Sachs a similarly potent intelligence. The crucial point is not whether Rhyme can continue to perform as a criminalist (or as a lover, or as a man) *in spite of* his extensive impairments, as Deaver's own comments might lead us to believe, but rather that Rhyme becomes who he is in these books *because* of them. Disability—and, I would add, pain, to the extent that Sachs experiences it from arthritis—is not eradicated through narrative closure. To the contrary: it is the ongoing foundation of work and self. Disability doesn't get solved in the Lincoln Rhyme series. It is what creates the necessary conditions whereby detectives imagine their way into creative solutions. There may be no clearer example throughout the novels I study in this book of how disabled detection territorializes space—how space *comes into being*, just as bodyminds interacting also become something, to and through each other.

In the process of rearranging spaces, crip detectives tease out the implications of analeptic imagination that Charles J. Rzepka describes as foundational to crime narrative. The pleasure of the text, in this schema, lies not in the drive toward solution in the future, but rather in being sustained in imagining the multiple possibilities of what happened in the past. Crime fiction readers, Rzepka argues, engage in "prolonged" "invention" (30) as we move "*ahead*" in a text to consider the "array" of stories about what has happened "*behind*" us (26; italics in original). This is temporal movement, but we can link the narrative to-and-fro of deciphering to the physical actions of detectives whose movement through the described spaces of the story is distinctly nonlinear. A limp like PI Fred Carver's becomes the embodied equivalent of that moment-to-moment recreation of where we just were and how we might continue on from here. Whether we identify with the crip detective or not, his atypical movement is the organizing principle of the dual stories he controls— that is, both the crime story and the novel itself. Getting to the end of the one means understanding the start of the other, but a good tale, as Rzepka suggests, will have offered us any number of options for how to navigate that journey in between. Disabilities of the sort I am exploring here enact corporeally the interpretive array, focusing attention in unexpected locations and shifting, by dint of the body's needs, what is deemed worthy of notice. In this sense, a detective like Carver powerfully resists the narrative lure of "inspired observation" (Rzepka, 158), as well as the expectation that detective stories have "plots that progress and resolve."[12] If we only solve narrative crime by moment-to-moment reinvention, Carver presents a related notion that we only get from here to there by remaking the world to accommodate our bodies.

There is, in matters of plot and scene, nothing particularly unusual about John Lutz's Fred Carver series. The novels, set in central Florida, have a stylized early-1990s *noir* feel with straightforward crimes—drug running, familial revenge, suspicious deaths at a retirement facility—and plenty of clichés about Disney World, dive motels, and Florida weather (all the titles in the series refer in some way to heat). Carver's cases tend to sprawl. The PI is often on the move, driving from one city to another to investigate, and information is most often elicited from conversation (rather than, say, eye-straining microfilm research); like any detective worth his salt, Carver engages people easily, and plots unfold largely through dialogue. That dialogue relies heavily on slang and hard-boiled diction (sometimes cringe-inducing), and the characters are stereotyped in the extreme: the Mexican-Italian lieutenant Alfonso Desoto is "ethnic matinee-idol handsome," suitable for "the role of romantic bullfighter" (*Scorcher*, 1987; 5) or "an Aztec coin" (40); a girlfriend with sparkling eyes and curvaceous body walks with an "elegant sway of her hips" (*Flame*, 1990; 65); the slimy, gap-toothed, cussing conversationalist of a cop McGregor wears bad suits and dandruff; leering villains sport knives, necklaces of earlobes, flame-throwers, and undercover molls. Onto this high-gloss set enters PI Fred Carver, whose left knee, shot in a convenience store hold-up when Carver was an Orlando policeman, is now "bent at a thirty-degree angle for life" (*Flame*, 123). In his way, Carver is as much a type as any other character, a "hard sonuvabitch" (3) who announces his self-assurance and enduring vigor with every difficult step.

I have been suggesting that the mobility-impaired detectives return us to the phenomenology of our bodies not because (or not *only* because) disability metaphorically represents vulnerability to crime but because crime fiction tends toward an embodied epistemology even when ideation and reasoning seem paramount. The pleasures of knowing, of writing history, may motivate us to keep turning the pages of an unfolding set of causations and effects, but accompanied by detectives whose work involves making so much *contact* with physicality, we become engaged in a process of figuring that goes beyond (or perhaps it is more accurate to say gets underneath) the trope of lone, white, able men dependably restoring order with their powerful minds. Indeed, the surprise is how often forms of making physical contact can critique, perhaps subtly and often from within, the established order of things. As formally conventional as the Carver novels are, impairment keeps disrupting attempts to pin it against a clean backdrop of ideological significance—to make Carver's leg equal "damage," to read it as the uncomplicated sign of a "fucked up"/"tough guy" dichotomy, (*Kiss*, 159) where the PI's hard edge only thinly conceals his woundedness and pain. As I will explore here, though Carver's relationships with Desoto and McGregor keep him connected to the law and so operating primarily inside the system, the movements of his body become subversive nonetheless. Slyly—perhaps unwittingly—he demonstrates what it might mean to learn the world by touching it. His limp and cane elucidate the complexity of those territorialities in which Carver comes into being as a certain kind of knowing subject.

There is no denying something improbable about Lutz's representation of the limp, as if one slightly bent knee annuls Carver's entire lower half; the leg is not paralyzed, and yet he treats it like a "completely lifeless appendage" (*Flame*, 45). Carver is mismatched and awkward, his upper body made lithe and strong by daily ocean swims, his lower body an impediment that must be "dragg[ed] ... around" (*Scorcher*, 12). Exertion is the crux, as Carver "hobble[s] to the window" (15) or "drop[s] his leg from the desk with a solid *thump!*" (2). These are not incidental descriptions. The combination of lean upper-body strength and lower-body proof of stamina mirrors the combination of skill and resolve Carver will bring to his work on cases. It is the repetition that really startles. Consider an eight-page sequence from *Flame* in which Carver "limped across the deep red carpet" (76), "limped out to the gift shop" (77), "limped down the hall" (78), "limped from the room ... limped over to the box ... limped back to the car ... limped up a blacktop driveway" (81–82), then spends "fifteen minutes of limping through low underbrush" (83) and "limping through the woods" (84). It is only the nondisabled reader (or writer) for whom Carver's body would become such a static object of fascination. At some early point in this sequence, "limp" ceases to pertain to walking at all and takes on some other resonance. As the narrator in *Flame* sums it up, "maybe things shouldn't be *too* easy; whence would come character?" (84). Carver's limping signals the perseverance of a sturdy man in the face of random, pointless violence.[13]

Scholars of literary disability representation have long understood that ill and impaired bodies are occasions for emotion, instigating pity, disgust, compassion, or contempt to quantify the moral standing of nondisabled characters. As Martha Stoddard Holmes has written, disability "is melodramatic machinery, a simple tool for cranking open feelings" (3). In crime fiction, where victimized but also villainous bodies are easily referenced through anomalies of form and function, the dysfunctional detective both intensifies the fright we want and makes the relief we feel at the hero's victory all the more satisfying. Lutz gets a good deal of traction in this way from Carver's bodily condition. Several scenes in *Kiss*, for example, trade on readers' acquiescence to clichés of infirmity and defenselessness. In an altercation with a pathological killer, for instance, the threat of "both legs ruined, of completely immobility, made Carver frantic with fear" (154), and when the dastardly Dr. Pauly destroys his cane, Carver panics: "*Jesus! This was how it was to be crippled! Really crippled!*" (235). Such hysteria is unearned: in realistic terms, Carver is far from "really crippled" even without his cane. But as an already impaired and therefore compromised man, he is easily disarmed—unmanned entirely—by its loss, and thus both feels and is depicted to be unduly infantilized or debilitated, as he "crawl[s]" (235) to his cottage, "lurche[s]" to a chair, "sway[s] this way and that" (236), "crawl[s] to the phone" (238), and later *drags* himself across the ground.

Surely Lutz could have done sufficient research into lower-limb impairments to be precise about the extent of mobility a man with one damaged knee might be capable of. But my point isn't to rescue Carver from greater disability. It is to resist an uncritical deployment of impairment to ramp up urgency and fear. The fact is that while the author and the villains (even McGregor the cop) collude in reacting to Carver's "worthless leg" (*Kiss*, 155) as an easy target for sadism and pity, Carver himself just keeps going, "up and limping as fast as possible," for instance, "into the shadows," "plow[ing] through thick shrubbery" (*Scorcher*, 130). The idea that Carver does feel vulnerable "without his cane," as he reiterates in *Hot* (176), simply reminds us that his body is an amalgamated entity, prosthetically extendable in all sorts of useful ways that, if he were deprived of them, would affect but obviously not *neutralize* him. It matters that from the first books in the series, the injury to Carver's leg has a determining relationship to where the PI does and does not go, that the impairment that forces Carver away from policing propels him into whole new informational and geographical depths once he acquires his PI license: he takes trips the cops cannot, pursues leads the cops must avoid, comes into intimate bodily contact with the victimized, the bereaved, and the guilty that would be debarred from him entirely as a policeman.

So much narrative attention to Carver's limp also sets in high relief the relationship between space and movement, highlighting actions whose relative ease a nondisabled reader might take for granted. Getting out of his roomy Oldsmobile convertible, Carver "struggle[s] ... with his cane" (*Scorcher*, 52). He "negotiate[s]" a marble floor "carefully" (53). Elsewhere he "dig[s] the cane hard" into a hotel carpet (*Flame*, 100), "use[s] furniture and the wall for support" (44), and later "swivel[s] his body, shoving his stiff leg with both arms ... and manage[s] to sit up" (45). He doesn't just rise; rather like Nero Wolfe, he "lever[s] himself to his feet" (1). Socks "requir[e] effort," and pants entail an elaborate choreography of "half sitting, half lying" (*Kiss*, 104–05). These motions situate us in a defamiliarized space, one in which we cannot assume *a priori* knowledge of how things work, how long they will take to complete, what our connection to them rightly is or how much control over the environment we can expect to have. Focus is redirected. It is not that impairment in this sense represents the ubiquitous possibility of crime in our daily lives, but that, given that reality, the capacity to do things otherwise, that flexibility in maneuvering ourselves that Carver has learned so adeptly, serve us no matter what bodily condition we may be in.

Space becomes material in this context. We don't just notice Carver's body; we must notice the dynamic relationship between that body and its environment. To return to Deleuzean territoriality, space becomes what it is because of the life happening there. Carver's impairment may function to reveal something about the detective's temperament, his character, but it also changes the very nature of nature, of elevation, distance, earth and floor. Unbeknownst to Lutz, perhaps, Carver's manner of limping all over the place redefines the places he is in, because they shift to accommodate him, they receive him and his cane; his movement through them defines their edges and their quality slightly differently. The beach, the woods, the car, the store, the stairs: these are no longer what they were once Carver and his cane redefine the quality of their textures. The cane that slips on gravel or a slick path, measuring the resistance of such surfaces as unaccompanied footsteps might not, might also hook an arm, extend a man's reach to pull a violent bully away from a man he is beating. Landscape is modulated by Carver's experience of himself as an embodied man; he is often figured gazing out at the ocean, sunlight glinting on waves, but that setting is not uncomplicated for a man who moves "awkwardly" on sand (*Scorcher*, 259), a man who is now a PI rather than a cop due to injury, a man who well remembers the pain of a gunshot, one who feels whole *when* he carries his cane (*Flame*, 253)—that signature announcement of enfeeblement and loss.

In a class of characters defined from Chesterton to Auster as upright and ambulatory, Carver is a hybrid figure. Without his cane he is no less a "fucking gimp" than with it (*Kiss*, 241); with it, he is not quite a normative man. His body gives the lie to the typical characteristics and kinetics of "a self-consciously and aggressively male genre," as Dennis Porter puts it (112), exactly as Lincoln Rhyme's does. And like Rhyme, Carver too seems to hold out a fantasy of release—not from disability, but from the pressure to surmount our own fleshly selves. Carver is so evidently everyone, "worthless" and "ruined," "trudg[ing]" and "clomp[ing]" through an ordinary life (*Scorcher*, 253). And yet, the "pattern of deep depressions and narrow drag marks" he leaves behind him on his way across the beach is entirely his own footprint (*Scorcher*, 252). In these books that work so hard to delineate types—"Latin," black guy, woman, villain, man's man, government agent, gimp—Fred Carver limps his way straight out of normalcy.

If there is something slightly parodic about Carver, with his muscular biceps, his sunrise erections, his improbably debilitating bent left knee, he is also a working PI with a cane, and in this he defies a stereotype. Here is that subversiveness named by Jakubowicz and Meekosha in reference to Lincoln Rhyme, the cerebral/embodied detective with an obvious impairment that doesn't impede his professional identity. Marshall Browne's D.P. Anders, an Italian Interpol inspector with an artificial leg, similarly confounds expectations—including and especially those of his opponents. If a compensatory logic were to hold in the context of mobility impairment, the crip detective would need to prove creative or intellectual success, some other form of physical beauty or proficiency to transcend the brute reality of stubborn flesh that cannot be willed into motion. Anders is clever, to be sure, and his author hides his thinking from us so that we are held in suspense about what the inspector is planning up to the novel's climactic last pages. But he doesn't think faster or more subtly (let alone more magically) than others he encounters; to the contrary, he is surrounded by shrewd and canny cops, politicians, women, and mobsters. But he does keep *at it*. Anders *should* give up—he is longing to retire, and after all, "the nation's apparatus of power was impregnable" (26)—but he doesn't.

In the first of a three-book series, *The Wooden Leg of Inspector Anders* (1999), Anders is a closer of sorts. Semi-retired from the Ministry of the Interior, he is assigned to unsolved major cases; as the novel opens, he has been called to an unnamed city in the south to close the file, in an entirely *pro forma* way, on the murder of another inspector, one who had been investigating the assassination of a judge. Initially, Anders conducts his interviews perfunctorily; he intends to deliver the report everyone expects, blaming the murders on a resurgence of political rebellion rather than uncovering the real culprit, which is effectively the stranglehold of corruption on Italian society by the mafia and crooked government officials. In this sense, Anders is more like Sarah Oatland than Rhyme or Carver; the perpetrators of the crime are known to us from the beginning, and the suspense of the tale is thus generated from wondering whether, and how, Anders and his wooden leg will be able to exact some form of vengeance. Steadily, as Anders spends more time with the particulars of the case—with the judge's widow, with other policemen trying to stay afloat against waves of complacency and deceit, with an ineffectual police commissioner and a treacherous mayor, with an aging leftie writer and a sensual middle-aged bar proprietress (Anders's particular interest is in women who've "lived")—he finds himself caught up in the promise of change, in the seduction of "revers[ing] the direction of the nation's life. To strike a major blow. To do real damage" (144).

Anders's leg is the physical emblem of a sensibility that "'come[s] up to the work'" in the face of a nation "'stink[ing] with the failure of good men, with good intentions'" (138). Impairment is his badge of honor. By the end of the novel, this "'public hero'" (135) will be "a national hero twice over" (222): once for suppressing a group of leftist anarchists, the conflict in which he lost his lower left leg decades before the action of *Wooden Leg*, and here, for blowing up a roomful of southern Italy's most brutal mafiosi. Like detective Matucci's blond hair or the widow De Angelis's quick glances and chain-smoking, the leg identifies Anders: he is the "middle-aged, low-ranking, crippled police officer" (37), the "one-legged cop from Rome" (184). But unlike those other features, the leg is far more symbolically freighted. It is a "'sad disability'" (102) that announces Anders's dedication and "'sacrifice'" (102) to an honorable cause; when a sergeant feels its "artificial complexities" during a pat-down, he "'commiserat[es]'" but clearly also feels respect (54–55). Defeating anarchist terrorism in the mid-1980s "cost [Anders] his leg, his career" (12), and now, "at the end of his career ... [a] stale hero following unheroic, manipulated paths. ... [a] man who might've done more with his life. *If* he'd had the courage" (31), Anders will manipulate one of his spare prosthetic legs, packing it with explosives, to regain a sense of purpose and pride.

As Ato Quayson has argued, disability can operate at "different levels of the text," so that "even if programmatic roles were assigned, these roles can shift quite suddenly" (25). I would put this slightly differently in the context of Anders's disability. It is not so much that roles suddenly change—what meanings get attached to the wooden leg stay constant over the course of the novel—but those meanings differ according to relationship and position with the text. The "wooden leg with its steel innards of working parts" factors far more significantly in Anders's adversaries' imaginations and in the workings of plot than it does in the actual life of the detective, for whom the prosthesis is just "an old acquaintance" (10) and his "stump" (as it is usually called) just a part of his body that he cares for with the same deliberate attention that he brings to everything he does, from sex to sabotage. To at least one lover, the stump is a fetish (she has "an astonishing sexual fantasy" about it [166]), but for the two who dominate this novel, it seems hardly to register once its significance—as either a source of physical pain or a site of political sympathy—is dispensed with. I would argue that the cyborg leg, that human–mechanical hybrid, matters more to the men in Anders's life than to women who see it being removed, and that it matters specifically as a *concept* rather than a material thing; men don't care what it looks or feels like, only what they can make it signify in terms of Anders's presence in the city. The wooden leg thus operates at descriptive, relational, political, abstract, and narrative levels. That it names the very book it figures in assures us of its structural importance. We cannot read the book without looking for it.

What, then, does "the wooden leg of Inspector Anders" matter to this world-weary inspector's reluctant re-entry into the world of political confrontation? In physical terms, Anders is represented most often as walking the streets of the city (in this he does resemble Benjamin's *flâneur*, though he hardly disappears into the crowd) or in bed with women. One activity brings pleasure, the other pain; one puts him in constant danger of being attacked by his enemies, the other is his most profound act of "connecting with another human being, with their unique experiences, labyrinthine memories" (158)—in other words, an embodied other consciousness. Anders is unabashed about being watched as he removes the prosthesis, and he is described as an ardent and poetic lover. When Anders, "momentarily unbalanced by his disability ... toboggan[s] on their perspiration off her generous stomach," Cinzia the bar-owner laughs "quietly, deliciously," not derisively (65)—and this is the only instance in the novel of any such effect of his asymmetry. If anything, being relieved of the prosthesis seems an important component of the relaxed freedom of Anders's sexual behavior. In contrast, walking produces pain. With the exception of occasional taxi rides (and one final trip with mafiosi to the site of his "resurrect[ion]" as a hero [29]), Anders walks to his interviews, and the walking causes his stump to chafe against the prosthesis; as the novel proceeds, his leg begins "burning slightly most of the time" (101). It is a vulnerable site—but no more so than *any* body part stressed by repetitive motion or subject to injury in confrontation with "mafia thugs" (119).

Bodies *knowing* each other, then, is what *Wooden Leg* asks us to consider—the corporeality of relationship and vice versa; and Anders putting his own biomechanical form into motion to converse, discern, interpret the inscrutable answers he receives from cagy interlocutors; and body parts transforming into the ideological banner of solidarity or opposition. As I indicate above, the leg in its totality becomes more important for the assumptions others make about it than for any practical limitations it presents. Walking is not so much a functional problem for Anders as it is a habit that exposes him to risk, not because his *prosthesis* makes him physically vulnerable but because others' knowledge of it gives them—or so they assume—a tactical advantage over him: "A man with an artificial leg, moving about the streets, must always be in some danger" (106). Yet Anders perambulates through the city unharmed until the moment he manipulates his own abduction. His enemies misappraise both the danger he is in and the consequence of his prosthesis to his total person: "Anders supposed that they thought it quite normal for a one-legged man to be also one-handed" (96). In fact, his appendage will become the instrument of destroying the city's ruthless cabal, gathered for an extraordinary, gruesome exchange of power in one room in a concrete auditorium. Anders only walks with a truly "pronounced limp" (180) when he has packed the artificial leg with explosives. Only then does he seem to be "walking with great difficulty" (191), "in a strange way, even for him" (194); only then does he become dangerous to himself; only then does he allow himself to be captured. In a set of provocative reversals, walking is the preamble to triumph, not damage.

Proximity is key in this novel of the dark machinations of corruption, venality, and exploitation. There is something curious about the text's many expansions and contractions of space—from Anders's movement across the city, where in his quiet, methodical way, he absorbs information, confounding others with his "'air ... of private thoughts'" (80), his "hidden agenda" (195), his enigmatic inwardness (resonating again with Nero Wolfe); to interiors of bedrooms, cafés, cars, offices, libraries where conversations go nowhere and stymy the progress of truth; to the tiny windowless bathroom inside an auditorium where bodies explode in parts, anatomized and unrecognizable. What enrages the presumptive mafia boss is that "'one man, a crippled, retired man,'" could come "'this close!'" to the core of their power (212). It is Anders's leg—the stump and the prosthesis together, but also apart—that manufactures the most dramatic of all movement.

When the bomb goes off, Anders is barricaded in a bathroom, completely naked (he has been stripped in preparation for disemboweling by a pig butcher): "the pink, obscene stump of his left leg, ... his balls swinging, his penis flopping" (217). He becomes a hero in the least dignified of circumstances—or perhaps the scene invokes rebirth, the unadorned bareness of a man in the process of shucking the lassitude and fatigue of resignation and regaining a sense of authenticity. The absence of the "artificial" leg would seem obviously expressive, in this sense, but I would also suggest that whatever resurrection happens in that bathroom is a disabled one: which is to say, Anders does not emerge from the flying apart of dozens of criminal bodies a "whole" man, but rather an off-center, off-kilter one, a man no more "complete" than he was when he clomped up a flight of stairs in "comical" fashion (217) just minutes before his prosthesis explodes.

Tsvetan Todorov writes that in thrillers, as opposed to classic detective whodunits, "everything is possible, and the detective risks his health, if not his life" (47). Plots whose momentum is driven by what might be about to occur rather than the conundrum of what has already happened imperil the sleuth in especially fearsome ways. It is no coincidence, I think, that mysteries with mobility-impaired protagonists deploy *suspense* more often than retrospective ratiocination, given the particular symbolic entanglement of paralysis and problems of locomotion with vulnerability. Paralysis, the limp, the mismatched legs—these expose sleuths to danger and lay bare the fiction that violence can be controlled, and repetitive images of stasis and death work as a measure of fear about that ultimate truth. As Lincoln Rhyme thinks, "When you lie on your back frozen in place month after month after month, time slows to near-death" (*BC*, 80). Hanne Willhelmsen, the lesbian detective who makes her first appearance as a crip-ex-cop in *1222*, wonders if she has "swapped a vital, ambitious life for an existence in waiting" (274).

But importantly, the permanence of mobility impairment in the novels discussed here does not actually bring about a deathly stasis, even if it also *sustains* disability as an ontological condition.[14] The detectives in question do not get better. Their injuries do not heal, they do not progress, and they do not resolve. Inspector Anders, mobile as he is, longs to stay put; at the end of *Wooden Leg*, he has taken a room in a boarding house where, seated at a table, he will complete a book about a poet-ancestor, "the intensely personal detective work of thirty years" (224). We associate movement with arrival and change; these bodies may do neither. They *do*, however, eat, ambulate, blink, sit, screw, shit, touch, talk, wiggle, and feel. They tell us what we should know. And they make knowing *matter*.

Notes

1 For more on the "reasoning machine" trope, cf. Rzepka, 138.
2 In those tales where immobility is a temporary situation, the effect is simply amplification of an already understood deductive superiority. There are many single instances of armchair detection by an otherwise ambulatory investigator. Call it sickbed sleuthing—as in Agatha Christie's "The Mystery at Hunters Lodge," where a bedridden Hercule Poirot nearly solves a murder without leaving his room, or the *Monk* episode "Mr. Monk Stays in Bed," in which Monk *does* solve a murder from his sickbed (2005; 4.3), or the *Murder, She Wrote* episode "Crossed Up," in which Jessica Fletcher (Angela Lansbury), laid up

with back pain, solves a murder she has overheard being planned on crossed telephone lines without getting out of bed (1987; 3.13).

3. "Anne Holt's Top 10 Female Detectives," theguardian.com, Wednesday December 8, 2010. http://www.theguardian.com/books/2010/dec/08/anne-holt-top-10-female-detectives.

4. https://www.bookbrowse.com/author_interviews/full/index.cfm/author_number/192/jeffery-deaver.

5. Just how big is he? In *A Family Affair* Archie says he weighs a seventh of a ton—just under 300 pounds (713). He resembles Jackie Gleason, 308.

6. Cf. in particular Nancy Mair's collection of essays from 1996 entitled *Waist High in the World*.

7. Perhaps this is why the final story, *A Family Affair*, brings the violence right into the brownstone, and why this is the one story where Wolfe openly admits that he is in a rage, out of control.

8. Carlon could not have read Charlotte Perkins Gilman's *Unpunished* (written in the late 1920s but not published until 1997), but there are intriguing resonances. The novel concerns the murder of a sadistic brother-in-law/step-father, Wade Vaughn. Jim Hunt is the detective on the case, but the real sleuth of the story is Jacqueline "Jack" Warner, paralyzed and disfigured in a car accident, who overhears details leading to the solution of the crime through a listening device installed in her house. (Mrs. Todd, an elderly, infirm woman who watches the goings-on at the Vaughn house from her upstairs bedroom, also plays a part.) Jack is restored to beauty and mobility through surgery at the end of the novel, but she is instrumental to Hunt's detecting from her disabled and not her normative embodied state. Thanks go to my colleague Catherine Golden, co-editor of the 1997 edition, for calling this book to my attention.

9. Just as, in the contemporary Deaf movement, the "problem" is not an inability to hear but a hearing person's unwillingness to learn Sign.

10. In this particular context, cf. the work of disability activist Mark O'Brien, who became known for an essay called "On Seeing a Sex Surrogate," published by *The Sun* magazine in 1990. The movie based on that essay, *The Sessions*, was released in 1999.

11. Mary Johnson's *Make Them Go Away: Clint Eastwood, Christopher Reeve, and the Case against Disability Rights* (2003) is the definitive text on this controversy.

12. Linda Wertheimer interviewing Susie Steiner on NPR, Weekend Edition Saturday, July 16, 2016.

13 The counterpoint to Lutz's obsessive recording of the "limp" might be Richard Deming's 1950s bodyguard Manville Moon (who acts as an unofficial sleuth in three books from the early part of the decade). Moon has an artificial leg from a stevedore accident, but though it is mentioned a few times in each novel, it hardly factors in his movement or characterization. See *The Gallows in My Garden* (1952), *Tweak the Devil's Nose* (1953), and *Whistle Past the Graveyard* (published in the UK as *Give the Girl a Gun*, 1954). Published by Prologue, a division of F+W Media, Inc.

14 To some extent, suspension in embodiment accords with a standard feature of the mystery genre in general, which is that its hero-detectives do not tend to age or change. Rex Stout is quoted by biographer John McAleer as saying that his Nero Wolfe tales "have ignored time for thirty-nine years ... I didn't age the characters because I didn't want to" (49). Stout's reasoning has to do with training readers' attention on the mysteries rather than the people solving them; plot, in much classic detective fiction, supersedes character. In this sense, the unchanging disability becomes a dependable trait, part of the costume that readers can expect and that signals the reassuring presence of a mastermind. As Julian Symons similarly suggests of Holmes's various quirks, "attributes ... are really substitutes for characterization" (71), and as Snyder and Mitchell have contended in a different context, "the disabled body ... solidif[ies] a form of visual shorthand. Its appearance prompts a finite set of interpretive possibilities now readily recognizable to audiences" (*Cultural Locations*, 164).

5

The Missing Arm of the Law

Though less numerous than their blind, deaf, mobility-impaired, or neurodiverse counterparts, investigators with injury to hand or upper limb play an important role in an inventory of disability and detection. They embody a not-quite tongue-in-cheek pun, after all: what kind of safety does a sleuth provide if he or she is *unarmed*? To lack such an appendage would seem the very antithesis of what is meant by *the long arm of the law*, with its implication that the powers of the police and criminal justice system cast a wide and reliable net over wrongdoers. As I have been discussing throughout these chapters, impairments of different body parts are embedded in cultural narratives that mediate questions of order and truth in ways that are unique to their symbolism. Hands, with their distinguishing opposable thumbs; arms, with their connotations of both strength and embrace—these are aspects of the embodied self that signify dexterity, acculturation, and command (from *manus*, "hand" as well as "power"): in a word, humanness itself. The synecdoche of hand to person, an idiom that took hold in English in the nineteenth century, makes handedness a practical requirement of humanity: *all hands on deck*, we say, and know what we mean. In this context, injury to hands and arms is not just a dangerous hindrance to wielding a gun; it strikes at the integral relationship between personhood, work, and civil society that has been figured for centuries by this uniquely human appendage.

Much philosophical attention has been devoted to the eyes as the conduits of soul and intelligence. But the hand—as the site of distinctively human gestures like praying, shaking hands, or raising a fist in solidarity and protest—has its own representational history. In the writings of Zeno, open and closed hands signified the arts of rhetoric and logic. Kathryn L. Lynch notes that Aristotle "compares the hand to the soul" and that Galen praised the hand as God's "special gift" to humanity (33, 34). When Milton in "The Reason of Church-Government" attributed prose written during the English civil war years to his "left hand," vatic poetry to his right, he not only invoked a ready analogy of part to whole; he also rendered the sides of the body in hierarchical terms ("left" comes from *sinistra*, which gives us *sinister*, opposed to "righteousness"). Throughout early modern religious polemic, hands were an "important icon of subjectivity and divine teleology," as Justin Pepperney explains (217), used to depict the spiritual agency of martyrs, the cruelty of the wicked, and the transcendence of God's blessing. From Mosaic "hand for a hand" justice to the laying on of Jesus's healing, hands are linked to morality and religious law; a hand is placed on the Bible to swear an oath, not any other body part, and to lend a helping hand is as much an ethical as a bodily act. As Rosemarie Garland-Thomson writes, "the art of divination from observing the hand understands the body as a sign of character and a fleshly version of the soul" (*Staring*, 122). In eighteenth- and nineteenth-century English fiction, hands became compacted emblems of race, class, and gender norms, as scholars have shown, registering in such novels as *Pamela* and *Bleak House* a deep anxiety about the social contract and human exceptionalism. The trope of the hand reoriented in American labor activist art, capturing the "revolutionary Zeitgeist of the 1930s" in paintings and photographs boldly spotlighting workers' arms and hands in images of "symbolic contestation" (Fraser, "Hands Off"). Justice, of course, is even-handed (if also blind!), while being *handicapped* is to suffer a life of burden and disadvantage.

In a different but related vein, damaged and severed hands have figured prominently in Western popular culture from the medieval origins of folklore to contemporary comic books, often in the service of parables that aim to restrict bad behavior. Consider the multitudinous versions of the madman-with-a-hook horror story with which many a youthful camper has been inculcated in the dangers of too much individuality (striking off into the woods alone) or too much sex (getting stranded in a car on Lover's Lane). Pulp fiction and sci-fi/horror television are rife with crawling hands, monstrous hands, and evil-doing transplanted hands.[1] There is Captain Hook, of course, and *The Addams Family*'s Thing, and the captivating Darth Vader of the *Star Wars* saga, whose severed hand—representing his disobedience and alienation from Jedi community—is at once hidden and announced by the heavy leather gloves he wears upon turning to the so-called Dark Side. (In retribution for his injury, Vader later severs *both* hands of his nemesis.) There is Vader's heroic son Luke Skywalker, whose own lost hand (in a lightsaber duel with his father) is redeemed by a strikingly lifelike prosthetic, but also the over-anxious Byron "Buster" Bluth of *Arrested Development* (Fox, 2003–06), who loses his left hand to an aggressive seal in a storyline that uses dismemberment as a rough gag about Oedipal castration. A "One-Armed Man" haunts fugitive Dr. Richard Kimble in ABC's "The Fugitive" in the 1960s. An alive severed hand distinguishes David Tennant's tenth Dr. Who from the other nine before him. And so on.

In *Hallucinations*, Oliver Sacks writes that the experience of phantom limb—that oft-invoked if little understood sensation of presence in the place where an appendage once was—is far more prevalent in the case of missing hands than legs or feet. He proposes that the subtle movements and coordination required of hands (in addition to how often humans use them) activate the brain in concomitantly complex ways, so that the parts of the brain responsible for manual dexterity may remain more receptive to the signals of damaged nerves than those associated with other parts of the body. It makes sense, given this intricate and highly stimulated system, that a disembodied hand would generate a creepy effect of undead animation where a foot simply wouldn't, and that characters without two working hands would connote a very specific form of compromised subjectivity. Hands are hard-wired, so to speak, in our perceptual sense of self. We keep them alive even when they've been separated from the whole. We invest them with a kind of conscious self-awareness, imagining that they carry on moving, thinking, even missing *us*, as when one-armed Dan Fortune muses that "what's missing hurts more than anything else, especially when you're alone at night. Sometimes I find myself lying awake and wondering if the arm is still alive somewhere and missing me" (*Act of Fear*, 1967).[2]

Wounded, scarred, misshapen hands make a battleground of a single body, if the appendage most connected with the "ultimate authority" of reason and intellect, to quote Lynch again, bears upon it the evidence of chaos and misrule (34). And yet both the artificiality of prosthetics and the empty fall of a sleeve ask us to consider how sure we are of humanity's priority in the first place. If hands separate humans from animals, their existence a ready reminder of the potential *handicraft* of human ingenuity, they are also always under threat of replacement, first by machinery and later by digital technology. Maybe more troubling, hands may actually be irrelevant to the status of human, as evidenced by the ongoing work of one-armed sleuths and their specifically order-restoring work. The loss of a hand is thus over-determined. It may signify a downward disorganization that the hybrid body of the sleuth exhibits but can never fully repair; or the threat of obsolescence (it is no coincidence that these texts repeatedly feature the mangled and/or auxiliary hand as a convenient trope of interpersonal and professional uselessness); or opportunity, for differently crafted selves, professions, and realities. If dexterity (from *dexter*, meaning "right hand") implies adroit skillfulness and mental aptitude, manual impairment may actually explode the link between justice and handedness by challenging what we require of symmetry and balance.

Perhaps more than any other condition I explore in this study, manual impairment in the context of crime is bound up with what is "missing," with empty space and questions of *fit*, which explains an emphasis in these texts on social worlds rather than individual sleuthing genius—even if the one-handed detective is the only one of his or her kind in the novel. Ours is a "romance with double-handedness," in Garland-Thomson's words (123), and even the most "cunningly made" prosthetic hand will reveal its artificiality—"every mechanical hand invokes a drama" (128). As PI John Kenneth Galbraith Jantarro declares of his own prosthesis in Simon Ritchie's 1989 *Work for a Dead Man*: "made to resemble the real thing, but in fact a tube of wires and levers and motors and myoelectric switches that more properly belongs in a factory than on anyone's shoulder" (6). P. D. James has claimed that the pleasure of crime fiction lies in the fact that "*human* ingenuity, human intelligence and human courage," rather than "luck or divine intervention," solve problems (174; my italics). Can an artificial hand—or worse, the claw *pretending* to be a hand—ever provide such "reassuring relief"? Given a tight symbolic link between hands and human authenticity and agency, that simultaneity of the crafted and the organic, the absence and the excess, sets the epistemic certainty of detection against the irregularity signaled by disability. Sally R. Munt writes that crime fictions "always return us to the beginning, to recover an original story" (196). The detective whose corporeal form seems so out of alignment, whose impairment signifies a disconcerting problem not just of being but of *belonging*, suggests something awry at the heart of the tale. Can a PI who visibly embodies both a clash of substance (flesh to steel) and various distortions of shape (the metal hook, the empty space) be entrusted with the care of someone else's selfhood?

The entanglement of hands and personhood may explain why this set of sleuths is more disturbingly uncanny than others. Does the sight or feel of a metal hook, a plastic hand, inevitably repulse? Or can it redefine what is "organic" to life experience? The unhanded investigator lacks a full set of those uniquely identifying marks that by the time of Poe and Doyle were synonymous "with criminal classification and surveillance," in Linda Schlossberg's words: i.e., fingerprints (261), which "promised to make the morally or socially deviant body legible" (261). Detection "is about the reading of bodies," writes Gill Plain (96), but detectives whose own bodies are themselves illegible, unable to be guaranteed as individual, self-same, knowable—or perhaps more threatening, only *partly* so, and so dangerously liminal—expose the inadequacy of explanatory modes and the normative grammar of social arrangement and power. They are composite forms, containing awkward thresholds, evidence of clashing juxtaposition, and the sleeve that dangles is a frustratingly never-to-be satisfied possibility. The sleuths in this chapter, acting as a kind of linguistic/corporeal *bon mot*, deform the very logic of modern civility. For what can the unhanded- or mechanically handed detective possibly demonstrate about truth? The shape of things to which such heroes quell upheaval is always already an upended chain of unmannerly being, as their own bodies make distressingly manifest.

But, as I have been exploring throughout this book, bodymind impairment is always an opportunity for delineating alternative realities and justice. Embodying both absence and pretense, manual impairment forces a kind of crip primal scene whereby our notions of humanity must be revised. If humanness is guaranteed by handedness but hands can be missing, severed, or harmed, where else, *how* else, can we locate our sense of ourselves? Donna J. Haraway famously declared in her 1991 "Cyborg Manifesto" that we are all chimerical hybrids, creatures "of both imagination and material reality" (7), organic and machine, amalgams of lived experience and social construction, inhabiting worlds that are at once "natural and crafted" (6), and far more imbricated with both animals and technology than our myths of human uniqueness can bear.

Scholars have long understood that the disabled body, with its technological extensions and accoutrements, its mechanical parts and functions, explodes notions of human distinction and wholeness along the lines of Haraway's cyborg revolution, and that rearticulating the body in terms of assemblage, interdependency, and hybridity can have radical ethical consequences for how we situate ourselves in relation to community. Missing and mechanical hands rewrite the rules, generating "an openness of the embodied self," in Margrit Shildrick's words, "to embodied others" (154).

For the manually disabled detectives, in fact, the questions of what happened and why are bound up with expectations of *regularity*—a word that recurs throughout the Fortune series I discuss below—and to be regular, as Fortune understands it, is to be "one of" (a family, a clan, a neighborhood) in ways that are at once filial and territorial: that is, defined by the spaces in which certain kinds of life experiences, desires and volitions, jobs and professional identities, occur. To be regular, of course, is to *have been* regulated, one's bodymind inculcated in the modes and formations of a particular environment. Place matters to all of the detectives I examine in this study, but the unhanded detectives are particularly associated with milieu, as questions of fit, form, and function become urgent in the aberrant context of compromised humanity. In the tension between sustaining order—by definition a balanced state of equilibrium—and the sleuth's skewed body, shape is key: not so much movement through space as the spaces occupied by people as they gesture, converse, interact with objects and others in moments of what Shildrik calls the "strange encounter" of difference (162). Describing what can happen when a disabled bodymind engages with one that isn't, Shildrik writes that "*potentiality*—in Deleuzian terms, the inherent power of assemblage—relies not on the comfortable fit, but on … asymmetries" (162). Asymmetry *between* people, asymmetry *of* a person: the shock of what isn't there that should be, or is there that shouldn't, creates not just fascination or fear but also opportunity for learning something about the many forms of intimacy, power, cruelty, justice. What is ultimately and intimately figured by handlessness—the stuff of nightmare, missing the limb of divine inspiration—is the hollow core of human priority.

John Brass is known to "most people" as the creator of that popular comic strip, "Georgie the G-Man" (4). So says the narrator of Henri Weiner's 1936

Crime on the Cuff, one Donald Hogarth, who "ink[s] Georgie and fill[s] in the balloons" (10) and doubles as a kind of body-guard and "right arm" (214, 237). The novel is set in Toronto, where Brass once served in the Department of Justice until he loses an arm to bootleggers "trying to dry up the Great Lakes back in 1928 for the government" (4). Like the debonair blind sleuths discussed in Chapter 2, "Brass is well known around town, a tall, thin figure in a gray double-breasted suit, with the empty right sleeve shoved into the side pocket" (4).[3] In this novel of kidnapping and murder—the only one of Weiner's to feature the one-armed sleuth[4]—Brass maneuvers people around him exactly as if he were framing them in the panels of his strip, culminating in a final speech in which he commands "'every one [to] sit down,'" saying, "'I've got a lot of talking to do'" (262). He is not a stereotypical genius detective, though his repeated assurances during the denouement that he'll "explain … later" (264) do seem to confirm Hogarth's earlier inkling that his boss "had something figured out" (65). What interests me is the connection between the arm and job of the past (the sleuth was literally top brass) and the new identity as one-armed crime-solving cartoonist. How do disability, low art, and the law come together in this tale?

Hogarth remarks early on that Brass doesn't talk much about himself, so that no one really knows how the boss has lost his arm. But that arm, rather like the purloined letter that (with a nod to Poe) "prove[s] that the best place to hide anything is in full sight of the searcher" (35), constantly announces itself in its absence. The "sleeve shoved into the side pocket" is another overburdened signifier, hiding the missing arm in plain sight. It is not so much that Brass's arm is the truer mystery, the more intriguing case to try to solve; in fact, Brass's uneven body is one of the least remarkable in the novel when compared to the kind of ludicrous exaggeration of "the runt" (32) and the "half-pint" (34), the bartender with one eye, the "too gaunt and boyish" women (45) or the "tallest and fattest detective captain" (18). But the process of Brass's transition from lawman to cartoonist and back again does make disability the agent of an altered—which does not mean *lessened*—relation to justice. Once an *actual* member of the Justice Department, Brass is now a kind of approximation, disabled and technically amateur—a caricature, we might say, except that he is the source of knowledge and not the butt of a joke. Between the pocket and sleeve (that armature of a civilized man made useless and macabre), and the creative hand that in making fun also inevitably remakes sense, Brass both literally and figuratively redraws the lines with a hand that had to learn for the first time how to manipulate its tools. The detective's body becomes an alternative locus of enforcement that explicitly contours reality according to the logics of cartoon, which might also be said to hide truths in simple graphics.

Although his new career is cast in rehabilitative terms—Brass studied art to "'develop [his] left arm'" (21) after amputation of the right—disability is presented in this text less through the normalizing tactics of recuperation than as a mode of social commentary. Among several others, references to Gustave Doré and Honoré Daumier, nineteenth-century French illustrators who were also political caricaturists, align the disabled Brass as a cartoonist along a genealogy of artistic satire. Brass learns how to draw as a consequence of having become disabled; his comic take on the world is thus portrayed as a direct consequence of having needed to learn new ways to hold a pen, to observe his surroundings and contour his perceptions. A comic book, a political cartoon, an unevenly embodied man, even a crime novel—these might all be said to arrive at the truth of a thing through distortion. If caricature aims to divulge some subtler quintessence behind comic prominence, then Brass's lopsided dexterity—the artistically gifted hand on one side and the pocket filled with an unexplained empty sleeve on the other—could be said to expose something tenuous, inadequate, even corrupt about the world this sleuth is charged with holding together. Rick Eden has argued that detective fiction is inherently satirical, its sleuthing protagonists "almost always outsiders in some sense," "superior" and "aloof," "not participants so much as unbiased observers" (285). By this logic, John Brass is a tripled caricature, his body, his profession, and the narrative he dominates poking fun in our trust that truthfulness is definitive, neat, and wholly present—and yet, all the while, steadily driving toward some place *disarmingly* revelatory and right.

In a novel that frequently mentions the "'normal and businesslike'" (203) process of tying up loose ends, Brass's remark that premeditated crime bears the "style" of its perpetrator "as individual as Cezanne's, Wagner's, or Bing Crosby's" (202) suggests not tidy resolution but rather the unpredictability of individual uniqueness. These are not wildly unstructured artists, to be sure, but the implication remains that detecting must be as agile and imaginative as the crime it hopes to solve. Given the symbolic conflation of hand and divine creation, Brass would seem to be at a severe disadvantage in pursuing villains understood to be capable of masterful, inimitable artistry. But here, too, the novel slyly proposes something awry in the usual way of regarding quality, beauty, or success. As both creator and sleuth, Brass represents not the generalizing tendencies of art criticism—or more precisely, the way in which a single word from a critic can establish a generalized opinion—but rather an emphasis on quirky distinctiveness. The famed art in this tale is the comic book "Georgie the G-Man," not the oils of Cezanne, its master craftsman not the able hand of God reaching toward that of Adam but a one-armed detective in a mismatched suit. Once the perpetrators of crime have been apprehended, *Crime on the Cuff* restores us to a boldly delineated but also uneven world. That empty sleeve may be "shoved" in its pocket with anger and shame—or simply impatience to get on with the project of drawing existence into being.

John Brass makes detection a matter of how we understand outline and shape. Crime solution, the novel implies, will always leave something out, the blank space between parts of the story—what's called the "gutter" in the idiom of comic books. John Trench's one-handed archeologist and amateur sleuth Martin Cotterell creates juxtaposition in another way, seeking "the bones of [a] case" (*Dishonoured Bones*, 1955; 161). The protagonist's impairment is far less significant as a plot device in this three-book post-war series than in other books I will address below, but it serves its purpose as an indicator of what happens when apparently unlike parts come together in some way. Where lower-limb impairments feature in detective fiction as markers of effort and "stride"—the detective's command of the spaces where crime takes place, as discussed in Chapter 4—upper-limb impairments interrogate normative spaces in a different way, asking what, in complex and modernizing societies, gets shoved up against what, and to what dangerous consequence. Trench's novels (published in quick succession in the mid-1950s) emphasize what Cotterell describes as the "'zestful brutality'" with which a society "treats its townscape and landscape'" (*What Rough Beast*, 1957; 189); a hillside marred by shale-extracting equipment, or a country village altered by mercantile expansion, are backdrops for crime motivated by class conflict and money in a changing socioeconomic context. Enter the archaeologist-sleuth whose profession reanimates the distant past and whose aluminum hand represents a set of material and conceptual clashes—as between mid-century interest in rehabilitative technology and the clumsy appendage that is "always covered" (*Bones*, 21), between metal and flesh, war and peacetime, the comforts and/or stagnation of the past and the innovations and mistakes of the present.

At the heart of these mysteries are "'changing conceptions of the universe'" (*Beast*, 68). There is crime—a tomb is raided for its "gilded seraphim" (178), an uncle impersonates a dead father so the son can avoid death duties, people die—but the sleuth is "'fighting for a landscape'" as much as he is the truth of any case since "'its landscape shows you what a country values'" (189). The fact that Cotterell himself with "his frayed tweed coat" and alloy hand seems "entirely native to the landscape" (*Bones*, 22) tells us that the indigenous is rightly defined in hybrid rather than pure terms—however nostalgic his author may be for the "unsought perfection" of British cathedrals (*Beast*, 24). In *Dishonoured Bones*, the local community is unsettled by the "monstrously menacing" shale extractor that looms on the horizon and "*walk[s]*" across the moors with uncanny lifelikeness (16; italics in original), but what is "not native" here has less to do with the blight of machinery on the landscape than with the economics of putting miners out of a job. The message in these books isn't quite so retrograde as to say that we should embrace "centuries of settled living" (*RB*, 55). (They have a 1950s optimism about the future.) But they do insist that rampant development is dangerous when it disregards the particulars of human experience and has no patience for "love and gentleness" (190). Cotterell's role in all of this, as the "decipher[er] of fragmentary inscriptions" (*Beast*, 149), is to embody these various themes of distressing formal incoherence while assuaging them with his rapid, cogent thinking and the "metal hand" (110) that problematizes the insistence that aesthetic—let alone ontological—perfection demands seamless wholes.

The curious thing about Martin Cotterell as a sleuth is that his own "truth," the fact of his prosthetic hand, is both shrouded by plot and "always covered" by gloves (*Bones*, 21). Readers observe the hand only through others, men who feel "a pang of shame, and angry sorrow and even a tiny prick of envy for the young men broken in the wars that [they] had missed" (21), or women who are "frankly interested" (*Beast*, 123). Covered, though, is not equivalent to covert, so that Cotterell's hand, gloved and resting on his knee, may signal a more "native" form of embodied reality than that of the able-bodied, prosperous men who populate these books with their unembarrassed physicality, their racy cars and presumptions of cultural capital. The rough generalizations and abstruseness of Trench's plots notwithstanding (one Australian blogger complains of *Docken Dead* [1953] that "it is an unusual experience to read paragraph after paragraph of a text written in English and yet to have only the vaguest sense of what the author intended to convey"[5]), the fact of their one-handed protagonist does suggest something interesting about a moment of social change, one in which neither the unearthing of fragments of the past nor the "improvements" of the present (*Beast*, 46) fully satisfy a longing for things to make sense. The "bones" of a case, as Cotterell arrives at them in states of contemplation—like holy relics, scraps of ancient language, shards of pottery or tools, a quarry cut into a hillside, a hand severed from its body or a plastic prosthesis attached to an arm—do not magically reveal or stabilize meaning. The artifact can only invite speculation; the rock is always a remnant of sorts. Bones are but a type of structure upon which the observer layers interpretation. "Truth," in other words, is only ever a story.

The injuries that take the arms of Brass and Cotterell happen off-page.[6] If there is something missing where a body part should be, the texts fill in the gap with other kinds of appendages—paintbrush, relic—with which the sleuth secures his place in the known community, but also extends himself beyond the perimeters of that location, Brass by publishing into the world and the future, Cotterell by delving into the earth and the past, both through acts of reshaping. Both Brass and Cotterell are trained to read patterns from parts and to approximate completion from across the gaps of what isn't there. What they suggest as detectives with impairments of handedness is that while crime may be an obvious disruption to the *design* of things, reinstating lawfulness does not inevitably require *fixing* or filling in the outlines. Cartoons lampooning the existing state of affairs will still get inked in; the honeycombed tunnels of quarries, residue of greed, might crush a murderer. The irregularity of the sleuths' own bodies, displaying civil upheaval from the small scale of crime to the grand scale of world war, inevitably prompts an explanation (I will return to this motif below), but neither sleuth seems inclined to acquiesce to a demand to stabilize their impairments in the excuses of story. In this sense what they embody is neither the persistence nor the disruption of norms of integrated masculinity and dependable class structures, but instead something more like *likelihood*, possibility, potential. Outlines, finally—like the chalk-drawn shape of a body on the pavement—are only that: intimations of what was there or what might come, hints that might never be fully explained.

With the appearance of Dan Fortune and Sid Halley, both in the late 1960s, the anxiety of *misfitting* that attaches to the trope of the missing hand becomes more obviously tied to the tenuous guarantees of belonging, the environments these PIs occupy more thoroughly characterized by tensions of class, race, and gender. Fortune and Halley are rough-and-tough risk-takers, professional sleuths with former ties to the milieus in which they now work, Fortune to the working-class neighborhoods of Brooklyn and Halley to the elite circles of British horse racing. Their injuries allow them to move unimpeded through the otherwise closely guarded circuits of these worlds. It is because they are *not* police that they can gain entry (to spaces, to conversations), and because they *are* impaired that they are at once fascinating and discounted, for who would bother to take on a man whose left arm "ended uselessly four inches below the elbow"? (Francis, *Come to Grief*, 1995; 22). Because neither exactly fits, the shapes of their bodies, interacting as they do with the forms that other things take—from caste and clothing to honor, memory, and justice—show us, in Caroline Levine's words, "that there is a great deal to be learned about power by observing different forms of order as they operate in the world" (23). The drama of handlessness is engineered to raise questions about how we decide who has the right to determine or defy certain social behaviors and identities.

In the twenty-book Dan Fortune series by Michael Collins (penname of Dennis Lynds), the gap of the missing arm is filled with the hero's penchant for speechifying: narrative itself is thematized. Collins's stock in trade is class injustice, and his use of crime writing as a "vehicl[e] for sociological observation" most directly explains Fortune's impairment.[7] Many commentators make the easy link between Fortune's empathetic style, his sensitivity to the havoc of poverty and racism, his introspection and broad social awareness, and the fact of his disability. The connection works two ways. The dramatic change to, and difference of, his body does seem to attune him to histories of exclusion and oppression writ large, both in his native New York and around the world. At the same time, disability is narratively functional, as one blogger suggests: a detective who can't engage in "fisticuffs … has to rely more on his intelligence and compassion."⁸ In this sense, Fortune is akin to those sleuths with mobility impairments whose cognitive ingenuity is often portrayed as a way to offset the limitations of their bodies. More significantly here, Fortune's disability becomes a repeated occasion for narrative—not so much because everyone wants to know how he lost his arm (the "what happened to *you*?" trope⁹), but because Fortune is cognizant of how quickly "story" can harden into "truths" that are far more delimiting that his physical impairment. It is this awareness of how stories might explain but also actually produce criminal behavior that makes Fortune an effective investigator.

Fortune's disability tends to feature as one among various forms of embodiment, many of which are written to emphasize the indistinctness of types, rather than to reify them. The author seems primarily interested in Fortune's loss of an arm not as a diminishment he must compensate for but as an instigator of ego-narration that is entirely in keeping with what "most of us" do to forge identities we can stand inhabiting (*Act of Fear*, 47). Indeed, Fortune is keen to remark on the fact that we *all* engage in self-exculpatory storytelling all the time; that kind of apology, he implies, conscious or otherwise, and thoroughly implicated in the unequal structures of social life, is practically synonymous with personhood. Where other sleuths' shame and anguish are all about their *actual* hands, mangled or prosthetic (I will return to this point below), Fortune says that he makes up stories about how he lost his arm "*not so much because* [he's] ashamed of the real way [he] lost it, but because how [he] lost it is part of [his] youth" (47, my italics). *Youth*, rather than disability, "is one of [his] troubles," and youth matters in these tales because they are fundamentally stories of origin, inquiries into the antecedents of socially constructed identities.

"How many of us," Fortune asks, "escape what we were born to, who we are, what we have?" (*Fear*, 155). His cases invariably involve crimes motivated by the desperation of feeling stuck: in the stultifying rage of poverty and the ethnic tribalism of urban neighborhoods; in the centuries-old trauma of colonialism and the struggles of immigration in the "unmelted" pot of America (*Blue Death*, 1975; 46); in the dead-end cycles of homelessness, gang violence, drug dealing, and the traffic of sex; in "a crummy world where a kid's dream can't come true" (*Chasing Eights*, 1992; 386). Collins's interest lies less in restoring any sort of order to the streets of New York's Chelsea (or later Santa Barbara) than in exposing the fates of "the people who never appear in the American Dream" (*Fear*, 154), and in wondering just how inevitable their trajectories may be. In this he owes something to the "radical critique of modern American society" typical of Hammett and Chandler's "incisive insights into modern life," as Stephen Knight describes these forebears (14, 116), but his plots emerge more obviously from the sociological theorizing and activist mood of the late sixties and early seventies, inflected by pop psychology. Fortune's world is one in which "so many people have a pet peeve. Something or someone or some group they have to hate" just for "something to do" (*Fear*, 165). The urgency of solving crime, then, has everything to do with understanding the hatred for what it is. "We all need identity," Fortune says in *Shadow of a Tiger* (1972), "pride in what we are" (182). In this context, crime is merely a misguided attempt to *be* someone.

The protagonist loses his arm as a "Chelsea kid bandit [who] fall[s] into the hold" of a ship he's looting (*Blue Death*, 130); when he returns to his neighborhood years later as a PI who knows his Buddhism and his Freud, disability is the badge of youthful indiscretion that helps him to fit in despite the suspiciousness of his license and his years away from home. Fortune is "not an outsider" in the clannish terms of neighborhood, but the combination of his leaving town and the fact of his having "been straight since that day"—that is, not a crook—casts doubt on his allegiances (*Fear*, 30). "They are not sure about me," he says; "they are not sure about me" (30–31)—because learning, reading, and "know[ing] more than the hiring boss" all "adds up," in 1970s New York, "to not being regular" (30). Sleuthing, in this milieu, is tied to guilt—that Fortune somehow escaped his circumstances, that he did not turn out like local gangsters who represent where all the boys of the neighborhood might have "[gone] off the track" (73)—and so to the injury that prompted a departure from home in the first place. Being irregular, then, encompasses the shape and functionality of Fortune's body as well as his geographical identity. Because Fortune has been *elsewhere*, his presence back in Brooklyn is disruptive. It demystifies the "way things are."

Both disability and crime are entangled in the coercive pressures of mythmaking, whether on personal, national, or global scales. Collins suggests that to understand crime we must search beyond the more obvious point that where we come from influences how we will someday behave. More insidiously, as I mention above, he indicates that the stories we tell about ourselves can have an annealing effect, rooting us in attitudes of antagonism, cynicism, and despair that in themselves motivate lawlessness. As Fortune explains of himself, he is the product of a father who abandons the family and a mother who "just had to have men to tell her that she was a woman" (180). Hating that mother, hating men perhaps even more, spurs Fortune to prove he can

> "be a big man ... You know what a kid does in Chelsea if he wants to be big ... he becomes a crook ... I was born in the slums, so I started stealing. I was pretty good. I supported my mother for a year. Then I fell into the hold of a ship I was looting ... I lost my arm from that fall. ... One night around 4 a.m. I suddenly got the message. ... My mother and father had ... made their own choices. ... Who the hell was I to sacrifice myself for them? ... I lost my arm stealing for them! I had gone out and done what my world told me to do. It had cost me my arm." (180–81)

In this revelation, Fortune's impairment is explicitly rendered as a mark of his parents' failings—of their sins, to invoke a very old supernatural symbolism—but also as an indictment of the very "established protocols" that produce and then condemn behavior as sinful in the first place: the social obedience, the striving (also the misogyny) of conventional masculinity. Trying to fulfill those expectations leads Fortune not to material success (his name is obviously ironic and emblematic) but to aporia, to the "missing," the "lost," the emptiness we all stare into, expecting substance but getting nothing, the absent arm. Both disability and crime, in this schema, are more than the mark (and/or consequence) of not fitting; they represent trying too hard in environments that cannot sustain us, that fail our basic needs.

The Fortune stories are thus told through a scrim of pointlessness, since everything—education, money, love, fighting for one's beliefs—buckles under the coercive pressures of capitalism, patriarchy, and American nationalism. The PI, moving his one-armed corporeality across these dreary landscapes, becomes the lone figure of efficiency, if not hope. Fortune might improve nothing, but he *does* something; he has no real moral advantage over the people around him, but he directs his energies in a kind of combustive way, seeking to break up the pious rigidities of contemporary life (even if, at the end of every book, we know it will reassert its priority all over again). The quality of irregularity that Fortune embodies, his one arm and his missing arm, is key to this enterprise. Ato Quayson writes that disabled characters can "institute significant disjunctures to the established protocols of the social domains in which they appear" (117). What he calls a "systemic uncanny"—"the chaos of fraught sociopolitical processes"—sums up Fortune's environments, both the ethnically and economically fractious world of late twentieth-century New York and the Hispanic/Anglo southern California that Collins renders as racially and thus geographically and socioeconomically bifurcated. Between "ritual authority and the manufacturing of docility and compromise," in Quayson's words (117), disability becomes a wedge, disrupting the belief that success comes from, and that action should be dictated by "'do[ing] what your society tells you to do to get ahead'" (*Fear*, 180).

One-armed Fortune is the very embodiment of his own claim that to eke out an existence in this world is nearly by definition to be "'dehumanize[d]'" (*Castrato*, 1989; 141). His unevenness is America's bad form and plot reduces to this logic: crime is driven by the impulse to be, or to stay, on the "inside." What is deemed legitimate in these systemic and relational contexts is portrayed throughout the Fortune stories as the exertion of enormous social control—the suppression of life's flow and pulsation, in Deleuzean terms, beneath the normative, fixative weight of law and government. Upholding the law with a "missing arm" and "empty sleeve" (*Eights*, 76–77), an "empty sleeve" and "missing arm" (124–25), an "empty sleeve" (177) and one arm—I rehearse the repetition deliberately—Dan Fortune manifests a sly joke about conformity as itself a void (the ship's hold, or "hole," into which he falls—and from which he reemerges in a kind of altered birth). "'Myths and legends hide the real world,'" Fortune says, "'the real power. It's one way those in power get others to do what they want'" (*Castrato*, 412). Of course, another way to put this is that myths and legends *are* the world, and fundamentally implicated in social ills. They stoke prejudice, and they incite the violence that erupts from a defeated realization that individual agency matters little in an unfair system—or, conversely, from a dangerous belief in entitlement.

When Fortune tells us that "[he'll] always be a stranger in [his] own country" (414), he's narrating himself as the outlier, rebuilding himself against a certain grain that is itself far from universally true or essentially given. He seems to have a knowing awareness of this even if the books he stars in do not entirely escape the lure of easy characterization (gendered, racialized) or simplified accounts of motive. What's important is that they also strive to render the meaning of their imagined worlds in terms of what's looked for but can't be seen, humanity's arrogant sense of itself lopped off. Dan Fortune is by lineage *Fortunowski*, so that even by name he represents selfhood amended to fit in (the ship's hold is also the round hole through which square Fortunowski cannot, without harm to himself, pass). The strange shape of a pinned-up sleeve makes everyone "uneas[y]" (*Eights*, 177), but dis-ease is what we all ought to feel, Collins implies, in "Modern America" (95), crushed beneath its promise of money, its Baudrillardian simulacra, its spurious grandiosity and jingoistic lies. We can rely on our dogged private cop for an importantly enduring presence (he is *there*, book after book, with his explanations of social hierarchy and corporate greed), but some part him—what we pin upon him as our agent of good—will always fade into absence.

The rarified but distinctly unethical domain of thoroughbred horse racing created by Dick Francis is dominated by matters of fit and function. As a jockey, Sid Halley is marked by size: "smallness had always been an asset for racing," he says in *Odds Against*, the first book of the series (1966); "neither had I ever really understood why so many people thought that height for its own sake was important" (34). Size has its advantages for detecting, too, since the "thing about being small" is that "no one is ever afraid of you" (86)—or in Gill Plain's words, Sid's "crime-fighting methodology is the hiding of steely resolve behind a mask of inoffensive, unthreatening anonymity" (127). Stature isn't all that matters to Sid's identity as a jockey. A racing accident that badly injures one hand also ends his career, and now the shape of that "wretched hand" (110) immediately identifies him: "the wasted, flabby, twisted hand" with "scars on [his] forearm, wrist and palm, not only the terrible jagged marks of the original injury but the several tidier ones of the operations [he] had had since. It was a mess, a right and proper mess" (37). Later, after Halley loses this hand (further damaged by a brutal crook), he sports an "ingenious false hand" that "work[s] via solenoids from electrical impulses in what [is] left of [his] forearm" and that "*look[s]* like a real hand ... to the extent that people sometimes didn't notice" (*Whip Hand*, 1979; 4, italics in original). People *do* notice, though, and the prosthesis is in turn an object of fascination both sexual and sadistic.

Other shapes and spaces are integral to Halley's post-racing existence: his ambiguous marital status, for instance (he is separated three years in the first book, later divorced), which dominates his thinking. Or his ongoing relationship with his father-in-law, in whose stately home he frequently stays, and because of whom he begins working in a detective agency, where he learns to investigate by reading divorce and missing persons files, "'soak[ing] up everything ... like a hungry sponge'" (*Odds*, 55). Steeplechasing, Halley's specialty, is defined by the unevenness of its course, requiring riders to jump a series of ditches and fences; the sight-line from atop a horse on one such course is key to solving the crime in *Odds Against*. Successful riding requires perfect form; form demands two hands through which a jockey "*talk[s]* to a horse" (*Grief*, 307; italics in original); symmetrical form, then, the grip of both hands, is paramount for successful communication. All of Halley's cases involve disruptions of contour, including sabotage to racing courses to race fixing to gruesome mutilation of horses. Halley drives a retrofitted Mercedes; he navigates the shoals of "class distinction" (*Odds*, 10) and "old school ... aristocrats" (*WH*, 21). A racing form is a tabulation of statistics and odds. What American cops call "priors," the Brits refer to as "form," which invokes the manner of doing a crime as much as the paper it's recorded on.

Form is thus a style as much as a material shape, as Halley's partner Chico suggests early on. "'That's just your form, Sid, mate. You don't want nothing,'" to which Halley agrees: "I wanted nothing. My form. My trouble" (*Odds*, 9). The tension here is that *form* as a habit has *nothing* as its content. What is the shape of nothingness? Disability, of course—that quintessential simultaneity of too-much and too-little, absence of wholeness (a word Halley repeats, compulsively) and excess of flesh, of fragile mortality. Halley's one-handedness inspires "revulsion and horror" (*Odds*, 75), feelings of waste and self-hate (*WH*, 16, 138), "helplessness and humiliation" (*Grief*, 332); it is coded as what shuts down wanting, a deterrent to self-sufficient masculinity, a source of "savage, petrifying fear" (*Grief*, 58) that renders him incapable of doing his job. Disability is a form of feeling, a way of eating or driving, a state of mind, and a process—the "slow, lingering birth" of the detective (*Grief*, 8). It establishes intimate connection, as with the disfigured secretary in *Odds Against* whose "sad travesty of [a] face," "ravaged" by a firework [68–69], cannot be hidden in a pocket like Halley's "useless, deformed left hand" (16). It prompts the depravity of crooks, who gleefully pounce upon "'this precious crippled hand of yours'" (31), further mutilating one hand in the first book and threatening the other in the second.

All this reference to forms suggests that the Sid Halley books, *formulaic* in their adherence to certain conventions of their genre, might also be interested in reworking the tropes by repeatedly dismantling and reconstructing a range of formal relationships and mechanisms. "Multiple and conflicting modes of organization," as Levine puts it (16), can explode expectation, "dismantl[e] unjust, entrenched arrangements" (18). In Halley's case, the injury that destroys his identity as a jockey both produces his new identity as PI and reveals the ableist and exclusionary bias of male codes of conduct. When Halley acknowledges that "other ex-jockeys became trainers or commentators or worked in racing in official capacities, [while] only [he], it seemed, felt impelled to swim around the hidden fringes" (*Grief*, 16), he sounds like a private eye, familiar in his disaffection, but also like a stereotypical disabled person, marginalized and excluded, weak and even untrustworthy. Invoking the one in the context of the other frays the edges of both clichés; in the collision of the two, something must give way, some normative certainty about what it means to perform, to be professional, to protect. How can the lone-wolf tec, fundamentally able-bodied and secure in his assumption of masculine toughness, also be small and impaired, full of "'fears and self-doubts ... shame and uselessness and inadequacy'" (*WH*, 259)?

Therein lies the paradox: undisabled, Halley would not be a detective, but disability, which is what makes him a detective, also defies the conventions of the genre. The fact is that Halley still inspires awe in the cruelest of criminals, who call him "Tungsten Carbide," "the hardest of all metals" (*Grief*, 283), epithets he earned as a jockey. Halley doesn't "regularly" ride—pun intended—but he *can* (and does in every novel); that he doesn't more often is a problem of "too much pride" (261) rather than actual physical insufficiency; it isn't Halley's technique that gets in the way, but his self-consciousness. When he bemoans toward the end of *Whip Hand*, "Why, *why*, couldn't I have two hands, like everyone else?" (257), the question seems at once beside the point—he doesn't *need* two hands, given his capabilities—and entirely to the point: if he had two hands, Halley would still be a jockey.

Perhaps it is these contradictions of form and function that prompt an obsessively reiterated dichotomy of use value against uselessness, as the irrevocably altered protagonist struggles to relearn himself in contexts where individual status as well as social relationships are strictly defined by how things look and how they are done. In this we can sense the author's own ambivalence about how to understand his hero's condition. In a genre equally defined by tension between "chaos and confusion" and the detective's ability to "effect meaning out of nonsense" (Schlossberg, 259, 255), Halley's disability becomes the ultimate test of just how much "de-forming" can be withstood before a thing loses existential coherence. The novels force this question, as in *Whip Hand*, when tough-as-nails Halley, taunted with a shotgun trained on his "good" hand, experiences "liquefying, mind-shattering disintegration," "a morass of terror" that breaks him "in pieces" at the prospect of further "humiliation and rejection and helplessness and failure" (100). It is not loss of life but the threat of "losing the other hand" that leaves him "stunned, ... ill. Disoriented and overthrown and severed from [his] own roots. Crushed into an abject state of mental misery. ... a feeling that [his] whole self had been literally smashed ... a psychic upheaval like an earthquake" (103–04). Hands *are* Halley—how he is known as a former racing champion, as the man who crashed, the reinvented PI, the man who's "damned good at looking into things" (*WH*, 21), "'a whiz'" at sleuthing (*Grief*, 72), but who carries "a deformity in the pocket" (*Odds*, 64) that can be exploited because there will always be "abnormal" men to "look carefully at a crippled hand and *then hit it*" (*Odds*, 59; italics in original). It is "the recurrent nightmare of ... no hands" (*Grief*, 332)—and, emphatically, the shame produced by that terror—that propels the protagonist, and the plots he leads, into motion. Everything focalizes to those hands: they make, undo, and remake Halley over and over in every case.

Whether it results from accident or violence, is Halley's impairment thus to be read as an aberration proving a fundamental incoherence that must be rectified by the agent of law, time and time again? Or as an always potential feature of humanity that, in belying "normal" form and function, *revises* how we might reorient our attitudes about embodiment, work, family, our own histories, or the pleasure of "two people fitting together in the old design" (*WH*, 225)? (Halley is an unexpectedly "gentle" love-maker.) Is *fit* a requirement of satisfaction in the world Halley has shaken off his post-injury self-loathing to protect? Plain argues that Francis's novels "occupy an uncomfortable boundary between the radical and the reactionary" (120). As I suggest above, Halley's cases are all about restoring form—the smooth operations of a racing syndicate, say, or a horse's very body, imperiled by frustrations of envy and greed. The crime-space of these scenarios is defined by clashes of status, of belonging, of desire; what it means to know the workings of this world, really "get" it, is constantly at stake. That Halley denies himself the pleasures of riding, that quintessentially formal activity, because he is worried about his *improper* form simply ignores that he can (even if he can't race); he has only to find a different mode of communicating with a horse through his altered body, through the reins, the pressure of his legs, his tone of voice. In this sense the novel is more radical than its reactionary hero, and detection will never recover the "old design" because the old ways were inherently inadequate, or corrupt, or simply one of many possible, and certainly not the best.

It is an established trope of crime fiction at least since the mid-century psychological turn of authors like Ross Macdonald and P. D. James that detectives *feel* as much as they *think*. Disability allows Francis to exaggerate inwardness, to ensure that we understand Sid Halley as a man with emotional depth, capable of unmanly terror, and not just a ratiocinative mind. But all that high-octane self-loathing and panic betray, I think, the author's own horror of losing his "grip." "In crime fiction," writes Ria Cheyne, "objects and appearances are always potential or actual signifiers of something other than themselves," and this is why the genre is "ideally suited to problematizing how we read—and misread—disabled bodies and minds in the wider world" (190). Halley may be the "'best snooper in the business now, so they say'" (*WH*, 62), but he reads *himself* very badly, which means his impairment is also being badly written. When he tells his father-in-law that "'everyone has an outside and an inside, and the two can be quite different'" (*WH*, 259), we are meant to identify with him—surely we all hope to mask our private insecurities with a confident exterior, as Dan Fortune also understands—as we also admire Halley's perseverance through physical damage. But the dichotomy is too exaggerated, Halley too quick to deny a trainer's assertion, watching him ride, that he "'looked just the same'" (*WH*, 198).

It's true that Halley has changed, and in one way these are tales of adjustment and accommodation, of change but also continuity, as Halley works, drives, rides, has sex, fights, plays chess, enjoys a whiskey, and becomes good—very good—at a new career. And yet he seems incapable of reconciling this talented and successful disabled self with the one he remembers and dreams about, the "whole" self unburdened by "wasted, useless deformity," "useless deformity" (*WH* 16, 138). At some point, we would imagine, Halley might stop rehearsing that line about how "'not many people look the way they are inside'" (*Grief*, 348) and align his sense of himself with his embodiment. But as soon as he becomes a man *not* wrenched apart by longing, mourning, lingering shame, and the ferocity these set in motion, he stops being Sid Halley, private eye. And so it *must* sound a thudding, revealing beat throughout these pages, that shame, across thirty years of publication—the "useless, deformed left hand" (*Odds*, 16), the "useless hand" (*Grief*, 8), the arm that dangles "uselessly" (22), a man's very identity "held in uselessness" (282)—in the very hand that guarantees his newfound authority and success.

Sid Halley's preoccupation with uselessness puts in high relief the interrelational dynamics of novels defined by their protagonists' line of work. Usefulness is, after all, a socially determined value, generated by systems of economic exchange in which disability has historically been deemed a burden and a drain on resources. To find their way back to a sense of legitimate personhood in that context seems to require an openness to alternative epistemologies that not all of the sleuths in this category can muster. When that happens—when knowing shuts down, and form obliterates being—a kind of existential clumsiness ensues and sleuthing takes on a quality of desperation. The more intense the need for *personal* recuperation in such a plot, the greater the degradation of crime. In this way, the spaces of crime become fraught with conflicting needs and the insulted body confronts its own inadequacies as metonymic of social and national misfortunes.

Such is the urgency of a short series by Stephen R. Donaldson (under the penname Reed Stephens) in the 1980s, where the rush of solving crimes and catching killers is matched, even exceeded, by the drama of redemption that disability provokes. The series is narrated by Mick Axbrewder (Brew), a recovering alcoholic and former PI, who has lost his license and self-confidence by mistakenly shooting a cop—his own brother—while drunk. Brew is meant to be our sympathetic hero—the intuitive, thoughtful if ignoble man brought low by addiction and one heart-wrenching but unintended bad act—and his travails take up a great deal of narrative space (he gets shot at the end of the second novel and spends the third hobbled by pain). But the *emotional* drama of the novels concerns PI Ginny Fistoulari's more than Brew's impairments: Fistoulari's left hand has been blown off by a bomb.

The character of Fistoulari, beyond any other detective discussed in this study (including the morose Sid Halley), raises the interrogation of usefulness to a hysterical pitch. Her impairment is marked as heroic, incurred by holding a bomb out of the window of the hospital room in which Brew's niece, rescued from a sex trafficking ring in their fictional Southwestern town, is recovering. But it is also insistently depicted as shocking. What might such reiterated terms as "stump" and "claw" reveal about crime as a matter of shape and form? In a discussion of manual impairment in horror cinema, Ian Olney writes that disability "throws into question the corporeal norms upon which the body politic is founded" (299). When the "classical" body becomes the "revolting" body, he argues, "what was a 'human' entity composed of indivisible, interdependent organs all working together to ensure the survival of the system is now a 'posthuman' collection of divisible, alien(ated) partial objects, each potentially unwilling to be subsumed into a unitary organism" (299). Fistoulari's handlessness is indeed explicitly coded as a kind of anarchic horror whereby stump and later prosthesis, invoking the very fearsomeness of a deranged, homicidal maniac the PI should be protecting against, become their own kind of narrative fetish.[10]

There could hardly be a more obvious statement that crime and disability alike disturb our expectations of fit. We can link such anarchy to locational space, to that "decaying city" in which, as Julian Symons notes, the PI circulates (304), like the fictional Puerta del Sol of these novels where Chicanos run "grungy little" businesses in the "old part of town" (8) and the whites live in the Heights, their men preying on young girls and the disabled for sexual thrills. In such an environment, Fistoulari's injury can be read as problematizing orthodoxy, evidence not of a violent element that must be excised from the whole and healthy social body but rather proof that "one nation, indivisible" is predicated on the marginalizing of bodies that do not conform. In this way she organizes the spaces in which she circulates according to what Deleuze would celebrate as "the Unequal itself" (qtd. in Shildrik, 162), her bodymind a graphic contestation of inequity and hierarchy.

Yet the narrative thrust in these books insists on the contrary, on reintegration, putting bodies back together again. *The Man Who Risked His Partner* (1984) is as much about the sleuth "find[ing] her way back to the woman she used to be" as it is the seedy underside of the town's gambling racket, according to her partner (170), who refers to "her stump" (102), "her stump" (106), "her stump ... her stump" (167)—that "dead piece of meat"—even as he urges her to take the case as an antidote to the morass of dependency and self-hate (4). This obsessive emphasis on *stump* alongside the drive toward various kinds of restitution—the need to get back to how things *were*—adamantly maintains wholeness, a certain kind of bodily and social shape, as the only legitimate conclusion to the job. When Fistoulari worries that she is "'not equipped to handle'" a dangerous protection gig (22), she does not just mean that her one-handedness weakens her ability to fight or lessens the intimidation she might provoke in the villain. She means primarily that *she* is lessened, existentially: she has "only ... one hand—and no self-confidence" (36), her other forearm is "a dead piece of meat" (59), and even the client can tell that she's "'going to pieces'" (185). Fistoulari is the "problem solver" of the outfit (*The Man Who Killed His Brother*, 1980; 59), but that cerebral talent, or tactic, deteriorates with her worsening mood. We are meant to side with Brew in reacting to his partner's existential crisis as out of proportion to her injury: she is *not* "'a cripple,'" as he retorts to one crook; "'she's just lost her left hand'" (185). And yet the story he narrates colludes with the crook's estimation completely, keeping "'the angry old cripple'" (126) before us and reminding us that the "attractive" woman who "could've been a society doll" (1) has become a "maimed ... cripple" (3), "'half human, not a person at all'" (234).

It is surely the strong integration of handedness and personhood that accounts for such mutilation disgust, which Donaldson both assumes and eroticizes. In *The Man Who Tried to Get Away* (1990), Fistoulari has not progressed very much, despite her realization at the end of the previous novel that if "'one hand and a claw [are] too much less than two hands,'" one hand and a claw are still "'a hell of a lot more than a hand and a stump'" (*Risked*, 279). This third in the series fairly collapses under the strain of the duo's damaged humanity. Here it is the "'half-ambulatory alcoholic'" (8) Brew, recovering "too slowly" (7) from his gun shot wound and frustrated by his lack of mobility, who needs a good case to restore his sense of purpose: "a chance to take care of [him]self" (10). Fistoulari, meanwhile, is now routinely wearing her "claw"—it will be named as such in *every single instance*—but she is far from reconciled to a new form of embodiment. She wears the prosthesis "like a handicap instead of something familiar" (6), Brew acknowledges, and it will take the length of the novel for us to understand just how right he is in saying that "everything [is] twisted."

Brew refers to their current gig, security at a secluded lodge during a mock-murder weekend (they are also hiding out from a drug lord, el Señor), as "[a] nursemaid job if ever there was one" (14). The language is telling. Donaldson writes crime in these books almost as a perversion of *caretaking*. Someone requests a bodyguard (but it's a screen for his own wrongdoing). Parents fail to watch out for their girls, who get drugged for sex. A young boy is killed delivering gambling profits. Ginny, protecting Brew's niece, gets her own hand blown off. In the third book, such failures of interpersonal dynamic—essentially formal collapses—reach their apotheosis in the marriage of a man named Hardhouse and his wife Lara. In this convoluted plot, the assembled guests at the lodge quickly get snowed in, the game turns deadly, Brew and Ginny are in danger from el Señor's hired gun, and as bodies start piling up, other shenanigans ensue. Hardhouse and Lara have kinky proclivities: he likes to "screw" "*damaged* women'" (314, italics in original)—Fistoulari's "'claw's the sexiest thing [he's] ever seen'" (180)—and Lara tells the wounded Brew that she "'likes having sex with crippled men'" because "'they're *flawed*,'" "'half a human being,'" and "'cripples can't say no'" (302; italics in original). Worse: they "'kill each other's lovers. That's what holds [their] marriage together'" (313). In such pronouncements, disability is a cartoonishly recognizable gauge for depravity, a measure of criminal triumph and taint.

In this closed-house mystery with a macabre twist (shades of Stephen King), space becomes almost inescapably involuted. What's intriguing in the context of crime solution is the way in which disability circulates. It motivates and disrupts relationships; it instigates wrongdoing, obstructs the sleuths' focus on their investigation, and spurs them on to transcend their pain and self-loathing to prevent further chaos. It reveals truths and masks them at once, forms and deforms networks of power and stature. "'How am I supposed to start liking myself again,'" Fistoulari asks Brew after she has slept with the pathological Hardhouse. "'I'm a *cripple* ... I can't even pay attention to my job. ... I need some reason to think I'm worth having around'" (184; italics in original). Having sex with her "claw" on signifies to Brew (who espies them at it) a turning point in his partner's recovery—because she is willing to expose herself with it to a man—but betrays to readers the depth of Fistoulari's need for a man's approval. The same action conceals the killer's truer intentions (he likes the claw for all the wrong reasons), all the while demonstrating the author's ableist fantasy of the disabled body as easily manipulated and therefore arousing. The prosthetic is less an object in this story than a mode of organization, bringing bodies together and thrusting them apart again according to the shifting formal dynamics of mayhem and law.

When Fistoulari tells Brew, at the end of one case, that she never realized how much she depended on her hands, the ostensible message is that we over-prize not just normative embodiment but also the mind—through our protagonist, we might realize how *unnecessary* it is to professional and personal well-being to be "whole," symmetrical, two-handed. The suggestion is that Fistoulari falls apart not so much because she becomes a disabled body, but because she realizes that she is a body *at all*, and has no resources, no ready body language, for coping with that change. Clinging (manual pun again intended) to a sense of herself as irremediably damaged, Fistoulari compromises other aspects of herself: her acumen as a detective, the enjoyment of her sexual self. Putting on the "claw" could operate in this logic as prostheses do in many personal narratives of disability—as a gesture of acclimation and redefinition. But Donaldson's plots do not actually align the taking on of disabled identity with renewed empowerment or an alternative epistemology any more than crime solution problematizes hopes of restored order or social coherence. Instead they deploy the troubled body in a lazy way, defining a certain narrative shape where descent into distraction, vulnerability, and unproductive self-pity is inevitably followed by transcendent resurrection into the sleuths' proper roles as defenders of the innocent and harmed.

Donaldson voices his attitudes toward mystery plotting through a novelist character in *The Man Who Tried to Get Away*, Connie Bebb. "'The true function of the mystery novel,'" Connie intones, is to "'search and analyze character ... to define the resources and restrictions which make one individual incontestably him- or herself and no one else. ... The best mystery novels ... searc[h] and analyz[e] the participants'" (77–78). Setting aside the cliché of the self-reflexive mystery (how often do fictional sleuths announce that only in fiction do crimes get neatly solved?), these remarks are interesting for what they reveal about Donaldson's treatment of hand impairment, since they imply that disability is deployed as a convenient identity-testing "restriction" and that being "incontestably" oneself thus actually requires two hands. Something like irreducible selfhood exists, these statements assert, but it can never be regained after significant injury to handedness, no matter how acclimated a person becomes to prosthetics. "'I don't like *cripples*,'" Ginny says to Brew at the close of the novel. "'I don't like being one'" (326). Handlessness is in the end a form of monstrous unraveling that is only approximately corrected by Fistoulari's gun, that other metallic appendage offered up as counterweight in the lopsided morality of these degenerating worlds.

For Sid Halley and Ginny Fistoulari, the sense of misfit that comes from manual damage is so distressing as to implode the supervisory function they serve. Both sleuths flirt with shame-induced depression so profound that they very nearly lose control of their cases altogether. The implication is that regulating the body coincides with holding social networks together, with the maintenance of proper and predictable relational ties; without *hands*, we are not simply impaired—we fall apart completely, with any and all sinister, insidious element prepared to take advantage. Embodying disruption, though (and perhaps in some way unintended by their authors), these detectives also suggest what Michael Davidson refers to as "the dark doppelgänger of [the] restorative trend" toward prosthetics and rehabilitation that quickly became "big business" in the wake of the Second World War (78–79). As two of the manually impaired investigators who sport prostheses, Halley and Fistoulari have the kind of composite physicality that simultaneously defies and endorses normative human form, evidence of ongoing trauma and treatment at once. In some sense, then, these bodies are constantly undoing what is done, reviving and collapsing, giving with one hand (but which one?) what is taken by the other (but is this law or revolution?). However depressed they may be about it, theirs is provocatively corporeal incoherence, yanking at the foundation of conventional novels trying hard to contain it.

Ria Cheyne writes that to be considered subversive, genre fiction need not deviate from its own generic norms, especially if those norms are precisely what allows a text to subvert something else, like "dominant perceptions of disability" (195). Cheyne argues that because detective fiction, "more than any other type of literature, encourages the reader to interpret bodies and behavior" (190), even the most conventionally plotted crime story can afford us the opportunity to "problematiz[e] how we read—or misread—disabled bodies," primarily through disruption of crime's generic association between disability and villainy. In a 1994 novel by Abigail Padgett, for example, called *Strawgirl* (which also features a neurodiverse investigator), the disfigured hand of Paul Massieu is what saves this father of a murdered girl from being wrongly convicted, as videotape of "the perpetrator's (undamaged) hands is displayed in court" (Cheyne, 190). Paul's scarred, misshapen hand, missing a finger—the very emblem of ethical deformity—exonerates him, Cheyne suggests, along with disabled bodies "in the wider world," from within the pages of an otherwise predictable novel.

It is significant, I think, that the post-war manually impaired sleuths are private detectives rather than amateurs or professional police. Drawing on the convention of the singular figure of the PI—proximate but not belonging to hegemonic power; fulfilling stock expectations of ironic banter, sexual availability, and jaded commentary on the futility and hollowness of contemporary life—the handless sleuths have the capacity to invoke but then move beyond the staleness of generic tropes; their very unevenness ironizes the idea that some more profound truth is to be located by, and embodied within, the autonomous enterprise of "private" detection. Consider John Kenneth Galbraith Jantarro, a one-armed Toronto insurance investigator in two late-1980s novels by Simon Ritchie (penname of Toronto law professor Simon Fodden). While falsely imprisoned for fraud, Jantarro loses his arm to "a couple of sadistic guards and an incompetent prison surgeon" (*Work for a Dead Man*, 6). He invokes this impairment frequently, but in self-mocking ways that undercut binary hierarchies and complicate taxonomies. Strapping on his .38 Chiefs Special, for instance, Jantarro says, "when I'm not wearing my prosthesis, it feels as if I've got two stumps" (142), and then, "deformed ... is a good way to feel if you must carry a weapon, I suppose" (143). What constitutes deformation here? Jantarro implies that having a gun for *any* reason is a violation of formal propriety. The conventions of the genre would read disability as the manifestation of disregard for the law, yet Jantarro's bodily form (and his jocular narration) synonymizes disability and the *rule* of law, gun and stump. The lopped-off limb is an over-determined sign of power, both the sadistic misuse of it and Jantarro's upholding of truth and justice. One is not so easily distinguished from the other—or more subtly, one is actually *felt* as if it were the other.

This is of course the precarious balance upon which so much crime fiction teeters, the slippage whereby collapse and conformity mimic one another in frightening ways, and the security of social regulation so readily devolves. Jantarro is, in this circumstance, reassuring. He carries that gun and has no qualms about using his prosthetic as a weapon. His injury at the hands of the law results in a "very large" settlement that "fixed things so I didn't have to work again unless I wanted to" (*Dead Man*, 14): money confers both social status and moral legitimacy upon him (his detecting is decent and selfless rather than mercenary). But Jantarro is also a provocative figure whose body moves through *Work for a Dead Man* in alternating states of completion and irregularity—his prosthesis is broken in an attack, so he is one-armed through much of the story—that defy this antic novel's own impulse toward correcting what goes off or wrong. These pages refer often to a "fake arm" and a "good arm," but do not offer a reliable framework for differentiating the ersatz from the real or for establishing how one might supersede the other.

In the triangulation of these terms—good, fake, and, by implication, missing—Jantarro "really" solves crime, figuring out who killed his employer (the titular "dead man," filling in what's "missing"), but his corporeal presence evacuates those terms of stable meaning, provoking epistemological crisis. Other characters in the novel, for instance, are deployed to foreground the contradiction that Jantarro embodies and the need to stabilize him in recognizable categories, as when one gives his "fake arm a squeeze" and another "[makes] sure it was [his] good arm that she squeezed" (16). That attempt to be definitive, though—precisely what we count on the detective for and seemingly guaranteed by language, sure distinctions between words—ultimately has nothing to do with Jantarro's sleuthing skills, despite the repeated reference to difference. "I held my hands out in front of me," Jantarro tells us at one point; "my right hand trembled and the plastic one moved back and forth like a metronome because all my nerves were jumping on their own and turning the myoelectric switches on and off" (91). One might argue that pronouns reveal an important hierarchy, the possessive signaling a fleshly arm Jantarro is willing to claim as his own and the article distancing him from what is inhuman but also eerily animated. But the description blurs the distinction between mechanical and organic in less uncanny ways, too, since the nerves are also Jantarro's, the plastic is attached to *his* flesh, and the myoelectric switches are controlled by *his* impulses. Later, when he says that he "spread [his] hands—plastic and real—to the width of the screen" and that "the newly refurbished plastic one didn't shake, but the flesh one did" (182), blurring gets even more pronounced. The human hand registers fear, the plastic one steadiness. I would argue that what we want from our sleuth, in the face of threat, is neither *one* of these reactions but *both*, the trembling that signals natural trepidation (as opposed to sociopathic calm) alongside the ability to maintain self-control. Jantarro does exhibit both of these, but in hybrid fashion.

Physical peril is a generic near-necessity, and *Work for a Dead Man* delivers, with Jantarro eventually locked in a glass pen with several very large Komodo dragons. Were he not temporarily without his prosthesis, the circumstance would lose its particular urgency. "The obvious stone for the job stood in front of me, mocking me," he says, "because it would have needed two hands to lift it, two hands to throw it, two hands to get freedom" (242). "My stump flailed around with the uselessness of perfect impotence" (232). But because "you learn to do a lot of things" differently when you're "one-armed," Jantarro can "conside[r] the possibilities" (233), and another rock quickly presents itself to him. The shift is clumsy, narratively speaking, but it makes the point: extricating himself from a life-threatening predicament requires not able-bodiedness but simply patience and some ingenuity. Where Sid Halley and Ginny Fistoulari obsess about uselessness, Jantarro takes the extra beat to fashion an alternative. The emphasis on considering possibilities strikes me as most significant where crime solution is concerned, since it invokes the disembodied ratiocination that defined the genre for nearly a century in the form of a man whose *body* necessitates unconventional creativity.

Jantarro is a smart, successful investigator. "'You've got to stop being surprised when I solve a case,'" he remarks to a police detective at the end of the story. "'It's happened often enough'" (238). But he seems to derive just as much satisfaction from his irregular physical form, his manipulations of flesh and mechanics: "[Bench] watched intently as I did up my belt one-handed. ... [He] handed me the arm, holding it gingerly as if he might break it. ... He paid close attention to how I fitted it over the stump, how I worked the straps. A curious feeling of pride welled up in me" (239). This is ableist curiosity at the supercrip dressing himself, to be sure, an unabashed instance of staring that Jantarro's pride plays directly into, where it becomes the job of the disabled person to teach the nondisabled about inhabiting non-normative space. Yet Jantarro's management—of the story, the stare, the technicalities of a prosthetic, his own physical outline, and the case itself—also works to subordinate Bench in a moment of suggestive intimacy between cop and PI where the anomalous body reverses the dynamics of authority and narrative control. Impairment of handedness obviously maximizes the drama of Jantarro's remaining dexterity, the startling quality that guarantees readerly awe. But there is a superfluous quality to this scene that also relocates what we understand of balance and capability, since this demonstration of manual skill is, finally, utterly inconsequential to Jantarro's closing of the case. More important may be the way disability holds the law in a kind of quiet suspension, crafting its own patterns of form and meaning.

More than any other collection of sleuths, the manually impaired detectives as a group question their right to belong or to be taken seriously, so completely do problems of handedness seem to annul ontological validity. This is surely why none of the detectives discussed in this chapter is without *both* hands, or why they have all lost hands to war or job-related injury rather than having a congenital impairment. They maintain some degree of legibility and belonging in an able-bodied world with their remaining "human" hand, and can thereby serve an evident pedagogical purpose—as many throughout these chapters do—of teaching nondisabled readers something of living with disability. (This is why we must watch Jantarro buckling himself up.) Asymmetry, I think, is imaginatively key. The fascination in these tales is for the simultaneity of the human hand, with its connotations of authority, intellect, and truth, and *something else*, be it metal, plastic, mechanical, or empty space, that threatens to negate the hand with which "[man] writes laws for himself"[11]—one side constantly contesting the other. In the body of the detective, opposites collide, law and unlaw, godly and base, perfection and distortion. What early moderns would have known as "doublehandedness"—deceit embodied in the vice figure of Ambidexter, for instance, whose feigned emotions can turn on a dime[12]—is provocatively tweaked by law-abiding, ambiguously handed investigators whose two halves come close, but not exactly, to canceling each other out.

If we take for granted all that is presumed by the awesome intricacy of the hand—in a word, human primacy of place—then damage to that signature appendage in the context of violence would seem to disclose a powerful cultural worry about the consequences of losing that superiority. The logic of prosthetics, too, seems to insist on correction, on the need to approximate if not replace the humanity that is defined by manual dexterity. But if crime fiction is itself always a comment on the fallacy of form, the fiction of fit, as I have argued here, so too is the one-armed/prosthetically endowed sleuth a comment on the insufficiency (even the fundamental ridiculousness) of our faith as well as our fears. The Deleuzian ambiguity, the dis-organized hybrid potentiality of prosthetic and absent handedness tell us that bodies and spaces can communicate in unfamiliar but finally generative—indeed, productively world-shattering—ways.

Unlike the various other conditions studied in this book, impairment of arms and hands carries with it no symbolic endowment to offset connotations of a damaged humanity—no special insight or inward concentration, no presumption of creative "madness," no particular bravery or heroism. I have been arguing that, whatever the specifics, disabled detection does much more than regurgitate the standard tropes, of course, but those ready cultural narratives of compensation nevertheless inform the way detectives are situated in their plots, pressured as they are by demands of superb deductive capability. Here, as it were unaided by recognizable symbolism, in fact freighted with horrified reaction to what Garland-Thomas calls "singleton hands" and their violation of "bilateral symmetry," of "cooperative interlaced functioning" (123), the manually impaired detectives provoke an especially heightened inquiry into the most basic source of knowledge: *how* we are human. I phrase it this way to stress the idea that we become ourselves not just in the substance of embodiment but in the subtlest methods and means of being, not just as we are interpellated into cultural expectations but in the myriad interactions of our bodyminds with the surfaces, depths, and angles of life. The hybrid handless tecs must know on their own, as it were, and in so doing liberate power from the norms of form.

Notes

1   https://io9.gizmodo.com/5727965/severed-hands-photos. Consider also post-war movies, such as Hollywood's *The Best Years of Our Lives* from 1946. Harold Russell, who lost both hands to a defective explosive while making a training film in North Carolina and won the Oscar for Best Supporting Actor, plays Navy sailor Homer Parrish.

2. Compare Karl Shapiro's poem "The Leg," where the amputated leg is imagined to carry on with a life of its own, so that by the end of the poem it is the *leg* missing the person rather than the other way around.

3. Brass surely owes something to *Saber of London*, a series from the 1950s about a British police captain named Mark Saber who works, in the program's original version, in an American homicide department. South African actor Donald Gray, who took over the role in 1955, had his left arm amputated after an injury during the Second World War.

4. Henri Weiner was one of the pennames used by Stephen Longstreet, born Chauncey Weiner, American author of over 100 novels, plays, and works of non-fiction.

5. Karyn Reeves, "A Penguin a Week" (Sunday, March 16, 2014). http://apenguinaweek.blogspot.com.

6. They are both signs of heroic do-gooding, loss in the name of law. When the omniscient (or third-person limited) narrators of these novels mention the armlessness, it is to let us know something important about the sleuth's moral status—or at least his loyalty to King and country.

7. Myrna Oliver, "Dennis Lynds, 81; Author Used Detective Novels to Explore Social Conditions," *The Los Angeles Times* (August 25, 2005). http://articles.latimes.com/2005/aug/25/local/me-lynds25.

8. The Thrilling Detective Web Site. http://www.thrillingdetetive.com/dan_fortune.html.

9. Disability, as many commentators have noted, occasions this question, demanding explanation to account for its very anomalousness; as Mitchell and Snyder put it, "disability usually provokes the riddle in need of a narrative solution" (*NP*, 61). Cf. Lois Keith's edited collection of personal writings by women with disabilities with the ironic title *What Happened to You?*

10. While metal and wooden hand prosthetic devices existed as early as the Roman era, hook prosthetics, particularly split-hook designs that approximated the movement of fingers and thumbs, were still very much in use after the Second World War. Contemporary biorobotics promises to "[push] the mechanical human body to new limits," according to one recent article from *Machine Design*. https://www.machingdesign.com/motion-control/more-meets-eye-future-bio-robotics-pdf-download.

11. Galen, *On the Usefulness of the Parts of the Body*, qtd. in Lynch, 33.

12. Cf. Thomas Preston's heroic comedy *Cambyses* (1569).

6

Detection and the Mind's Private Eye

In a conventional narrative frame, the challenge of the physically disabled detective may be summed up as one of quelling the fearsome chaos of crime by insuring the impervious, extensive authority of law and reason: a Cartesian equation of mind over body. Physical disabilities capitalize on an important duality at the core of the character of the detective, who is at once a forceful, compelling mind positioned to tackle the unexpected in a dazzling as well as protective fashion, and a vulnerable, wounded self who dramatizes the familial, social, political breakdown he or she may be charged with redressing. What Ralph James Savarese calls a "perverse reconciliation" of that dualism, however, whereby physical disability is often assumed to be associated with cognitive impairment (42), indicates the way in which problems of mind are coded as the consummate insult. When PI Joe Binney announces, for example, that he's "'deaf, not crazy'" (*Die Again, Macready*, 206), he attempts to excuse a "mere" bodily fault by refusing its association with a worse fault, one that taps into a potent and age-old terror of madness.

This chapter asks what happens when disability affects the mind of the detective, when he or she has such varied conditions as autism, obsessive-compulsive disorder, epilepsy, Tourette's syndrome, schizophrenia, or something rarer like *alexia sine agraphia*, even the psychic ability to locate the dead. Where a detective's anomalous body easily suits the logic of compensation and may be "overcome" by intelligence and the power to outwit—making it the symbolic indicator of cognitive genius—the perception of a "broken brain" will have different consequences for how fully a detective may be trusted or empowered to get the job done. To what sort of law and order can the *neuro-disordered* sleuth return us, given our equation of mind with self and the enormous stigma associated with mental illness? Because problems of mind estrange the detective from the communities in which crime is solved, the severity of threat associated with crime *and* the fact that the sleuth can actually understand it may be heightened. The criminal and the detective are aligned in this sense not because the sleuth may be prone to certain acts of recklessness or rebellion, but because both represent ways of thinking that defy the norm—an eeriness at the very core of self. The stranger is not just in the house; the stranger is within.

I have argued throughout this book that whatever its role may be in concretizing the conservative values inherent in detective fiction, disability also works in more expansive ways to rearticulate how we understand the mapping of knowledge across a range of bodily and intersubjective spaces. As the genre in its broadest definition has moved away from the figure of the lone genius, recent authors have turned to psychiatric issues as a way of focalizing the unusual modes of cognitive processing that we expect from a great detective, but often in a manner that invites us to consider what *else* is involved in thinking—which is to say, the many cripistemologies I have elsewhere examined that engage bodyminds in dynamic relation with their environments. While the idea that solving crime requires some truly out-of-the-ordinary thought might seem to isolate the neurotec as an aberration (not just specially endowed with smarts but *weirdly* so)—especially when traditional law enforcement is rendered utterly ineffectual—the opposite is also true, as sleuths' apparent peculiarities become regularized (which is not to say "fixed") over the course of a case. The invitation extended by the stories to be discussed here is to reconsider not only how we know, but what we mean by knowing in the first place.

Michael Bérubé argues that narrators with intellectual disabilities "open a window onto a reinterpretation" of both "narrative as such" and "self-consciousness" (160). Such is the effect in particular of Mark Haddon's hugely popular *Curious Incident of the Dog in the Night-Time* (2003), Jonathan Lethem's *Motherless Brooklyn* (1999), and a host of other narratives featuring detectives whose mode of accessing information is atypical. In *Curious Incident*, Haddon's fifteen-year-old protagonist Christopher narrates his investigation of the death of a neighbor's dog, which is entangled with what Christopher himself refers to as behavioral difficulties and the discovery of a terrible familial deception. Haddon has insisted that Christopher is not to be read as autistic, but his statement that *Curious Incident* is "a novel about difference, about being an outsider, about seeing the world in a surprising and revealing way"[1] raises questions about the relationship between disability and diagnosis. To construe Christopher as a metaphor is to try to figure out what he represents, and thus also to make Christopher himself (and so disability) the mystery of the novel, as is borne out by the trouble several characters have with making sense of his behaviors and especially by the critical scramble that ensued after publication to name Christopher's condition. The novel itself, however, confusing absolute distinctions between types of detective and the urgency of its various investigations, collapses the idea that disability is a puzzle that must be solved in order to be tolerated. The question of whether or not Christopher's habits of mind are like or unlike any "normal" person's recedes behind the greater conundrums of family dynamics, love and sexuality, even the London Tube system.

This is one aspect, then, of narratives in which detectives are characterized by apparent psychological difference: they not only defy diagnosis; they make the question of diagnosis irrelevant, and throw "mystery" back onto the world. Is the "barking, grunting, spasmodically twitching hero" of Lethem's *Motherless Brooklyn* simply a caricature of a gruff, hard-boiled detective (to quote Publisher's Weekly), or worse, of someone with Tourette syndrome—or is his "freakishness" a cannier representation of pathways to truth?[2] Does the question of realism in this novel matter because Tourette's is named, or—as in *Curious Incident*—is it the provocation to regulatory norms of public behavior that should interest us? The issue in these novels is epistemological, of course, but with stakes raised. To forget; to forfeit one's nuance for names, words, facial expressions; or to know too much, to *feel* too much, to be unable to ignore an object out of place or to resist the imposition of another's emotions and motivations: these are heightened instances of the porousness of personhood and the fluidity of knowledge, and it becomes the job of the detective to put together some kind of truth in the context of fundamental ambiguities about identity, reality, and the social whole of which he or she is only one part. The sleuths to be discussed below are a disparate bunch, representing a broad spectrum of cognitive styles, but they have in common an emphasis on knowledge as a condition of multiplying alternatives that originates in both embodied emotion and the relational networks within which the sleuth exists.

The spatial dimensions of matters of mind are significant here. In the more occult of the series—Charlaine Harris's Harper Connelly books (2005–09), in which Harper, struck by lightning, can sense the location and final moments of dead people (in addition to suffering severe headaches and pain in the leg where the lightning hit); and L. L. Bartlett's Jeff Resnick novels (2005–16), in which Resnick has visions of crimes after fracturing his skull, along with migraines and nausea—the affective quality of detection becomes a *literal* act of putting oneself in another's position, granting these investigators a form of identification that goes well beyond powers of observation or deduction; it includes sensing the geography of crime. Both *Curious Incident* and *Motherless Brooklyn* imbricate place with the requirements of crime-solving, skewing the familiar tableau of private eye perambulating the cityscape via their protagonists' unique psycho-affective relationship to where they grow up, and who else populates those neighborhoods. A slew of detectives with amnesia lose not only memory but also their sense of rootedness in a hometown, a workplace, continuity with the self that occupies a certain milieu, so that solving the crime coincides with repositioning themselves in their own geospatial histories.[3]

Crucial to these texts, then, are questions of where cognition happens—where in the world, so to speak, and where in the body. The typical detective may be "gargantuan" in knowledge, as Irving Zola writes, but sleuths whose conditions both amplify and lessen certain moves of mind radically restructure what it means to be an intelligent tec. The clustering of so many novels and television shows featuring detectives with cognitive disabilities and mental illness in the early 2000s may reflect a cultural shift away from psychological explanations for our moods and habits in favor of neurological and genetic ones: the ascendancy of medicine over psychoanalysis. But there's more at work here than a simple blow to the head or the privileging of neurochemical over interpersonal causation, even if some texts do foreground the controversy of pharmaceutical drugs or suggest purely physiological etiologies for their protagonists' issues. What emerges throughout these stories, in the coincidence of crime and atypical cognition, is both existential uncertainty *and* experiment, a need for the weird to be packaged as explicable but also a willingness to test the limits of acceptable selfhood. Stories that situate cognitive or emotional impairment as the agent of recompense would seem to throw the moral implications of the system upside-down. But this is exactly the point, as I will argue: to imagine the form of justice that might be guaranteed by madness.

Madness, of course, has long been depicted as the only *sane* response to a world of wild unpredictability (as in Shakespeare's *Twelfth Night*, where Sebastian says that either he is "mad,/Or else the lady's mad" [3.4.108], as if *somebody* has to be, given the antics going on around him). R. D. Laing famously protested in the 1960s that conditions like psychosis and schizophrenia were behavioral responses to environment rather than biological pathologies and needed, accordingly, to be treated not by psychopharmacology but by conversation and an awareness of the subject's familial and social context. Derrida argues in *Writing and Difference* that mental illness cannot articulate itself from within the language of reason, that reason cannot be contested from within its own discourse. Félix Guattari, Gilles Deleuze's longtime collaborator, takes such a premise a step further in *Chaosophy*, declaring that schizophrenia is induced by the operations of what he called "institutions and groupuscules, that is to say ... all kinds of power relations" (9); shouldn't "the mad people themselves" (83), Guattari asks, rather than the institution of psychoanalysis, act as the "machines" of revolution and re-creation? The Mad Pride movement brings such ideas literally to the streets, staging protests, concerts, walking tours, "bed pushes," and other events to destigmatize mental illness, raise awareness about both insufficient and involuntary treatment, and celebrate so-called extreme mental states as legitimate identities rather than diagnoses.[4]

The investigations I'll explore in this chapter raise questions about the degree to which our understanding of personhood is embedded in the capacity to tell a certain kind of story. They thus exploit the tension between the formal expectations of detective fiction, which presumes identifiable truths even if closure is often complicated as unreliable, and disability as a state of being that violates formal expectations in bodies, minds, and narrative. Richard Ingram has recently argued that both psychiatry *and* the anti-psychiatry movement endorse the ability to create sequential, linear narrative as the hallmark of mental wellness. Whether we identify as psychiatric consumers or survivors of a "pernicious" establishment, Ingram suggests (244), conforming to narrative is key—whether the narrative is one reified by such instruments as the American Psychiatric Association's *Diagnostic and Statistical Manual of Mental Disorders* (the DSM, now in its fifth edition) or simply by an implicit cultural injunction to command one's own story as a way of making sense of self. The ability to "make sense," writes Ingram—the very hallmark of a legitimate detective, we remember—becomes a "moral imperative" exerting a powerful regulatory function on subjectivity. We need "a critique of narrative," he argues, "as a technology that positions psychiatric patients as senseless bodies, dependent on mental health professionals who are presumed to know the true nature of their patients' 'mental disorders'" (244).[5]

So who are the "weirdo problem-solvers," as Cory Barker calls them in his review of the 2012 premier of TNT's *Perception*, and what is the status of the narratives they occupy and the ones they produce about the cases they work? How do we understand stories in which the very source of sense-making might defy expectations about coherence, integrity, and wholeness? How does a sleuth whose condition may be diagnosed in terms of a fractured connection to "reality" maintain authority over what *really* happened? The phenomenon that Sharon L. Snyder and David T. Mitchell refer to as narrative "safekeeping," whereby disability experience is framed by able-bodied "beneficence" and "every white coat means well" (*Cultural Locations*, 181), takes on new meaning in the context of *dis*-able-bodied law enforcement, in which the neurotecs proliferate possible realities far more than they contain a single one. Medicalized or depathologized, hewing to narrative tropes or narrating against convention, these protagonists occupy a complicated social location—or to put this differently, they *are* a complicated location, manifesting collisions between pattern and chaos, predictability and the utterly unanticipated, security and danger. What this means for crime stories, I think, is a version of the point Bérubé makes throughout *The Secret Life of Stories*, that intellectual disability is not simply represented as a character trait but instead mobilized as the very "condition of possibility for the text" (72). Realities clash and detectives slip in and out of verifiable planes of existence. Some sleuths channel the emotions of victims and perpetrators while others have difficulty feeling at all. Some can't remember a thing. Others can't forget. The conditions to be studied here don't get in the way of unraveling the mystery. They *are* the way.

Lionel Essrog, the private-eye narrator of Jonathan Lethem's highly acclaimed *Motherless Brooklyn* (1999), has Tourette syndrome. He is one of four orphans taken under the wing of Frank Minna, a small-time Brooklyn hood running a car service that fronts for a detective agency. The novel is detective fiction by homage—Lethem is known for his genre-bending mash-ups, and the investigation of *Motherless Brooklyn* is carried out through wildly associative, absurd utterances that violate just about every accepted tenet of crime writing—and Lionel narrates himself as much as he does the action of the mystery he tries to solve, which is Minna's murder. This metafictional dimension is cited by many reviewers as integral to the novel's handling of the obsessive, explosive verbalizing of Tourette's, which is praised as a canny metaphor for the formal constraints of detective fiction, the inwardness of first-person narrative, the rough-edged authenticity of Brooklyn as compared to Manhattan's glib homogeneity, the whorls of consciousness, language, and the human condition. Lethem has been likened not only to Joyce, Nabokov, and Faulkner for his pyrotechnic wordplay, but also to Chandler and Dickens for his keen portrayal of the subtleties of social organization, and to the latter for his interest in the losses and loneliness of childhood.

My interest here has less to do with Lethem's frankly metaphorical portrayal of Tourette syndrome (which he has acknowledged as "the kind of exaggeration ... that fiction thrives on"[6]), than with the specifically tactile quality of the protagonist's verbal and physical tics as these participate in Lionel's pursuit of Minna's killer. Tourette's is at once bodily and discursive in this novel—a duality that coincides with the fact that investigation is, too—and both useful and obstructive. Lionel's "bloodhoundlike obsessions" (143) are advantageous to detection, and people's inability to recognize Tourette's for what it is means that, frequently written off and ignored as "crazy" (84, 107, 300, and elsewhere), Lionel can hide in plain sight. On the other hand, Lionel is eruptive—not an advantage on a stakeout—and "an investigator who supplie[s] plenty of [his] own distractions, too many" (218). How, then, can he be a convincing "lead detective" (143)? How does touch mediate the collision between neurology and detection in Lethem's version of an epistemological genre? How is meaning at once contextual, corporeal, and interpersonal?

As in any hard-boiled mystery worth its salt, the urban scene of *Motherless Brooklyn* is an involute, stifling world of inscrutable motivation and random action, devoid of meaningful paradigms. Family is a makeshift affair. Minna's criminal activities are "discontinuous" (167) and the jobs Lionel and the other "Minna Men" do for him bear a "trademark of total inexplicability" (169). This is a world of circularities, where the ragtag staff of a detective agency disguised as a car service actually work as drivers when they're bored, before taking on the personal and serious case of Minna's death, before turning the "'corrupt and inept'" (101) detective agency into a bonafide car service by the end of the novel. "Consensual reality is both fragile and elastic" (44), Lionel remarks, sounding like a postmodern Marlowe or Spade. "Context is everything" (1). James Peacock argues accordingly that "Lionel's verbal tics are ... an idiosyncratic form of cognitive mapping" in that "they give him a defined role within Minna's tiny sphere of operation" in Brooklyn (75). Place, community, and Tourettic utterance exist in a thickly entwined, mutually constitutive relation that holds Lionel in place, Peacock suggests, keeping him stuck in a "nostalgically conceived past" (78). In this reading, it's only when Lionel breaks out of Brooklyn, concentrating his energies (read: subduing his ticcish impulses) to get himself to Maine, that the mystery of Minna's death can finally conclude. To "complete the mourning process" and "move forward" (78), Lionel has to "de-contextualiz[e]" (79), in Peacock's terms: leave something of his Brooklyn-bound Tourretic self behind and fully realize his role as private eye.

Lionel's own manner of talking about his tics, though, configures space in ways that are less bounded by actual geographical limits and more concerned with forms of interconnection, and in this sense, he's a sleuth because of Tourette's, not in spite of it. Both Tourette's and all the criminal activity of the novel occupy an intermediary area between compulsion and intention, environment and embodiment. Why we do what we do? There's the pure linguistic abstraction and aural filigree of Lionel's vocalizing, and language as truly corporeal, words "translated into physical performance" and often barely held in check by a "tongue wound in [his] teeth," "swallowed ... back like vomit" (47–48). Is one more meaningful, more purposeful, than the other? How do we square helplessness with creativity or criminality with intent? Is the difference between one verbal string and another—compare how Yankees slugger Bucky Dent becomes "Luckylent," "Duckybent," "*Lexluthor*," "Lunchylooper, Laughyluck, Loopylip ... *Lockystuff*" (51) with "Mr. Minna's" turning into "*misdemeanors*" (33) in the mouth of a doctor with an accent— one of purpose or control? Agency versus reception? Audience and setting? Lionel's "oddness" can quickly become uninteresting, depending on "the atmosphere" (31). Tics may be involuntary (Lionel shouting out "Eat me,

Bailey!") or echolalic riffs triggered by conversation: "'Maybe his name's in the book,' said Tony. ... 'Or maybe in Frank's book—you got that? Frank's address book?' ... Under my breath I said, *Franksbook, forkspook, finksblood—*'" (96). They may seem uncontrolled—"I raised my hands in surrender, then snatched an imaginary fly out of the air" (96)—or full of need to make a certain kind of contact: "I grabbed Tony back, my hands exploring his collar, fingers running inside it like an anxious, fumbling lover" (78). And it's this last, the analogy of lover (one that recurs again and again), that establishes a kind of holism in all the proliferating signification, and suggests how Lionel's neurological condition becomes a phenomenological mode of detecting.

If the question here is "who ha[s] to make sense of everything?" (169), Lionel's response is, *he* does—by sending out his tics to "course over the surface of the world, tickling reality like fingers on piano keys" (1). There's something of desire and "tenderness" (another word that repeats) in these modes of knowing, in the artistry and re-creation that emerge from points of physical contact. Lionel explains that "counting and touching things and repeating words are all the same activity," that Tourette's "is just one big lifetime of tag" (5). Tag might imply that truth—the it-ness of this mystery—will be endlessly deferred, that postmodern detection is nothing but gesture. But tag is also inherently physical and relational: it has no meaning unless one person taps another. Otherwise the game would be pointless motion, effort redoubling upon itself and effecting no change. A game of tag might seem to deny mystery's imperative of a single endpoint, much like Lionel's verbal sentences, but it also establishes meaning in the relay of identity (who "it" is) initiated by touch.

In "caressing" and "nudging" the world (1), then, in his many acts of "massage" that are also forms of "interpret[ing]" (1), Lionel redefines knowing as a process of expansive bodily contact. It may be that we can't say what a thing *is* with making a metaphor—tag, massage, piano—but the search for meaning that those metaphors represent necessitates touching. Lionel describes one of his early tics as "bouts of kissing," helpless "lunge[s]" at fellow inmates of St. Vincent's Home for Boys (45) while he desperately, "sometimes as tears of pain [run] down [his] face" (46), tries to disguise this behavior as a game. He doesn't precisely grow out of this form of touching: tapping Minna's shoulder, or Gilbert's nose, or running his fingers under Tony's collar—these are "regular gesture[s]" (6), familiar steps in a "ticceography" (79) that orients Lionel vis-à-vis others and what he needs to know of or from them. Tourettic touching is "negotiating a new understanding" (220) between people, *is* detecting: "the making and tracing of unexpected connections a kind of touchiness, an expression of the yearning to touch the world, kiss it all over with theories, pull it close" (178). Lionel says at the end of the novel that "assertions are common to [him]," "common to detectives," and also, "of course, a version of Tourette's. A way of touching the world, handling it, covering it with confirming language" (307). This is how he intervenes in a purposeful way, unravels the tidy fabric of social decorum, cuts through senselessness, "restore[s] order" (9).

Writing in 2009 about a "new strain" of Anglo-American fiction in which "the novel of consciousness ... has transformed itself into the neurological novel, wherein the mind becomes the brain," Marco Roth worries about the literary effects of explanatory physiological "reductionism." In a post-psychoanalytic era in which analysis, once "taken to offer the most authoritative account of personality," has been replaced by neurology, less "friendly to the informal psychological explorations of novelists," a form that was once "open to the whole range of human language" becomes a stiflingly diagnostic one. What was once the radical experimentation of modernism becomes "mere biological contingency," which closes off meaning and denies the "ordinary" reader any imaginative identification with diagnosable characters. *Motherless Brooklyn*, Roth argues, perpetrates a terrible self-indulgence, "marginaliz[ing]" its own "experimental impulse," its admittedly astute perceptions, as mere "abnormal psychology."

Whatever Lethem's intention may have been in using Tourette's to get at something intrinsically Brooklyn, or Lethem, or more generally social, Roth is guilty here of reifying ableist distinctions between normalcy and pathology by suggesting that a novelized neurological condition—no matter how apparently metaphorical its representation is—can never be more than a factual oddity, something *those* people have that bears no relation to the ordinary firing of *my* neurons. A resistance to disability in the novels Roth discusses (he includes autism and *Curious Incident*) is ultimately a disdain for disability itself, a failure both to consider and to value, as Bérubé has argued, what cognitive disabilities mean for the creation of story, which is a way of understanding how—or more acutely, *whether*—subjectivity can only be realized through narrative.[7] It's one thing to resist *Motherless Brooklyn* as an ableist fantasy of what it might be like if everybody got to say or do whatever we feel the urge for, no matter how socially disastrous.[8] It's another to object to Tourette's *as Tourette's* as a foreclosure of intellectual expansiveness. That move, it seems to me, diminishes the novel in a different way, refusing to be engaged by the philosophical provocation of neurodiversity, to take Lionel seriously as "evidence of life's unpredictability and rudeness and poignancy" (57).

A reader might legitimately object to Lethem's occasional suggestions that there's a little Tourette's in everyone as an irresponsible flattening of what are ultimately significant differences. But situating ourselves on a continuum of human behavior is neither a reckless nor an apolitical act. And there are other invitations here. What would happen to our notions of *truth*, for instance, if we challenged social imperative when it "border[s] on sheer Dada" (172), rather than succumbing to it? Or if, like Lionel, we plucked at the threads of "the reality-knitting mechanism people employ to tuck away the intolerable, the incongruous, the disruptive" (43)? Even as the locus of "interruptions of interruptions" (195), Lionel is the emotional and ethical ground of this mystery, the one who avenges the death of the only father he's ever known. When he says at the end that he has "visit[ed] the labyrinth that runs under the world, which everyone pretends is not there" (310), we can read him as a Virgilian figure who risks the depths of human transgressiveness without losing himself. Indeed, part of Lionel's appeal is precisely how fully *himself* he is. The novel allows us to figure out for ourselves, in Lionel's company, just how true it is that we're "'all freaks'" (49). "'You're strange to me,'" says Kimmery, Lionel's girlfriend, but then again, "everyone is so strange'" (219). At the same time, "'nothing's wrong with you,'" she says. "'That's my whole point'" (212).

Discussing Mark Haddon's *Curious Incident of the Dog in the Night-Time*, Bérubé asks how a detective story can be told—how an investigation can be led—by a *"teenager who cannot distinguish significant from insignificant detail"* (134; italics in original), since by definition good detecting requires such distinctions. Bérubé argues that "intellectually disabled characters ... bend the narrative around themselves so as to warp our expectations for degrees of detail or continuity" (134), and suggests that a novel like *Curious Incident* trades on provoking readers' impatience about sticking to the "point," just as the TV character of Adrian Monk (to whom I will turn below) also does. What's significant in these instances is how these sleuths' cognitive habits redirect our understanding of the criteria by which we determine what anything means.

As Christopher himself says, referring to the process of connecting stars in constellations, "this is really silly because it is just stars, and you could join up the dots in any way you wanted" (125). Myrdene Anderson and Floyd Merrell make this same claim differently in *Semiotics and Dis/ability*, writing that "everything is in some way like and … also different with respect to everything else," a philosophical position that would necessitate "a flattening of any and all hierarchies" (271–72). *Curious Incident* is specifically a *mystery* novel, I would argue, because "join[ing] up the dots" is what both detectives and metanarratives do, and Haddon is interested in complicating the latter by means of the former. Mysteries of all sorts abound in the text, from who killed the Shears's dog Wellington to the nature of time to the puzzle of idiomatic expressions to the very definition of disability, and Christopher—with his somewhat stereotyped aptitude for esoteric math and science problems and his inability to grasp the nuances of emotion—becomes both an extremely articulate instructor and a naively astute interrogator. As Bérubé points out, Christopher is "narratively self-aware" (136), which means that he tells his story with a high degree of responsibility about accounting for his take on things, which in turn means that even the "obvious" is scrutinized and explained in ways that deny rather than confirming its legitimacy. This is why "learning difficulties" and "special needs" are deemed "stupid" classifications, since "everyone" has them in one form or another (43), and why heaven makes no sense, because (as Christopher says with deadpan logic) "if heaven was on the other side of a black hole, dead people would have to be fired into space in a rocket to get there, and they aren't or people would notice" (32–33).

The implication that anything can be anything depending on how you connect the dots, along with the possibility that "all the facts that you take for granted [are] completely wrong" (80), may seem surprising acknowledgements from a narrator who doesn't like metaphor, but they are tied to Christopher's detecting skills. In his insistence on breaking down uncritical assumptions (like his hero, Sherlock Holmes, he is especially impatient about belief in "the supernatural" [74] as a go-to answer for anything that defies ready explanations), Christopher denies us the comfort of simply leaping toward what's easy because already "known." For all the apparent rigidity of his cognitive style, he is the surprising locus of enormous freeplay, as putting some pressure on conventional norms tends to demonstrate their absurdity. As the detective in this story, Christopher's methods of processing thus lead us not to fixed meanings but to ambiguity, revision, and the unpredictability of emotion.

At the novel's pivotal turn, for example—the shocking discovery that his father has lied to him about his mother's death, that his mother is alive—Christopher leaves home to find her in London. On the Tube, he sees an "advert" for travel to Malaysia promising "*A world of difference*" (179; italics in original). Detecting thus leads to actual travel, which leads to the promise of more travel, which entails an encounter with difference.[9] But according to whose perspective? In relation to what center of "same" is Malaysia "other"? Christopher understands this completely: it's why he tells us that "a thing is interesting because of thinking about it and not because of being new" (178). Meaning is framed (literally, like the advertisement in the train) rather than essential, in other words—or to put this in Deleuzean terms, the spatial dynamics of interaction make it so; we are always *becoming* in contact with our environments, rather than existing as fixed identities within unchanging locations. Where is "home," in this regard, if "Father [is] there and he told a lie and he killed Wellington" (176)? Is home 451c Chapter Road, London NW2 5NG, an utterly unfamiliar place, even though Christopher's mother is there? Between the Swindon of Father and the London of Mother, both of whom are now frightening sources of unpredictability and untruth, Christopher must recalibrate his "Chain of Reasoning" (42). He is far from intractable, which his ventures into these estranged milieus of mystery and metropolis are clearly intended to prove.

The tendency to attribute Christopher's sequential thinking solely to logic, moreover, deprives his intelligence of its emotional dimension, as Stuart Murray has argued (183), and discounts the degree to which Christopher's cognitive habits—rendered here as detection—are founded in relationships. Take Christopher's supposition that the fact that Mr. Shears "didn't want to live in the same house as Mrs. Shears anymore," even though married people "have to promise that [they] will stay together," means that "he probably hated her and … might have come back and killed her dog to make her sad" (43). This makes surprising sense. In fact, it's nearly *right*, because it's Christopher's father who kills the dog in a fit of pique, jealous that Mrs. Shears (with whom he's become involved) "'care[s] more about this bloody dog'" (122). The decision to "find out more about Mr. Shears" (43) to learn what happened to Wellington isn't just good detecting, then (given the man's proximity to the victim of the crime). More than that, it betrays Christopher's sensitivity to emotional motive, whatever trouble he may also have with facial expressions.

A preference for orderliness and ritual over the unexpected makes Christopher's voyage to London an anxious one, although he understands that detecting will require that he be "brave" (35). But what most frightens Christopher through the second half of *Curious Incident*, I think, is less this harrowing spatial relocation than the fact that his father has lied to him and proven himself to be capable of an awful violence. Christopher is not in any physical danger from Ed Boone, as readers understand, and I would argue that the purpose of this sense of threat is not even to make the point that we can be hurt by those in whose care we entrust ourselves. Strictly speaking, Ed takes better care of Christopher than anyone. It's just that, as Christopher says in a different context, "people ... do things that you don't expect" (143)—and *that* is the point. The unexpected death of Wellington prompts Christopher's sleuthing, which becomes an unexpected arena of resistance to the pressures of normative emotional and cognitive behavior. To quote Murray again, "the central generic spaces of the crime narrative become locations for ideas of disability that refute the reductive, and rather outline the cognitively disabled as a complex space of human subjectivity" (181). As Christopher is led further and further afield from the safe space of the familiar, sleuthing and disability alike are presented as forms of challenge to what we thought we knew about human behavior, and to *how* we thought such things in the first place.

The last decade has brought a spate of protagonist-sleuths with pronounced psychological issues to television. "All decent detectives suffer from OCD," says DCI John Barnaby in *Midsomer Murders* ("The Flying Club," 2014; 16.4). With series like *Monk* (2002–09), *House* (2004–12), *Bones* (2005–17), *Psych* (2006–14), *The Mentalist* (2008–15), *Unforgettable* (2011–14), *Black Box* (2014), *Perception* (2012–15), and *Grimm* (2011–17), TV has become a purveyor of storylines about neurodiverse investigators whose conditions are written as instrumental to their mystery-solving abilities.[10] Such shows surely indicate a Hollywood penchant for imitating plotlines that work. Cory Barker reacts accordingly to *Perception* (about a paranoid schizophrenic neuroscientist who assists the FBI): just one more show, he writes with ironic ennui, about "singular, kooky individual[s] … Who Can Solve Everything But Themselves!" Esther Breger has a less forgiving response, warning in *The New Republic* in 2014 that "mental illness as superpower" is "one of pop culture's most noxious tropes," and Lesley Smith agrees, referring to the phenomenon as "chic tic." But others have suggested that these shows destigmatize just by featuring protagonists with mental illness living more or less regular lives, and by uncoupling mental illness from both monstrousness and moralized taint.[11]

The point I will argue about *Monk*, as a quasi-police procedural and one of the progenitors of the trend, is that the series redirects our attention away from the problematic mental health trope of mad creativity toward other forms of being, relating, and knowing. Adrian Monk, former San Francisco PD detective-turned-consultant, has a peripheral connection with the agency he assists. Smith dismisses this as the "brilliant oddball as criminal consultant genre," but I will suggest otherwise, that the affectionate, respectful relationships Monk establishes with both traditional law enforcement and his various personal assistants create lateral, hybrid frameworks in which top-down power is displaced and different forms of collaboration are positioned as vital to social order. His story implies the necessity—and, importantly, the value—of *help*, and of some *other* manner of thinking and observing that the neurotypical detective would be incapable of on his or her own. To decry this as *only* clichéd fantasy, the go-to binary logic of emotionally "crippled"/cognitively "gifted," is to minimize the revisionary effect Monk's disability has on traditional epistemologies.

Monk, created by Andy Breckman and starring Tony Shalhoub, aired on USA from 2002 to 2009. The series was both enormously popular and critically acclaimed, garnering eight primetime Emmy awards in as many years and earning Shalhoub three Outstanding Lead Actor awards. Monk becomes a consultant after a breakdown necessitates his retirement from the police force. He is described as having OCD (though certain of his tendencies hue more closely to a common conception of Asperger's syndrome); a long list of phobias—including germs, heights, crowds, snakes, milk, mushrooms, vomiting, and dentists; and obsessive behaviors like touching parking meters or lampposts. The severity if not origin of his condition is linked more or less explicitly to two emotional traumas: one, the abandonment of the Monk family by the father, when Adrian was a child; the other, the death of his beloved wife in a car-bomb explosion.

The *Official Episode Guide* explains that Doyle's Holmes stories were the inspiration for both the hero and the plotting style of *Monk*: "'Monk is ... a modern-day Sherlock Holmes,'" says show creator Breckman; "'people who know Sherlock Holmes recognize all the components of *Monk*'" (2). Like his predecessor, according to Breckman, Monk is "'superintuitive,'" "'quick, brilliant, analytical,'" with an "'amazing ability to see the things'" that others can't (5)—and also "too different, too smart, too eccentric" for audiences to "identify with" (6). But while Breckman might have wanted to invoke the "'fun ride'" of a Doyle story rather than Agatha Christie's "'intricacies of plot,'" I would argue that his hero is far more overtly the heir of Hercule Poirot, that other genius detective obsessed with symmetry and straight lines.[12] Both cut their toast into squares; neither can tolerate soft-boiled eggs of different sizes. They sleep neatly on their backs with crisp sheets pulled up to their chins. They are fussy and prudish, similarly disgusted by the messier inevitabilities of human existence: smells, bodily functions, exposure to weather, and noise. Poirot is the more gallant of the two, but both are marked by their habits in ways that compromise social status and prohibit full inclusion in the life going on around them. A certain pathos thus attaches to these sleuths: they know too much about the depths of human degradation and are preoccupied by attempts to defend against their own. In this sense, I think, both Poirot and Monk function as exaggerations of common tendencies rather than clinical portrayals of something diagnosable, and we are *strongly* invited to identify with them.

As the *Guide* tells it, Monk is "'nuts'" (2), a sleuth who "'can barely function in the world'" (5). But Monk cannot be reduced to a "'cluster of symptoms'" (6) any more than he is simply "someone magical" (15); to describe him in these terms is to make him a caricature, to minimize the subtler dynamics of what is dramatized in actual episodes, which rarely rest on the passive entertainment of a man made helpless by psychological disorder. The show's creators wanted a fusion of mystery and comedy, but if Monk's condition provides the latter, it is not slapstick ridicule; the humor of the show most often emerges from the interstice between Monk's (mis)understandings—of social niceties, of vernacular, of cultural identities—and behaviors or apparent truths that a neurotypical viewer might gloss over as unremarkable.[13] In the process of being minutely clarified, what is normal becomes ludicrous (just as in *Curious Incident*) rather than more explicable; what might have seemed natural or obvious appears elaborately constructed.

When a group of law students proposes that Monk sue the SFPD under the ADA for wrongful termination ("Mr. Monk and the Missing Granny," 2004; 2.13), the sleuth has a moment of alarmed self-consciousness. "Am I ... disabled?" he asks. *Monk* is not a series to delve especially deeply into the legal or existential thickets of such a question, but that it is posed at all suggests some interrogation of how we know ourselves. Monk is hardly timid about announcing his limits, preferences, or opinions, but "disabled" as an identity category is not part of his habitus, and the moment is fraught with contesting definitions. Is it *obvious* that Monk is disabled according to ADA parameters—impaired in a way that affects daily activities? Does it matter? Any number of minute decisions on which a case will turn seem packed into that single query; what does it do to Monk's own or anyone else's understanding of him if he wears the label? When we next see Monk failing the reinstatement exam because of his compulsive erasures of pencil marks on the Scantron form, the implication is twofold: not only that Monk *is* disabled, and the protection of the law means nothing if he can't manage the responsibilities of the job (like handling a weapon), but also that such institutional gatekeeping disadvantages non-normative modes of processing. Does any viewer really doubt that Monk could "ace" the test if it were delivered in a way that would account for him?

Scenes from *Monk* frequently linger over aspects of the hero's behavior that would seem either unrelated to solving a case or liable to derail an investigation by bogging the team down in frustratingly extraneous concerns. What can feel like digression, however, is always central to the plot, not just in the interest of creating dimensional characters but because it emphasizes all that gets revealed when we pay a different kind of attention. Consider the following from "Mr. Monk and the Rapper" (2007; 6.2) in which Monk is asked to weigh in on a debate about an unfinished song (Natalie [Traylor Howard] is Monk's personal assistant in seasons 4–7):

RAPPER: I'm still working on these lyrics. Tell me which you like better, though [rapping]: "club-hopping, game-chopping, … booty-popping." *Poppin'*? Or *bangin'*?

....

MONK: *Poppin'* or *bangin'* … First off, thank you for asking … what does *poppin'* mean again?

RAPPER: *Poppin'* is just like, you know, like, really *crackin'*, like, you feel me? Like, just, like when the booty is just like [tracing a shape with his hand] … *ah* … and *ah* … you feel me?

MONK: I feel you. Uh, and, what does *poppin'* mean again?

RAPPER: I just told you! It's like really *crackin'*.

NATALIE: They both mean "good," Mr. Monk.

MONK: Yeah, *poppin'* or *bangin'* … oh … wow. Pressure! Um, *I-I-I-I* I think it'd be a lot easier if I actually met the girl … I'm gonna to have to go with *bangin'*. Nah, no, wait, um, this is hard because they're both so evocative. Is it *poppin'* or *boppin'*?

STUDIO
ENGINEER: Let's just take a break.

....

MONK: Is it *crackin'* or *cracklin'*?

The scene is comical because Monk is so hopelessly square ("'terminally unhip,'" in Shalhoub's own words [*Guide*, 6]), and it's a send-up of the seriousness of insider lingo. But it also suggests, more philosophically, that the effort to pin something down, to stabilize the meaning of the thing, will inevitably devolve into circularity: "popping" is "cracking" is "banging," which could also be "bopping" or "crackling." Monk's attempt to get at some core truth by appealing to "reality"—meeting the girl—produces only more words, more possibilities, *evoking* but not confirming.

As the scene goes on, viewers might also begin to wonder, with our sleuth, about subtle gradations of difference, and to want to know, exactly, what is what. Perhaps we wonder if it matters, or who's telling us we should care. Perhaps we begin to revel in the proliferation. Perhaps, as Robert A. Rushing has argued of *Monk*, repetition itself is the point, the source of the pleasure we take in "the entire genre, with its endlessly repeated formalist tics" (150). Attunement to *difference*, though, is what makes Monk a good detective,[14] so that his effort to distinguish between one slang term and another is both utterly beside the point and entirely to the point (in this episode, the solution hinges on Monk's realization that a car bomb was timed to standard rather than daylight savings time: a literal difference of an hour). Such moments are not ancillary comic relief, then; they are exemplary of how Monk's mind works and why he's good at his job: nothing is obvious and everything is subject to scrutiny, exactly as Christopher Boone also declares. It is well known to lovers of mystery that Sherlock Holmes explains in "The Adventure of the Naval Treaty" that the detective must be able to sort essential from irrelevant facts. Monk is explicitly *not* Holmes in that his method doesn't just separate the significant from the extraneous in a hierarchical sense—a question of *what* we notice. Rather, it engages him in conundrums of definition—*how* we notice.

This is why the sleuth becomes temporarily ineffectual in "Mr. Monk Takes His Medicine" (2004; 3.9). Telling his shrink, "I'm just so tired, tired of being … *me*," he starts a course of the fictional Dioxnyl, which (totally improbably) turns him overnight into the sports-car-driving, Hawaiian-shirt-wearing, other-people's-food-eating, self-named "the Monk." The drug seems to liberate Monk from his severely inhibiting phobias, which are in effect a matter of paying too much attention—he is playful, able to laugh and touch—but it also compromises his focus. In the apartment where a woman has reportedly committed suicide, "the Monk" glances quickly at an apparent suicide note and says, "There's something wrong with this note …," but he can't discern what it is. The problem is one of concentration, the loss of that "autistic intensity," as Lennard J. Davis puts it, "that aids his detective work" (*End of Normal*, 32). Davis explains that "with OCD … suffering comes from being in an environment that pinpoints the kinds of things you are doing as unproductive and worthy of stopping" (33)—Rosemarie Garland-Thomson's notion of disability as a matter of *misfitting* between bodymind and milieu. A medicated Monk, by fitting in with his surround, would be a more convenient one, while the unmedicated version can figure out what's wrong with the note but also lets a suspect escape because he cringes at touching a crowbar.

But Monk doesn't ultimately quit the medication just because it hampers his powers as a detective. I disagree with Davis that Monk is portrayed as happier on meds; perhaps more crucial to his crime-solving than his distracted state is the fact that no one around him actually likes "the Monk," and it is in part the loss of the collective that prevents Monk from doing his job well. At the end of the episode, when Monk is off the drug and back to "normal," his assistant Sherona (Bitty Schram, seasons 1–3) asks, "Is it you?" Later, when Monk says, "You understand that if I toss these out you'll never see the Monk again," Sherona responds by throwing the pills into a dumpster herself. "Missed ya," she says, touching his arm, to which Monk replies, "I missed me too." The implication is not so much that Monk's sleuthing requires the suffering of illness as it is that Monk needs the close if unlikely bonds he's formed with others, and that being medicated out of disability actually harms those relationships. The intriguing questions of the episode are thus ontological and relational—less "who is the Monk on meds?" than "can Monk be himself without community?"

This is the unexpected inquiry of "Mr. Monk Can't See a Thing" (2006; 5.4), where the additive conceit of OCD+blindness opens to intriguing possibilities about how *else* to function, which is also a question about interrelationality. In this episode, Monk is temporarily blinded by chemicals thrown in his face. He is initially terrified by his new condition, and Shaloub hams up the stumbling and groping (he's swooping "like a bat in a cave," he says, while walking into walls). Immediately, though, other senses kick in, and Monk goes about solving the case as he would any other—his signature style is simply not to let go of a detail—relying on aural and tactile rather than visual clues. Blindness is at once irrelevant to Monk's detecting capabilities in this scenario and a source of relief, since it also grants him temporary reprieve from anxiety ("I'm glad I didn't see that," he says when Natalie reacts to a few rats in an alley[15]). Monk's gifts do not become *enhanced* through blindness; they simply adjust to a different mode of sensory engagement with the environment.

Monk's psychiatrist Dr. Kroger (Stanley Kamel), however, has other ideas:

DR. KROGER: Adrian, I have to tell you I'm a little concerned. Now, there are five stages of grief and I think you've already leapfrogged over at least the first three of them ... I think that you're using this condition as an excuse to cut yourself off from the real world even more than usual ... I just refuse to believe that you're happy, genuinely happy, having lost your *eyesight*.

MONK: It's the best thing that ever happened to me.

DR. KROGER: Oh, OK, fine, well then, why don't we get some earplugs and some nose plugs and then you can just cut yourself off completely from the world. Or, maybe, we could arrange to have you put into a coma!

It may be right that Monk hasn't had long to adjust to a radical alteration of lifestyle or sense of self. But the doctor's escalation from blindness to *coma* reveals a powerful bias. He cannot fathom that Monk might legitimately appreciate his new condition, and in accusing his patient of clinging to blindness as a dangerous form of isolation, equates it with complete withdrawal from society—worse, complete withdrawal from *consciousness*. Chastising Monk for narcissism and cowardice, he endorses two stereotypes: that disabled people are lonely and self-indulgent and that accepting disability instead of fighting it is tantamount to failure.[16]

Blindness may be played for laughs in this episode, but quite contrary to Dr. Kroger's warning lecture, it changes very little about how Monk interacts or does his job. Far from isolating him, it makes him that much more relaxed in physical spaces he doesn't have to see, and the people closest to him do as much adjusting (in their own fashion) as Monk does. What Dr. Kroger misses but the show invites us to consider is that even the excessively rigid Monk—"afraid of change, and … afraid of not changing" ("Mr. Monk Takes His Medicine")—is capable of adaptive plasticity. Thus one episode suggests that dealing *normatively* with Monk's condition, through drugs, will mar his unique attentiveness and undermine the relationships that support him, while the other portrays *disability* as effecting both a productive cognitive shift in his gathering of clues and confirmation of those same relationships.

John Scaggs writes that "it is the very flexibility of the [police] procedural that allows it to be appropriated" (102)—or "hijack[ed]" (104)—by authors concerned to interrogate the dominant white male heterosexuality of the genre. Because law enforcement is a "*social* world," he writes (103; italics in original), detectives with non-normative identities can "find [themselves] in the teamwork of police procedure" (103) even as their presence calls into question the values of this "traditionally masculine workplace" (102). Scaggs does not mention disability (an omission that should hardly, at this stage in my own study, be surprising), but his claim for the revisionary effect of difference within the seemingly intransigent conservatism of the form is precisely my point about *Monk*, whose hero—despite being more than once denied reinstatement to the force—works within a collective that must constantly adjust itself to accommodate a range of ways of being. To put this differently, despite Monk's strong desire to get back onto the force—his uniform hangs in his closet still, after many years—his skill and fragility are imbricated in his relationships in ways that trouble the system from within.

Lionel Essrog, Christopher Haddon, and Adrian Monk are acutely aware of themselves as individuals whose interpersonal styles defy normative protocols, particularly as their behaviors activate the physical space between self and other. Christopher and Monk do not like to be touched, and manipulate the environment to keep others at bay; Lionel reaches out (perhaps too often for the comfort of his friends), craving contact. In reacting to their environments, they also create their environments—revealing "a world jumping with tics waiting to happen," as Jennifer Fleissner says of Lionel (390), or organizing both objects and feeling-states through systems of number, color, or line. Lionel is stimulated by his surroundings toward spontaneous improvisation, Christopher and Monk more prone to corral perceptual chaos through exaggerated regularity. But as I have tried to show, both forms of engaging the surround are integral to information processing and thus to how these sleuths carry out their work.

In a 1998 article called "The Extended Mind," well-known in philosophical circles, Andy Clark and David J. Chalmers write that "cognitive processes ain't (all) in the head!"[17] The theory of extended cognition, as they explain it, posits that objects in the world—say, the letter tiles of a Scrabble game—are not simply objects of action; to the contrary, in that manipulation of such objects "is part of *thought*," the objects themselves become extensions of cognitive process. In the example of "Otto," who has Alzheimer's disease and writes down information he needs to remember in a notebook he carries with him everywhere, Clark and Chalmers argue that Otto and the notebook constitute a single but extended system, a "coupling of biological organism and external resources"—which means, in turn, that "there is nothing sacred about skull and skin" in terms of how we conceive of self and knowledge. The notebook is for Otto what memory might be for someone else, "reliably there when needed, available to consciousness and ... to guide action."

I invoke Otto's notebook because the concept of extended cognition is pertinent to the emphasis on object-use for many of the detectives under discussion here: the maps and drawings of facial expressions, for instance, that Christopher uses to navigate geographical as well as emotional terrain; or Monk's compulsive arranging of objects in orderly patterns; or even Lionel's echolalic riffings, elaborated semantic conversations with speech in the world. These are instances not just of emotional cathecting, we might say—objects invested with unconscious meaning—but of perceptual apprehension whereby "parts of [the] surroundings can be considered part of ... cognitive processes" (Romdenh-Romluc, 85). In Howard Engel's 2006 novel *The Memory Book*, we have an actual Otto: PI Benny Cooperman. Benny doesn't have Alzheimer's, but a severe blow to the head leaves him with significant cognitive impairment. Recovering in the hospital, he is encouraged by the nurses to keep a memory book, which functions exactly as Otto's does: as an extension of memory and intention beyond the limits of the body, facilitating thought.

The medical situation in *The Memory Book* is partly autobiographical. Like his protagonist, Engel experienced a rare and strangely paradoxical condition called *alexia sine agraphia*, or "word blindness" (Engel's from stroke rather than head trauma). In this so-called disconnection syndrome, damage to the link between the language centers of the brain and a small area of the visual cortex impairs recognition of written words (*alexia*)—but not the capacity to write itself (thus, "without *agraphia*"). Like his character, Engel could "see letters perfectly well," as Oliver Sacks explains in an afterword, but "not interpret them" (240), and so underwent a long rehabilitation to learn to read again by breaking words into smaller blocks and slowly "puzzl[ing]" them out (243). Since Engel's capacity to process language remained intact, he was also able to circumvent the *alexia* through other mechanisms of both receiving and producing writing—being read to, as an obvious example, but also tracing words with a finger on a table or back of his hand, or even with the tip of the tongue against the roof of his mouth. Such are the "new ways of doing things now that the old ways are unavailable," in Sacks's words (247), that so often accompany an acquired disability—importantly, newly embodied ways of processing language.

The Canadian Engel had been a prolific mystery author, with a dozen Cooperman novels in print before the stroke.[18] Basing *The Memory Book* on the event of the stroke was the culmination of Engel's laborious effort to relearn language from the alphabet up as well as a testimony to the experience of hospital life, with its temporary intimacies, the boredom, the sense of dislocation from "self." What Sacks refers to as the "of-necessity unorthodox way of writing" (247) instigated by *alexia* becomes in the novel both an impediment and an incentive to Benny Cooperman's work as a detective. Benny is his own client—not for the mystery of his cognitive condition but for how he acquired it. His memory severely impaired, Benny gradually pieces together that while working a case in Toronto, he was hit on the back of the head, left for dead, and subsequently discovered beside the body of a woman in a dumpster. But how to solve a crime when you're in no physical shape to leave the hospital and your memory is so faulty that you can't hold onto names or facts from one moment to the next? The answer is a kind of hospital-bed mystery in which, like several of the sleuths I discuss in terms of paralysis and mobility impairment, Benny investigates from his room in rehab and gathers information from "operatives" (such as his girlfriend Anna) in the field. But the novel also seems compelled by the enigma of how identity can be organized by a storyteller purportedly unable to maintain the continuity of his tale. In this sense the novel's murder mystery is subordinated to questions of cognitive process and how we might "surprise" ourselves with our own "ingenuity" when circumstances demand that we adapt to an unexpectedly "peculiar life" (78).

As a crime writer, Engel knows that "there's no time for PIs in books or movies to lie about, recovering" (43), and this is ultimately the novel's central generic intrigue: what sort of detective novel is it if the narrating sleuth "is no longer a fair and accurate observer" (49), with "no strong belief in any of [his] opinions" (63) and a "mind made of Swiss cheese" (28)? There might be something of hard-boiled cynicism or postmodern ambiguity in such remarks if they were metaphorical, but they're literal; *a propos* of details, Benny admits that "big or little, important or frivolous: [he] was capable of forgetting them all" (53). Here then is an unreliable narrator-sleuth who violates Holmes's injunction that a good detective is effective at sorting, with a twist: Benny can't remember the details in the first place, and although he writes them down to remember, he can't then read what he's written. Beyond the novel's obvious pedagogical intent (which is to describe what it's like to recover from brain injury), another question gets raised in the tension between straightforward crime solving and the difficulty of pressing toward knowledge when the mind can't reliably retain or access any. Benny tells us that he can't read any faster than six lines of print in fifteen minutes. The first tangible clue in the case happens on page 67. Benny must "decod[e]" words "one a time, ... returning to the beginning of the sentence to make sure [he hasn't] lost the sense" (46). This is a story that overtly complicates the genre's premium on a steady accumulation of clues and realizations. If we set aside the inconsistency of a wholly coherent tale replete with precisely remembered dialogue and legitimate theorizing narrated by a man who says he can't keep two ideas in his mind at once, what emerges is an indirect challenge to the all-knowing authority of the law—which might explain why the ineffectual cops in this novel are outdone by a PI with a "disorganized head" (71).

The primary mechanism of Benny's response to his "new memory," so "full of ... filigrees of twisted silken strands" that it needs a "latticework of aids to criss-cross [his] experience and expectation" (78), is the memory book, in which Benny records everything from the names of cousins that pop into his consciousness to fragments of memory to specific details as he "pick[s] up the pieces" of the investigation (42). In the context of crime, there's something paradigmatic in the disjunctive feature of this cognitive device, in the fact that Benny has no difficulty writing anything down but then struggles to reread it. Inherent in this mystery is a powerful disconnect between action and comprehension that demands painstaking reconstruction to locate the origins of motive and purpose. "Something not right; look again," Benny thinks, trying to read a novel. "Sharpening my focus" (46). He could be talking about detecting in general. The radical disruption of ordinary processing that results from Benny's brain injury is in some ways no disruption at all—if we accept the memory book as an extension of cognition—but *alexia* also enforces slowing way down, attending to a feeling that something isn't "right," starting over from the beginning. This is a sleuth who obstructs his own investigation, spending as much time trying to decipher what he's written down as a clue as the meaning any such clue purportedly contains. Implicitly, then, the novel destabilizes itself as the conveyor of truthfulness by presenting self-generated text as what comes between the detective and the knowledge he seeks; we are always our own worst enemies, managing to undermine our efforts to restore ourselves to self-possession and forward movement—or to put this differently, there is no such thing as equivalence with oneself; we keep going back to the beginning of the sentence to start again.

But *The Memory Book* does not fully sustain such intriguing implications. The fact that the details of the case are unearthed routinely, even swiftly, by a highly compromised sleuth who spends most of his time sleeping and attending rehab begs the question of why a big city force like the Toronto PD is unable to make headway until Benny, despite being "diseased in the mind" (105), gets the case "'moving again'" (224) two months later. The suspension of disbelief is high, since we are asked to trust a narrator who repeatedly says he's disoriented and confused, who tells us that he forgets information moments after learning it, but whose story is lucid and whose recall for details within its frame seems exact. The challenge for the author is how to maintain fidelity to the experience of head injury in a genre that demands "sense, logic, and deduction" (97)—a conundrum that produces a book somewhat wrenched by competing formal requirements. Crime fiction and medical mystery do not, in this case, precisely align.

Throughout the story, too, Benny expresses frustration about "'getting back to work'" (83): "I wanted to get on with my life. Anything less was makeshift and unsatisfactory" (17), "I wanted to get on with my life [but] I was still not in any shape" (42). Such comments concede to ableist expectations of productivity. Can a meaningful life not be had from within the womb-like atmosphere of the hospital, that "good, warm ... benign, friendly, and safe" place (88) that nonetheless "induces" a "general passivity ... in its inmates" (90)? More urgently, is legitimate selfhood possible given the hierarchizing impulse that separates the "'lucky ones'" (72) from "'people worse off than you'" (17) who might be really "sick" or even "out of [their] mind[s]" (25)? Here, I think, *The Memory Book* betrays its author's commitment to a normalizing definition of social value, where success is measured in terms of legible speech, rational thought, and a secure, ongoing, professional stature. Benny might arrive at truth more slowly than any other narrator-sleuth, but he does get there—down to the Poirot-style summation at the end that maneuvers the killer into revealing himself.

In his afterword, Sacks describes Howard Engel's "daily struggle to transcend" the "impact" of *alexia sine agraphia* as one of "heroic determination and courage" (247), language that indicates allegiance to an ableist expectation of progress and improvement. *The Memory Book* has the potential to embrace the unorthodox, but it ends at a wedding, the very locus of normative conceptions of time, relationality, and worth—"all about our best hopes for the future" (236). Although Benny might embody unconventional forms of dislocated knowing, the novel itself marches on toward closure.

Key shifts in the case in *The Memory Book* come to Benny through dreams. While changes to emotional temperament and intelligence after brain injury are well-documented—and while dreams might indicate nothing stranger than inferential, intuitive thinking as counterpoint to Benny's theoretical reasoning—I would argue that when one Toronto detective quips, "'Can't you work in a Ouija board?'" (225) and another asks, "'Where can *I* get hit on the head like that?'" (226), they imply that something supernatural has happened to Benny as a result of head injury. And, although readers are privy to the hard work of Benny's efforts to read and retain information, we are not entirely disabused of that notion. *The Memory Book* seems to want to have it all ways: verisimilitude to the real consequences of brain trauma without sacrificing the command of the sleuth who can "manipulate" "all the strings ... from [a] hospital room" (105) and has uncannily accurate "feeling[s]" (225). Ultimately, Benny is every bit as "'amazing'" as the best of them. "'You worked it all out,'" Detective Boyd marvels. "'And you did it from the hospital'" (228). (Cue exclamation point.)

The blow to the head, a staple of noir thriller, doesn't always result in occult capabilities, of course, but Howard Engel's impulse to recompense Benny's trauma with something *extra* suggests that no matter how popularized neuroscience has become, the workings of the brain continue to inspire fantasies of the paranormal. In the Jeff Resnick series, head injury in effect multiplies the consciousness of the sleuth through a kind of haunting. Seriously wounded in a mugging, former insurance investigator Resnick recuperates with family in Buffalo. There he discovers that a disturbing consequence of being hit on the head with a baseball bat is physic insight. In the first book of the seven-book series, *Murder on the Mind* (2005), Resnick's receptivity to emotion links him to the killer, so that he sees images of the victim from the murderer's perspective. By the second book it's clear that Resnick can sense the feelings and experiences of a range of people, sometimes by touching an object connected to that person and at others through more random clairvoyant sensations. He uses his past insurance work as a calling card (literally—he hands out old business cards as a cover for asking questions), but he is not a PI; instead, he pursues investigations with a kind of helplessness: getting to the truth of the matter is the only way to quell the physical and emotional toll of "this psychic shit" (he has frequent migraines) (*Dead in Red*, 2008; 156). And, gradually, people in town start hearing about Jeff Resnick's "sixth sense."

What interests me in the handling of Resnick's injury is not so much the idea that physical trauma to the brain could release psychic ability—as if that were just one more in a list of other complications, like memory loss, changes to a person's emotional tenor or resilience, or the risk of seizures, all of which Resnick also has—but rather the intensely emotional content of the sleuth's "visions." We learn that he has sustained a "classic coup-contrecoup injury" (*Murder*, 18), where the opposite side of the brain from the point of impact is severely bruised, which explains the blinding headaches and nausea. It does not explain in any physiological way the augmenting of what has apparently been a "'latent talent'" (88) since childhood, the images and "funny feelings" (134) whereby Resnick accesses information. He wonders in the first book if "emotions [were] the psychic key" (89), an inkling that's in full force by later books. "I tap into strong emotions," he explains at the start of *Room at the Inn* (2012), "whether I want to or not—and sometimes knowledge follows" (2).

That last disclaimer aside, what he calls his "damnably annoying empathic abilities" (*Dark Waters*, 5) are *precisely* how knowledge is acquired. Resnick can stand in someone's footprints and glean that person's emotion, run a hand along a bedspread and "instantly [pick] up residual anger" (*Room at the Inn*, 174), walk into a room and sense "the smooth walls and ceiling ... practically vibrating" with the traces of whatever was felt there (*Bound by Suggestion*, 2011; 7). In *Dead in Red*, he spends twenty minutes touching the steering wheel of a suspect's car and is "bombarded" by a "plethora of thoughts and feelings"—an image of shoes that "blast[s]" his mind, a "sensation of joy" that "swoop[s] over [him] like a sirocco," a "horrible weight" that "presse[s] against [his] soul"—in short, a "maelstrom" that leaves him panting and shaking (170–71). He claims in *Murder on the Mind* that he has to do "some real, hard-nosed digging" to "solve the case" (134), but the fact is that every investigation of every novel is conducted largely through the visions, dreamscapes, "'hallucinations'" (30), "inner radar" (45), "mental picture[s]" (75), "second sight" (130), "sixth sense" (252), and hunches of this human "'Geiger counter'" (119).

The exceptionality we expect of detectives is made both physical and supernatural in the figure of Jeff Resnick. Without head injury, Resnick is a divorced, unemployed, wholly unremarkable insurance investigator. With head injury, he is suddenly interesting: a brain-damaged man beleaguered by migraines and an overwhelming emotional sensitivity that helps him solve brutal crimes. It's a trope of the genre that the lone sleuth doesn't share information with police, a tendency that casts the dependability of the law into significant doubt. The Resnick novels exaggerate that form of social critique by locating "truth" not in fact-finding but in emotional forms of knowing that the investigator worries will seem illogical, even "crazy" (a word that recurs throughout the series). Worth noting, I think, is the connection here between crime solution—the restitution of order, at least temporarily—and a kind of emotional intelligence that is explicitly if not always willingly interrelational. It's one thing to know something he hasn't witnessed (such as where his brother put the luggage claim checks), and quite another to keep getting "caught up," as Resnick often puts it, in the swirl of powerful feeling experienced by the victims, perpetrators, and witnesses of murder. This literalizes the idea that you have to think like a crook to catch crook, but more; it implies that woundedness lowers one's guard in scary but ultimately protective ways. Resnick doesn't ratiocinate his way toward solution, he *feels* his way, and in turn becomes a conduit for an emotional intensity that is styled across the novels as vital for both individual and social well-being.

When Resnick insists, "'I *know* what I *know*'" (*Murder*, 229), we can assume that the denouement of the novel will bear out his instincts. He is not exactly clever (in fact, the novels make no claim for conventional smarts); he is instead a *mind's-eye-witness*. In some works, discussed throughout this study, we can trust that the detective *will* know, eventually, what happened in the past, in others that she or he *already* knows, and is simply awaiting one more clue before a final reveal. Resnick calls upon those forms of knowledge, but through "flash forwards" (*Dark Waters*, 2013; 231), he also *already* knows what is *going* to happen. In this sense, the Resnick novels play out a fantasy of knowing that, in some magical way, transcends all boundaries of time, place, person, and logic. The figure of Jeff Resnick assures us that *someone* can actually feel what we might feel, the whole gamut of human emotion from vicious triumph to abject sorrow. In an apathetic world, at least one person is truly empathetic—at least one person might be driven by bodily compulsion to stick with the case, to seek justice, to make it right again. When we ask for someone to see what we mean, it won't just be a figure of speech. Someone else will contain the urgency of our truths.

Christopher Boone is a literalist, and he hates metaphor, which he calls "a lie" (15). And yet Christopher understands that all language is metaphor—including "metaphor" and "Christopher"—along with the fact that just about anything we say is a lie, since we are never telling *literally* the whole truth. And when he describes "look[ing] up into the sky" and imagining "molecules of Mother up there" or "coming down as rain in the rain forests of Brazil" (when he still believes that she was cremated; 33–34), he is of course creating imagery, a kind of poetry, that remakes anything from weather to casual conversation according to his way of fathoming the world. And perhaps each of the sleuths included here is fashioning metaphors of truth in their unique ways of approaching the stuff of thought. The visions of suffering that Harper Connelly experiences after her lightning strike; the schizophrenic hallucinations that impel neuroscientist Daniel Pearce toward solution of a case in *Perception*; even the Polaroid photos taken to communicate reality to Leonard Shelby (Guy Pearce) from an immediate past he can't remember in the film *Memento* (2000)—these are all both real to the individual sleuth and forms of metaphorical compression that reveal meaning in sideways fashion.

In *Perception*, Daniel's hallucinations (only intermittently managed through medication) condense personal memory and elements of the case at hand, just as dreams are also palimpsests of now and then, containing both the urgencies of private desire and the randomness of sense impression. That Daniel (Eric McCormack) does not always realize his hallucinations are just that, invisible to anyone but himself and projections of his own consciousness, suggests that being a "private eye" means not just freedom from the constraints of law and state but something more intensely inward. Crime is rendered here as a psychological phenomenon that can only be worked out by someone with a sharp and explicitly personal understanding of what it is to feel disordered and out of control. Mental illness in this short-lived series has less to do with amplifying-by-contrast the sleuth's deductive intelligence than with his capacity to identify; Daniel's hallucinations are the narrative, neurological equivalent of Jeff Resnick's psychic impressions to the degree that they stimulate a sense of inhabiting another's emotional and perceptual truth. In both cases, of course, some *other* reality is created through the "metaphor" of—call it delusion, apparition, vision. These detectives become psychically creative nodal points, combining, layering, and reconstituting the past.

In the case of Leonard Shelby, whose blow to the head produces anterograde amnesia (the inability to form new memories), crime utterly disrupts the sleuth's continuity with his own experience. To figure out who killed his wife and injured him in the process, Leonard must surround himself with, even tattoo onto himself, messages to guide him: where he lives, who people are, whether or not he should trust them, what he takes to be the facts and clues of the case. These are not precisely the same as Benny Cooperman's memory book, since Leonard in effect *never* remembers; each reboot of consciousness starts the process over again. In this sense his photos, with their accompanying explanations—even the prompts written into his body—are not so much extensions of cognition (since they spark no *re*-cognition) as a kind of recipe that Leonard understands but does not feel himself to be the author of. What it means to Leonard to "know" anything about the case he is trying to solve is always a matter of learning it as if for the first time through a steady accretion of information. "Facts, not memories," he tells a man named Teddy (who may or may not be trustworthy). "That's how you investigate." But the factual is obviously suspect, since the statements Leonard writes down to tell himself what's what—"Don't believe his lies," "She'll help you out of pity"—are based solely on his impressions, which lack of immediate memory makes highly manipulable.

Where we expect a good detective to uncover the real, Leonard is a sleuth who is literally writing reality as he lives it. For all that his body seems to materialize facts in the ink of its tattoos, what's recorded there merely captures the belief of a moment, which in determining future choices makes every subsequent course of action a matter of considerable risk. I would argue that the film thereby raises more provocative questions about ethical decision-making than about the fiction of stable identity (indeed, critically acclaimed as it was, *Memento* strikes me as heavy-handed in the game it wants to play with memory and narrative coherence). It's suggested at the end of the movie that Leonard caught and killed the perpetrator of his injury a year before, and that he is now *knowingly* misleading himself so as to prolong his quest—as if, without memory of a past, his only viable mode of existence is momentum toward a future. That suspension in limbo, the not-knowing of the middle of a case, makes the brain-injured Leonard an exaggeration of the other sleuths I have discussed here: a storyteller whose incremental progression toward an elusive goal requires the willingness of others to engage on his terms, and whose awareness of *what happened* will forever circle back to the facts only as he has devised them.

If its director is to be believed, the crimes that initiate *Memento* have identifiable solutions.[19] What's spooky in the film's violence is not whether the detective will outwit the villains but the fact that, even if he does, he'll never fully know it. This is a peculiar conundrum, but it gets at something all of the sleuths considered here represent, the slippery nature of knowing at the core of a genre we turn to so often for the pleasures of resolution—*and suspension*. These detectives are paying attention *all wrong*, we might say, attending aslant, misunderstanding the obvious, riffing on the trivial, listening to what isn't even there. But in coming at crime through the oblique, the digressive, the imagined, and the felt, they *are* doing something. Christopher Boone's seventy-page excursion to his mother in London doesn't gum up the flow of a narrative that is trying to reach its destination; it *is* the narrative, and the answer to the crime is not in fact on the other side of that journey. Indeed, it is *solution* that propels Christopher into motion, which makes intriguingly explicit an idea that lurks at the heart of most crime fiction, that moving forward usually only brings us back, but the comforts of home are never constant or reliably known. This is the effect, finally, of all the eruptions, omissions, and repetitions of the mad detectives: they show up normality for the illusion it is—a costume, ultimately empty, like Monk's police uniform hanging in his closet.

Notes

1   Cf. Haddon's own blog: http://www.markhaddon.com/aspergers-and-autism.
2   https://www.publishersweekly.com/978-0-385-49183-9.
3   The opposite problem—not amnesia but an inability to *forget*—defines PI Brenna Spector in Alison Gaylin's 2014 *Stay with Me*. Cf. also Patrick Radden Keefe's

piece in *The New Yorker* about a specialized unit of London's Metropolitan Police Service comprised of officers "who shar[e] an unusual talent: they all [have] a preternatural ability to recognize human faces"—so-called super-recognizers whose talent is rendered as "uncanny" and "preternatural."

4 For a few different takes on the Mad Pride movement, cf. Amelia Abraham, "Remembering Mad Pride, The Movement that Celebrated Mental Illness," *Vice* (November 18, 2016). Web. https://www.vice.com/en_uk/article/7bxqxa/mad-pride-remembering-the-uks-mental-health-pride-movement; Gabriel Glaser, "'Mad Pride Fights a Stigma,'" *The New York Times* Fashion & Style (May 11, 2008). Web. http://jfactivist.typepad.com/jfactivist/2008/05/mad-pride-fight.html; and Joseph F. Kras, "The 'Ransom Notes' Affair: When the Neurodiversity Movement Came of Age," *DSQ* 30, 1 (2010). Web. No pagination. http://www.dsq-sds.org/article/view/1065/1254.

5 Arguing the opposite point, however, are any number of autobiographers for whom both sanity and selfhood reside in story. Nancy Mairs is not unique in making such claims as this from *Plaintext*: "I have to write. If I avoid that mandate, I end up trying to kill myself." Consider also the title of Paul John Eakin's 1999 volume *How Our Lives Become Stories: Making Selves*.

6 http://www.americansc.org.uk/Online/Online_2011/Lethem.html.

7 To scoff at the possibility of Benjy narrating all of *The Sound and the Fury* (as Roth does) is not just to demean Benjy but to miss the opportunity to rethink the very operations of narrative itself.

8 Cf. "A Conversation with Jonathan Lethem," *Indiana Review* 22, 2 (2000): 31–42.

9 Bérubé examines the full seventy pages of this journey as evidence of the novel's disruption of how we determine what is properly foreground and what ought to remain in the background, such that lingering in apparently pointless detail of this episode becomes significant not just to Christopher's character but also to the narrative we're reading—one that reorients how we pay attention, because Christopher "habitually notice[s] things that neurotypical people miss" (133).

10 Film, too, exploits the trend. *The Caveman's Valentine* (2001) stars Samuel L. Jackson as Romulus Ledbetter, a homeless man with schizophrenia. When Ledbetter finds a boy frozen to death, he works with his own hallucinations to determine the boy's killer. In *Mercury Rising* (1998), Miko Hughes plays nine-year-old autistic Simon Lynch, who cracks a governmental secret code.

11 In *Homeland* (SHO, 2011–), where a recurring plotline involves whether or not CIA agent Carrie Mathison will take her medication or not (she has bipolar disorder), morality has simply been replaced by psychopharmacology and the sleuth is sick rather than possessed.

12 For more on Sherlock Holmes and the ways in which his mysteries challenge conventional tropes, cf. the introduction to this book, "Sleuthing Disability."
13 Cf. Cefalu, "What's So Funny about Obsessive-Compulsive Disorder?"
14 While I disagree with Rushing's analysis of *Monk*—particularly what I take to be his reading of Monk's psychological condition as a kind of metaphysical perversity, representative of a world that is "obsessive-compulsive, persecutory, [and] unwilling to let us be in peace" (93)—I am intrigued by his contention that the series enacts, in both the characterization of its obsessive hero and in scenes that depict apparently meaningless repetition, the very thing that makes us want to read, or watch, mysteries over and over again—even when we know the outcome. "Our engagement with classic detective fiction," Rushing writes, "is fundamentally an obsessive-compulsive urge to repeat" (91).
15 "Let us call fortunate blindness," writes Naomi Schor, "one of the great myths of blindness" (85).
16 Colin Moriarty claims that "you would think [blindness] would change him for the worse, scar him for life. Yet, he makes the best of it, making it a positive attribute." This kind of redemptive logic structures disability as tolerable if we can learn something from it.
17 http://www.consc.net/papers/extended.html. Accessed July 31, 2017.
18 Engel's 2008 memoir reveals that he was also born with what he calls "an unfinished left hand" that "looked more like a paw with tiny ball-like fingers" [2], although this corporeal anomaly does not appear in the Cooperman series.
19 Cf. the interview at creativescreenwriting.com: https://creativescreenwriting.com/remembering-where-it-all-began-christopher-nolan-on-memento/.

Epilogue

In a November 2018 Opinion piece in *The New York Times*, British novelist Nicola Griffith laments the dearth of disability fiction that could pass what has become known as the Fries Test. Like the so-called Bechdel Test for gender representation (to pass it, a story must contain at least two women who talk to each other about something other than a man), the Fries Test, named for activist and writer Kenny Fries, measures the representation of disability. In Fries's words: "Does a work have more than one disabled character? Do the disabled characters have their own narrative purpose other than the education and profit of a nondisabled character? Is the character's disability not eradicated either by curing or killing?" Unlike the Bechdel Test, the Fries Test does not require that disabled characters talk to each other. They do not have to be named. To quote Griffith, "it is a very low bar."

Many of the works I have studied throughout this book would not pass the strict outlines of this test. Most of them, even those by writers obviously motivated to counteract common stereotypes of disability (such as the Connor Westphal series), feature only one disabled character—the protagonist detective. Many of those detectives are portrayed with obvious and unapologetic pedagogical goals—educating nondisabled readers about disabled experience. And some of them, most notably Lincoln Rhyme, do undergo corrective procedures that lessen the severity of their conditions. Hundreds of books, then, with prominent and disabled characters doing interesting things (solving crime!), yet failing a basic test of social awareness. Griffith's powerfully articulated essay makes the point that the status of disability representation lags troubling far behind queer fiction in presenting readers with stories that challenge the "corrosive" effects of prejudice. "Think about all those stories that are missing," she urges us. "Without those stories, implicit bias will continue and the cycle will renew itself endlessly." To reprise the question I asked in the introduction to this book, then, *are* disabled detectives rewriting the assumptions of ableism?

The answer, at least in part, lies in the emphasis Fries places on *narrative purpose* of one's own. Disability functions in the novels and dramas I include here in complicated ways. Certain narratives do deploy conventional metaphorical tropes, even flirting with caricature; the preponderance handle disability with greater subtlety. Even instructional aims, I would suggest—demonstrating the complexities (or frankly, the ease) of living with impairment—can have a benefit, especially in older texts written for uninitiated audiences. But as I have been arguing, it is at the *epistemological* level of narrative that disability becomes most compelling in the context of crime detection, engendering heterodox modes of conceptualizing the world precisely at the moment when the fabric of that world seems most frayed, most vulnerable. By definition of genre, disabled detectives are engaged at the very heart of their stories, and as I have proposed, the sort of "order" to which the disordered bodymind of a disabled detective returns us is also by definition an altered, alternative one. However we understand the nature of fictional mystery, whether we construe its goal to be resolution or repetition, closure or the thwarting of endings, to install disability at the core of a genre characterized by troubling its own rigid parameters is to open toward the possibility of something other than clichés and norms.

As I also explain in the introduction, this study has not aimed for comprehensiveness, nor, precisely, for taxonomic specificity. Crime fiction as a whole has inspired very many excellent and thorough explanations of the distinctions between its various kinds. My intention has not been to dismiss the importance of such differences in how we experience stories, although I have subordinated them here to allow disability concerns to emerge most fully, and I do argue that disabled detectives *on the whole* enact revisionary forms of embodied and relational thinking regardless of structural and stylistic particulars. But of course there is more to explore about how disability works in a police procedural as opposed to a spy novel, in a domestic mystery as opposed to a noir thriller, to say nothing of disability as it affects characters other than the sleuths themselves. And what of disability in crime film? Graphic novel and crime comic book? Disabled detectives are disproportionately white; what further intersectional analyses can we bring to bear on this topic? I have not examined in detail how United States and British disabled detectives differ—indeed, my contention in some chapters is that disability effectively constitutes a third term, a third location—but given the well-known post-war split that gave us the American hard-boiled as opposed to the classic British mystery tradition, there is more to be said about how national perspectives at various historical moments mediate disabled sleuthing. And what of other archives—evidence of disability detection in literature worldwide?

Literary disability studies is itself far from a unified field, and scholars will inevitably have different takes on the characterizations and narrative structures I examine in these chapters. Indeed, I hope this study will encourage other disability scholars to reexamine crime fiction generally as an especially rich source—though maybe unexpectedly so—of positive and compelling stories about what disability can be and do. The point isn't an instrumental one; that is, I hope to have done more than simply present disability in yet another functional guise, a quirky fulcrum around which nondisabled meaning happens. In concentrating on dynamics of space, especially Deleuzean space, I have been interested in disability as a process of coming-into-being that upsets the status quo of the genre's narrative templates, offering readers a range of "different means" (quoting Cherokee author Jean Hager once more) for grabbing hold of what matters. There are nearly as many ways to explain the enormous popularity of crime fiction as there are forms of the genre. I have chosen here to emphasize the pleasure afforded by knowing that someone knows, and suggest in the introduction that, importantly, the disabled sleuths show us "how else we can know." But they do more: they show us how else we can *be*. And who we already are.

Works Cited

Adams, Rachel, Benjamin Reiss, and David Serlin, eds. *Keywords for Disability Studies*. New York: NYU Press, 2015. Print.

Anderson, Myrdene, and Floyd Merrell. "End Notes: Semiotically Digesting Dis/ability." In *Semiotics and Dis/ability: Interrogating Categories of Difference*, ed. Linda J. Rogers and Beth Blue Swadener. Albany: State University of New York Press, 2001. 267–72. Print.

Barker, Cory. "*Perception* Appears to Be a Little Too Calculated." July 12, 2010. Web. http://www.tv.com/news/perception-appears-to-be-a-little-too-calculated-29062/

Bartlett, L. L. *Murder on the Mind*. [2005] N. Greece, NY: Polaris Press, 2011. Print.

———. *Dead in Red*. N. Greece, NY: Polaris Press, 2008. Print.

———. *Bound by Suggestion*. CreateSpace Independent Publishing Platform, 2011. Print.

———. *Room at the Inn*. CreateSpace Independent Publishing Platform, 2012. Print.

———. *Dark Waters*. Frankly Graphics, 2013. Print.

Bauman, H-Dirksen L. "Toward a Poetics of Vision, Space, and the Body: Sign Language and Literary Theory." In *The Disability Studies Reader*, ed. Lennard J. Davis. 1st edition. New York: Routledge, 1997. 315–31. Print.

Bauman, H-Dirksen L., and Joseph J. Murray. "Deaf Studies in the 21st Century: 'Deaf-Gain' and the Future of Human Diversity." In *The Disability Studies Reader*, ed. Lennard J. Davis. 4th edition. New York: Routledge, 2013. 246–60. Print.

Baynton, Douglas C. "Deafness." In Adams et al., *Keywords*. 48–51. Print.

Bérubé, Michael. *The Secret Life of Stories: From Don Quixote to Harry Potter, How Understanding Intellectual Disability Transforms the Way We Read*. New York: NYU Press, 2016. Print.

Bolt, David. *The Metanarrative of Blindness: A Re-Reading of Twentieth-Century Anglophone Writing*. Ann Arbor: University of Michigan Press, 2013. Print.

Bramah, Ernest. "The Coin of Dionysis" and "The Knight's Cross Signal Problem." In *Four Max Carrados Detective Stories*. 1914. The Project Gutenberg eBook. Web. No Pagination. http://www.gutenberg.org/cache/epub/12932/pg12932-images.html

Brandt, Allan M. "AIDS in Historical Perspective: Four Lessons from the History of Sexually Transmitted Diseases." In *Sickness and Health: Readings in the History of Medicine and Public Health*, ed. Judith W. Leavitt and Ronald L. Numbers. 3rd edition. Madison: University of Wisconsin Press, 1997. Print.

Breger, Esther. "TV Needs to Stop Treating Mental Illness as a Superpower." April 24, 2014. Web. No pagination. https://newrepublic.com/article/117515/black-box-abc-and-tvs-mental-illness-problem

Browne, Marshall. *The Wooden Leg of Inspector Anders*. New York: Thomas Dunne Books, 1999. Print.

Brueggemann, Brenda Jo. *Lend Me Your Ear: Rhetorical Constructions of Deafness*. Washington, DC: Gallaudet University Press, 1999. Print.

Caeton, D.A. "Blindness." In Adams et al., *Keywords*. 34–37. Print.

Carlon, Patricia. *The Whispering Wall*. New York: Soho Press Inc., 1969. Print.

Caspary, Vera. *Laura*. [1943] In *Women Crime Writers: Four Suspense Novels of the 1940s*, ed. Sarah Weinman. New York: The Library of America, 2015. 1–186.

Castle. ABC. 209–16. Created by Andrew W. Marlowe. "That 70s Show." Written by David Amann. Dir. John Terlesky. April 21, 2014. Season 6, episode 20.

Cefalu, Paul. "What's So Funny about Obsessive-Compulsive Disorder?" *PMLA* 124, 1 (Jan. 2009): 44–58. Print.

Chambers, Tod. "Sick Detectives." *The Lancet*, 364. "Medicine, Crime, and Punishment" issue (December 2004): 56–57. Web. www.thelancet.com.

Chandler, Raymond. "The Simple Art of Murder." [1946] In *The Art of the Mystery Story: A Collection of Critical Essays*, ed. Howard Haycraft. New York: Carroll & Graf, 1983. Print.

———. *Trouble Is My Business*. [1939] New York: Vintage, 1992. Print.

Chesterton, G. K. "A Defence of Detective Stories." [1902] In *The Art of the Mystery Story*, ed. Howard Haycraft. New York: Carroll & Graf, 1983. Print.

Cheyne, Ria. "Disability in Genre Fiction." In *The Cambridge Companion to Literature and Disability*, ed. Clare Barker and Stuart Murray. Cambridge, UK: Cambridge University Press, 2018. 185–98. Print.

Christianson, Scott R. "Tough Talk and Wisecracks: Language as Power in American Detective Fiction." *Journal of Popular Culture* 23, 2 (Fall 1989): 151–62. Print.

Christie, Agatha. "The Cornish Mystery," "The Adventure of Johnnie Waverly," "How Does Your Garden Grow," in *Poirot's Early Cases*. Canada: FONTANA/Collins, 1977. Print.

———. *Appointment with Death*. [1938] New York: Berkley Books, 1984. Print.

———. *Cards on the Table*. [1936] New York: Berkley Books, 1984. Print.

———. *The Murder of Roger Ackroyd* [1926] and *Dumb Witness* [1937], in *Agatha Christie* (four novels). London: Peerage Books, 1984. Print.

———. *Hallowe'en Party*. [1969] New York and London: Harper, 2011. Print.

———. *Three Act Tragedy*. [1935] New York and London: Harper, 2011. Print.

Clark, Andy, and David J. Chalmers. "The Extended Mind." *Analysis* 58 (1998): 10–23. Print.

Cohen, Michael. "The Detective as Other." In Klein, *Diversity and Detective Fiction*. 144–57. Print.

Collins, Michael. *Act of Fear*. [1967] New York and London: Overlook Duckworth, 2013. Print.

———. *Shadow of a Tiger*. New York: Dodd, Mead & Company, 1972. Print.

———. *Blue Death*. New York: Playboy Press Paperbacks, 1975. Print.

———. *Castrato*. New York: Leisure Books, 1991. Print.

———. *Chasing Eights*. New York: Leisure Books, 1992. Print.

Davis, Lennard J. *Enforcing Normalcy: Disability, Deafness and the Body*. London and New York: Verso, 1995. Print.

———. *The End of Normal: Identity in a Biocultural Era*. Ann Arbor: University of Michigan Press, 2013. Print.

Deaver, Jeffrey. *The Bone Collector*. [1998] New York: Signet, 2014. Print.

———. *The Coffin Dancer*. New York: Pocket Books, 1998. Print.

———. *The Vanished Man*. New York: Simon & Schuster, 2003. Print.

———. *The Steel Kiss*. New York: Grand Central Publishing, 2016. Print.

Deleuze, Gilles, and Félix Guattari. *A Thousand Plateaus: Capitalism and Schizophrenia*. 2nd edition. Minneapolis: University of Minnesota Press, 1987. Print.

Derrida, Jacques. *Writing and Difference*. Reprint edition. Chicago, IL: University of Chicago Press, 1978. Print.

Dove, George N. *The Reader and the Detective Story*. Ann Arbor, MI: Popular Press, 1997.

Dubois, Page. "Oedipus as Detective: Sophocles, Simenon, Robbe-Grillet." *Yale French Studies* 108. Special Crime Fictions issue (2005): 102–15. Print.

Eden, Rick. "Detective Fiction as Satire." *Genre* 16 (Autumn 1983): 279–95. Print.

Edwards, Martha. "Constructions of Physical Disability in the Ancient Greek World: The Community Concept." In *The Body and Physical Difference: Discourses of Disability*, ed. David T. Mitchell and Sharon L. Snyder. Ann Arbor: University of Michigan Press, 1997. 35–50. Print.

Elias, Gerald. *Devil's Trill*. New York: Minotaur Books, 2009. Print.

———. *Death and the Maiden*. New York: Minotaur Books, 2011. Print.

———. *Death and Transfiguration*. New York: Minotaur Books, 2012. Print.

Engel, Howard. *The Memory Book*. New York: Carroll and Graf Publishers, 2006. Print.

———. *The Man Who Forgot How to Read: A Memoir*. New York: Thomas Dunne Books, 2008. Print.

Erdmann, Terry J., and Paula M. Block. *Monk: The Official Episode Guide*. New York: St. Martin's Griffin, 2006. Print.

Esmail, Jennifer. "'I Listened with My Eyes': Writing Speech and Reading Deafness in the Fiction of Charles Dickens and Wilkie Collins." *ELH* 78, 4 (Winter 2011): 991–1020. Print.

Fleissner, Jennifer L. "Symptomatology and the Novel." *NOVEL: A Forum on Fiction* 42, 3. Theories of the Novel Now, Part II (Fall 2009): 387–92. Print.

Francis, Dick. *Odds Against*. [1966] In *Four Complete Novels*. New York: Avenel Books, 1984. Print.

———. *Whip Hand*. New York: Berkeley Books, 1979. Print.

———. *Come to Grief*. New York: Berkeley Books, 1995. Print.

Fraser, Max. "Hands Off the Machine: Workers' Hands and Revolutionary Symbolism in the Visual Culrue of 1930s America." *American Art* 27, 2 (June 1, 2013). Web. No pagination.

Fries, Kenny. "The Fries Test: Disability Representation." Nov. 1, 2017. https://medium.com/@kennyfries/the-fries-test-on-disability-representation-in-our-culture-9d1bad72cc00. Web. Accessed November 26, 2018.

Galloway, Terry. *Mean Little deaf Queer*. Boston, MA: Beacon Press, 2010. Print.

Garland-Thomson, Rosemarie. *Staring: How We Look*. Oxford and New York: Oxford University Press, 2009. Print.

———. "Misfits: A Feminist Materialist Disability Concept." *Hypatia* 26, 3 (2011): 591–609. Print.

Gilman, Carlotte Perkins. *Unpunished*, ed. Catherine J. Golden and Denise D. Knight. New York: The Feminist Press, 1997.

Gilman, Sander. *Fat Boys: A Slim Book*. Lincoln: University of Nebraska Press, 2004. Print.

Goffman, Erving. *Stigma: Notes on the Management of Spoiled Identity*. [1963] Reissue edition. New York: Touchstone, 1986. Print.

Griffith, Nicola. "Rewriting the Old Disability Script." Nov. 14, 2018. https://www.nytimes.com/2018/11/14/opinion/telling-new-disability-stories.html. Web. Accessed November 26, 2018.

Guattari, Félix. *Chaosophy*. New York: Semiotext(e), 1995. Print.

Haddon, Mark. *Curious Incident of the Dog in the Night-Time*. New York: Doubleday, 2003. Print.

Hafferty, Frederic W. "Disability in the Media: The Evolution of a Deaf Detective." *Disability Studies Quarterly* 9, 2 (1989): 40–43. Print.

Hafferty, Frederic W., and Susan Foster. "Decontextualizing Disability in the Crime Mystery Genre: The Case of the Invisible Handicap." *Disability and Society* 9, 2 (1994): 185–206. Print.

Haraway, Donna J. "A Cyborg Manifesto: Science, Technology, and Socialist-Feminism in the Late Twentieth Century." In *Manifestly Haraway*. Minneapolis: University of Minnesota Press, 2016.

Holmes, Martha Stoddard. *Fictions of Affliction: Physical Disability in Victorian Culture*. Ann Arbor: University of Michigan Press, 2004.

Holt, Anne. *1222*. [2007] New York: Scribner, 2012. Print.

Hoppenstand, Gary, and Ray B. Browne. *The Defective Detective in the Pulps*. Bowling Green, OH: Bowling Green State University Popular Press, 1983. Print.

Ingram, Richard. "Reports from the Psych Wars." In *Unfitting Stories: Narrative Approaches to Disease, Disability, and Trauma*, ed. Valerie Raoul, Connie Canam, Angela D. Henderson, and Carla Paterson. Waterloo, ON: Wilfred Laurier University Press, 2007. 237–45. Print.

Jackson, Hialeah. *The Alligator's Farewell*. New York: Dell, 1999. Print.

Jakubowicz, Andrew, and Helen Meekosha. "Detecting Disability: Moving beyond Metaphor in the Crime Fiction of Jeffrey Deaver." *Disability Studies Quarterly* 24, 2 (Spring 2004). Web. No pagination.

James, P. D. *Talking about Detective Fiction*. New York: Vintage Books, 2011. Print.

Jay, Martin. *Downcast Eyes: The Denigration of Vision in Twentieth-Century French Thought*. Berkeley: University of California Press, 1994. Print.

Jimenez Heffernan, Julian. "Pamela's Hands: Political Intangibility and the Production of Manners." *Novel* 46, 1 (2013): 26–49. Print.

Kayman, Martin. "The Short Story from Poe to Chesterton." In Priestman, *The Cambridge Companion to Crime Fiction*. 41–58. Print.

Keefe, Patrick Radden. "The Detectives Who Never Forget a Face." *The New Yorker*, August 22, 2016. Web. No pagination. https://www.newyorker.com/magazine/2016/08/22/londons-super-recognizer-police-force

Keith, Lois. *What Happened to You? Writing by Disabled Women*. London: New Press, 1996.

Kendrick, Baynard. *The Odor of Violets*. New York: Little, Brown & Co., 1941. Print.

———. *Blind Man's Bluff*. New York: Dell, 1943. Print.

———. "The Silent Whistle," "Melody in Death," "The Murderer Who Wanted More." In *Make Mine Maclain*. New York: William Morrow & Company, 1947. Print.

Klein, Kathleen Gregory. *Diversity and Detective Fiction*. Bowling Green, OH: Bowling Green State University Press, 1999. Print.

Knight, Stephen. *Crime Fiction since 1800: Detection, Death, Diversity*. 2nd edition. New York: Palgrave Macmillan, 2010. Print.

Krentz, Christopher. *Writing Deafness: The Hearing Line in Nineteenth-Century American Literature*. Chapel Hill: University of North Carolina Press, 2007. Print.

Kuppers, Petra. "Performance." In Adams et al., *Keywords*. 137–39. Print.

LeBesco, Kathleen. *Revolting Bodies? The Struggle to Redefine Fat Identity*. Amherst and Boston: University of Massachusetts Press, 2004.

Lefebvre, Henri. *The Production of Space*. [1974] Trans. Donald Nicholson-Smith. Oxford: Blackwell Publishing, 1991.

Lethem, Jonathan. *Motherless Brooklyn*. New York: Vintage, 2000. Print.

Levine, Caroline. *Forms: Whole, Rhythm, Hierarchy, Network*. Princeton, NJ: Princeton University Press, 2015. Print.

Lewis. ITV. 2006–15. Created by Chris Burt and Stephen Churchett. "Counter Culture Blues." Nick Dear (story) and Guy Andrews (screenplay). Dir. Bill Anderson. April 12, 2009. Series 3, episode 4.

Lewis, Victoria Ann. "Crip." In Adams et al., *Keywords*. 46–48. Print.

Linett, Maren Tova. "Blindness and Intimacy in Early Twentieth-Century Literature." *Mosaic* 46, 3 (2013): 28–42. Print.

_____. "Deafness, Communication, and Knowledge." Chapter 3. In *Bodies of Modernism: Physical Disability in Transatlantic Modernism*. Ann Arbor: University of Michigan Press, 2017. Print.

Livingston, Jack. *Die Again, Macready*. New York: St. Martin's Press, 1984. Print.

_____. *A Piece of the Silence*. New York: Signet, 1986. Print.

_____. *The Nightmare File*. New York: Onyx, 1986. Print.

_____. *Hell Bent for Election*. New York: St. Martin's Press, 1988. Print.

Loftis, Sonya Freeman. "The Autistic Detective: Sherlock Holmes and His Legacy." *Disability Studies Quarterly* 34, 4 (2014). Web. No pagination.

Longmore, Paul. *Why I Burned My Books and Other Essays on Disability*. Philadelphia, PA: Temple University Press, 2003. Print.

Longstreet. ABC TV. 1971–72. Created by Stirling Silliphant.

Lutz, John. *Scorcher*. New York: Henry Holt & Company, 1987. Print.

_____. *Kiss*. New York: Henry Holt & Company, 1988. Print.

_____. *Flame*. New York: Henry Holt & Company, 1990. Print.

_____. *Hot*. New York: Henry Holt & Company, 1992. Print.

Lynch, Kathryn L. "'What Hands Are Here?' The Hand as Generative Symbol in *Macbeth*." *The Review of English Studies* 39, 153 (February 1988): 29–38. Print.

Macdonald, Gina, and Andrew Macdonald. "Ethnic Detectives in Popular Fiction: New Directions for an American Genre." In Klein, *Diversity and Detective Fiction*. 60–95. Print.

Mairs, Nancy. *Plaintext*. Tucson: University of Arizona Press, 1986.

Marcus, Laura. "Detection and Literary Fiction." In Priestman, *The Cambridge Companion to Crime Fiction*. 245–67. Print.

McAleer, John J. *Royal Decree: Conversations with Rex Stout*. Ashton, MD: Pontes Press, 1983. Print.

McBain, Ed. *Let's Hear It for the Deaf Man*. Garden City, NY: Doubleday & Company, Inc., 1973. Print.

McClain, Kathryn, and Grace Cripps. "The BBC's Sherlock: A 'Sociopathic' Master of the Social Game." In *Who Is Sherlock? Essays on Identity in Modern Holmes Adaptations*, ed. Lynnette Porter. Jefferson, NC: McFarland & Company, Inc., 2016. 95–110. Print.

McHale, Brian. *Constructing Postmodernism*. New York: Routledge, 1992. Print.

McHugh, Susan. "Seeing Eyes/Private Eyes: Service Dogs and Detective Fictions." In *Animal Stories: Narrating across Species Lines*. Minneapolis, MN: University of Minnesota Press, 2011. Print.

McRuer, Robert, and Merri Lisa Johnson, eds. Special "Cripistemologies" Issues of the *Journal of Literary and Cultural Disability Studies*, 8, 1 and 2 (2014). Print.

Memento. Newmarket Films. 2000. Written and dir. Christopher Nolan.

Messent, Peter. *The Crime Fiction Handbook*. Oxford: Wiley-Blackwell, 2013. Print.

Midsomer Murders. ITV. 1997–present. Created by Anthony Horowtiz. "The Flying Club." Written by Michael Aitkens. Dir. Luke Watson. February 5, 2014. Season 16, episode 4.

Milton, John. "The Reason of Church-Government." In *The Complete Poetry and Essential Prose of John Milton*, ed. John Kerrigan, John Rumrich, and Stephen Fallon. New York: Random House, 2007.

Mitchell, David T., and Sharon L. Snyder. *Narrative Prosthesis: Disability and the Dependencies of Discourse*. Ann Arbor: University of Michigan Press, 2000. Print.

Monk. USA Network. 2002–09. Created by Andy Breckman.

———."Mr. Monk and the Missing Granny." Written by Joe Toplyn. Dir. Tony Bill. February 6, 2004. Season 2, episode 13.

———."Mr. Monk Takes His Medicine." Written by Tom Sharpling and Chuck Sklar. Dir. Randall Zisk. August 20, 2004. Season 3, episode 9.

———."Mr. Monk Can't See a Thing." Written by Lee Goldberg and William Rabkin. Dir. Stephen Surjik. July 28, 2006. Season 5, episode 4.

———."Mr. Monk and the Rapper." Written by Daniel Dratch. Dir. Paris Barclay. July 20, 2007. Season 6, episode 2.

Moretti, Franco. "Clues." In *Signs Taken for Wonders: On the Sociology of Literary Forms*. London: Verso, 1983. 130–56. Print.

Moriarty, Colin. "Monk: 'Mr. Monk Can't See a Thing' Review." IGN, July 31, 2006. Web. http://www.ign.com/articles/2006/07/31/monk-mr-monk-cant-see-a-thing-review

Munt, Sally R. *Murder by the Book? Feminism and the Crime Novel*. London and New York: Routledge, 1994. Print.

Murder, She Wrote. CBS. 1984–96. Produced by Peter S. Fischer, Richard Levinson, and William Link.

Murray, Stuart. "Neurotecs: Detectives, Disability and Cognitive Exceptionality in Contemporary Fiction." In *Constructing Crime: Discourse and Cultural Representations of Crime and "Deviance,"* ed. Christiana Gregoriou. New York: Palgrave Macmillan, 2012. 177–89. Print.

Oliver, Myrna. "Dennis Lynds, 81; Author Used Detective Novels to Explore Social Conditions." *Los Angeles Times*, August 25, 2005. Web. http://articles.latimes.com/2005/aug/25/local/me-lynds25

Olney, Ian. "The Problem Body Politic, or, 'These Hands Have a Mind All Their Own!': Figuring Disability in the Horror Film Adaptation of Renard's 'Les mains d'Orlac.'" *Literature/Film Quarterly* 34, 4 (2006): 294–302. Print.

Ott, Bill. "Immigrants, Rednecks, and Cowboys: New Mexico Sleuths after Hillerman." In *Crime Fiction and Film in the Southwest: Bad Boys and Bad Girls in the Badlands*, ed. Steve Glassman and Maurice J. O'Sullivan. Bowling Green, OH: Bowling Green State University Popular Press, 2001. 24–36. Print.

Padden, Carol. "Communication." In Adams et al., *Keywords*. 43–45. Print.

Page, Jake. *Stolen Gods*. New York: Ballantine, 1993. Print.

———. *Deadly Canyon*. Albuquerque: University of New Mexico Press, 1994. Print.

Panek, Leroy L. "Post-War American Police Fiction." In Priestman, *The Cambridge Companion to Crime Fiction*. 155–71. Print.

Peacock, James. "'We Learned to Tell Our Story Walking': Tourette's and Urban Space in Jonathan Lethem's *Motherless Brooklyn*." In *Diseases and Disorders in Contemporary Fiction: The Syndrome Syndrome*, ed. T. J. Luistig and James Peacock. London and New York: Routledge, 2013. Print.

Pepper, Andrew. "Black Crime Fiction." In Priestman, *The Cambridge Companion to Crime Fiction*. 209–26. Print.

Pepperney, Justin. "'Cruel Handling: Reading Hands in *Actes and Monuments*." In *Acts of Reading: Interpretation, Reading Practices, and the Idea of the Book in John Foxe's Actes and Monuments*, ed. Thomas P. Anderson and Ryan Netzley. Newark: University of Delaware Press, 2010. 208–32. Print.

Perception. TNT. 2012–15. Created by Kenneth Biller and Mike Sussman.

Plain, Gill. *Twentieth-Century Crime Fiction: Gender, Sexuality and the Body*. Chicago, IL and London: Fitzroy Dearborn Publishers, 2001. Print.

Price, Margaret. "The Problem of Bodyminds and the Possibilities of Pain." *Hypatia* 30, 1 (2015): 268–84. Print.

Priestman, Martin, ed. *The Cambridge Companion to Crime Fiction*. Cambridge, UK: Cambridge University Press, 2003. Print.

Quayson, Ato. *Aesthetic Nervousness: Disability and the Crisis of Representation*. New York: Columbia University Press, 2007. Print.

Reaves, Karyn. "A Penguin a Week." March 16, 2014. Web. http://apenguinaweek.blogspot.com

Reddy, Maureen T. "The Feminist Counter-Tradition in Crime: Cross, Grafton, Paretsky and Wilson." In *The Cunning Craft: Original Essays on Detective Fiction and Contemporary Literary Theory*, ed. Ronald G. Walker, June M. Frazer, David R. Anderson. Macomb: Western Illinois University, 1990. 174–87. Print.

Rée, Jonathan. *I See a Voice: Deafness, Language and the Senses. A Philosophical History*. New York: Holt, 2000. Print.

Ritchie, Simon. *Work for a Dead Man*. New York: Charles Scribner's Sons, 1989. Print.

Rodas, Julia Miele. "On Blindness." *Journal of Literary and Cultural Disability Studies* 3, 2 (July 2009): 115–30. Print.

Romdenh-Romluc, Komarine. "Agency and Embodied Cognition." *Proceedings of the Aristotelian Society*. New Series, 111 (2011): 79–95. Print.

Ross, Barnaby. *The Tragedy of X*. [1932] New York: International Polygonics, Ltd., 1959. Print.

———. *The Tragedy of Y*. [1932] New York: Avon Publications, Inc., 1941. Print.

———. *Drury Lane's Last Case*. New York: Popular Library, 1933. Print.

———. *The Tragedy of Z*. Hamburg: The Albatross, 1934. Print.

Roth, Marco. "The Rise of the Neuronovel." *n+1*. Issue 8: Recessional (Fall 2009). Web. No pagination. https://nplusonemag.com/issue-8/essays/the-rise-of-the-neuronovel/

Rushing, Robert A. *Resisting Arrest: Detective Fiction and Popular Culture*. New York: Other Press, 2007.

Rzepka, Charles J. *Detective Fiction*. Cambridge, UK: Polity Press, 2005. Print.

Sacks, Oliver. *Hallucinations*. London: Vintage Books, 2013. Print.

Samuels, Ellen. "Critical Divides: Judith Butler's Body Theory and the Question of Disability." In *Feminist Disability Studies*, ed. Kim Q. Hall. Bloomington: Indiana University Press, 2011. 48–66. Print.

———. *Fantasies of Identification: Disability, Gender, Race*. New York: NYU Press, 2014. Print.

Savarese, Ralph James. "Cognition." In Adams et al., *Keywords*. 40–42. Print.

Sayers, Edna Edith. *Outcasts and Angels: The New Anthology of Deaf Characters in Literature*. Washington, DC: Gallaudet University Press, 2012. Print.

Scaggs, John. *Crime Fiction*. London and New York: Routledge, 2005. Print.

Schlossberg, Linda. "*Trent's Last Case*: Murder, Modernism, Meaning." In *Formal Investigations: Aesthetic Style in Late-Victorian and Edwardian Detective Fiction*, ed. Paul Fox and Koray Melikoglu. 2nd edition. Stuttgart, Germany: ibidem-Verlag, 2014. Print.

Schor, Naomi. "Blindness as Metaphor." *differences* 11, 2 (1999): 76–105. Print.

Shakespeare, William. *Twelfth Night*, ed. Bruce R. Smith. New York: Bedford/St. Martin's Press, 2001. Print.

Shildrik, Margrit. *Dangerous Discourses of Disability, Subjectivity and Sexuality*. New York and Hampshire: Palgrave Macmillan, 2012. Print.

Siebers, Tobin. "Disability as Masquerade." *Literature and Medicine* 23, 1 (2004): 1–22. Print.

_____. *Disability Theory*. Ann Arbor: University of Michigan Press, 2008. Print.

Snyder, Sharon L. "Unfixing Disability in Lord Byron's *The Deformed Transformed*." In *Bodies in Commotion: Disability and Performance*, ed. Carrie Sandahl and Philip Auslander. Ann Arbor: University of Michigan, 2005. 271–83. Print.

Snyder, Sharon L., and David T. Mitchell. *Cultural Locations of Disability*. Chicago: University of Chicago Press, 2006. Print.

Smith, Lesley. "'Perception': Chic Tic." July 8, 2012. http://www.popmatters.com/review/160765-perception/Web. No pagination.

Soitos, Stephen. *The Blues Detective: A Study of African-American Detective Fiction*. Amherst: University of Massachusetts Press, 1996. Print.

Stagg, Clinton H. "The Keyboard of Silence," "Unto the Third Generation," "The Money Machines," "The Flying Death," "The Thousand Facets of Fire," "The Gilded Glove," "The Ringling Goblets." In *The Problemist: The Complete Adventures of Thornley Colton, Blind Detective*. Landisville, PA: Coachwhip Publications, 2010. Print.

Stearn, Queenie. "The Sound of Silence." *British Medical Journal* 296, 6630 (April 1988): 1179. Print.

Stephens, Reed. *The Man Who Killed His Brother*. New York: Ballantine Books, 1980. Print.

_____. *The Man Who Risked His Partner*. New York: Ballantine Books, 1984. Print.

_____. *The Man Who Tried to Get Away*. New York: Ballantine Books, 1990. Print.

Steward, Dwight. *The Acupuncture Murders*. New York: Harper & Row, 1973. Print.

Stout, Rex. *Before I Die*. [1947] In *Trouble in Triplicate*. New York: Viking, 1949. Print.

_____. *Fourth of July Picnic*. [1957] In *And Four to Go*. New York: Viking, 1958. Print.

_____. *The Silent Speaker* [1946], *Might as Well Be Dead* [1956], *If Death Ever Slept* [1957], *A Family Affair* [1975]. In *Seven Complete Nero Wolfe Novels*. New York: Avenel Books, 1983. Print.

Sue Thomas: F.B.Eye. "Pilot," Parts 1 and 2. PAX Network. Written by Dave Alan Johnson and Gary R. Johnson. Dir. Larry A. McLean. October 13, 2002. Season 1, episodes 1 & 2.

Symons, Julian. *Bloody Murder: From the Detective Story to the Crime Novel*. 3rd revised edition. New York: The Mysterious Press, 1992. Print.
Thomas, Sue, with S. Rickly Christian. *Silent Night*. [1990] Columbiana, OH: Sue Thomas Ministries, 2010. Print.
Thoutenhoofd, Ernst Daniël. "Philosophy's Real-World Consequences for Deaf People: Thoughts on Iconicity, Sign Language and Being Deaf." *Human Studies* 23, 3 (July 2000): 261–79. Print.
Todorov, Tsvetan. *The Poetics of Prose*. Trans. Richard Howard. Oxford: Blackwell, 1977.
Trench, John. *Docken Dead*. [1953] New York: Penguin Green Cover, 1960. Print.
———. *Dishonoured Bones*. New York: Macmillan, 1955. Print.
———. *What Rough Beast*. London: Macdonald, 1957. Print.
Van Dover, J. Kenneth. *At Wolfe's Door: The Nero Wolfe Novels of Rex Stout*. 2nd edition. Rockville, MD: James A. Rock & Company, 2003. Print.
Warner, Penny. *Dead Body Language*. New York: Bantam Books, 1997. Print.
———. *Sign of Foul Play*. New York: Bantam Books, 1998. Print.
———. *Blind Side*. Palo Alto, CA: Perseverance Press, 2001. Print.
———. *Silence Is Golden*. Palo Alto, CA: Perseverance Press, 2003. Print.
———. *Dead Man's Hand*. Boonsboro, MD: Hilliard Harris, 2007. Print.
Weiner, Henri. *Crime on the Cuff*. New York: William Morrow & Co., 1936. Print.
West-Pavlov, Russell. *Space in Theory: Kristeva, Foucault, Deleuze*. Amsterdam: Rodopi, 2009. Print.
Woodcock, Kathryn, and Miguel Aguayo. "Adjustment to Deafness." In *Deafened People: Adjustment and Support*. Toronto: University of Toronto Press, 2000. Print.
Zimmerman, R.D. *Death Trance*. New York: William Morrow and Co., 1992. Print.
———. *Blood Trance*. New York: William Morrow and Co., 1993. Print.
Zola, Irving. "'Any distinguishing features?' The Portrayal of Disability in the Crime-Mystery Genre." *Policy Studies Journal* 15, 3 (March 1987): 486–507. Print.

Index

Adams, Jane A., Naomi Blake mysteries 41–42
alexia sine agraphia, in Engel, Howard 187–88
Alzheimer's disease 186–87
amnesia 168
   in *Memento* 195
amputees. *See* manual impairment; mobility impairment; paralysis
Anderson, Myrdene, and Floyd Merrell 176
autism spectrum disorders 174
   in *Monk* 179–80
   in Sherlock Holmes 13–15

Barker, Cory 179
Bartlett, L.L., Jeff Resnick series 168, 191–94
Bauman, H-Dirksen L., and Joseph J. Murray 62, 71, 82, 90
Bauman, H-Dirksen L., "Poetics" 84, 85, 86, 91
Baynton, Douglas 67
Bérubé, Michael 166, 175, 176, 197 n.9
Best Years of Our Lives, The (1946) 162 n.1
blindness, Chapter 2
   as absence of knowledge 26–27
   and companion dogs 36–38
   and Deleuzean space 29–30, 35, 40, 46
   and intersubjectivity 44, 47–48
   as mystical insight 25, 27–28, 33, 47, 50, 51–57
   ocularnormativity 27
   and Oedipus 18–19
   and staring 28–29
Bolt, David 26–27, 28, 32, 33
brain injury. *See* Bartlett, L.L.; Engel, Howard
Bramah, Ernest, Max Carrados stories 26–28, 58
Brandt, Allan M. 72

Breger, Esther 179
Browne, D.P., *The Wooden Leg of Inspector Anders* 122–27
Brueggemann, Brenda Jo 61, 69

Caeton, D.A. 27
Carlon, Patricia, *The Whispering Wall* 107–11
Caspary, Vera, *Laura* 3, 23 n.3
Castle (ABC) 23 n.6, 41, 61
Chambers, Tod 11–12
Chandler, Raymond 50
   Philip Marlowe 82
Chesterton, G. K. 99
Cheyne, Ria 12, 151, 157–58
Christianson, Scott R. 82–83
Christie, Agatha 15–16
   Appointment with Death 23 n.11
   Cards on the Table 23 n.14
   "Cornish Mystery" 17
   Dumb Witness 18
   The Endless Night 23 n.10
   Hallowe'en Party 17, 23 n.14, 23 n.15
   Hercule Poirot 16–18, 69, 71, 180
   "How Does Your Garden Grow" 17
   "Johnnie Waverly" 17
   Miss Jane Marple 6
   The Murder of Roger Ackroyd 23 n.10, 23 n.14
   "The Mystery at Hunters Lodge" 127 n.2
   Three Act Tragedy 18
Clark, Andy, and David J. Chalmers 186
cognition 186–88, 195
cognitive impairment. *See* Chapter 6; *specific conditions*
Cohen, Michael 3
Collins, Michael, Dan Fortune series 133, 136, 142–47
Connor Westphal series. *See* Warner, Penny
cripistemology 9–10, 101–02, 166, 179, 200

Dan Fortune series. *See* Collins, Michael
Daniel Jacobus books. *See* Elias, Gerald
Davidson, Michael 157
Davis, Lennard J., *Enforcing Normalcy* 62, 69, 79
   End of Normal 183
deafness, Chapter 3
   deaf gain 67, 82
   and lip reading 63–65, 86
   as mode of translation 73–75, 76, 79–80, 82, 89–91
   otonormativity 64–65, 78
   and sign language 63–64, 78, 80, 85–86, 88, 90–91
   and spatial dynamics 62, 84, 90, 92
   and speech 64, 69
   and vision 67, 70
Deaver, Jeffrey 97
   Lincoln Rhyme series 98, 111–17, 127, 199
Deleuze, Gilles 8, 62, 136, 146, 153, 162, 177, 201
   and Félix Guattari, *Thousand Plateaus* 8–10
   territoriality 8, 30, 117, 121
Deming, Richard 129 n.13
Derrida, Jacques 169
Diagnostic and Statistical Manual of Mental Disorders 169
Donaldson, Stephen R., Mick Axbrewder series 152–57
Dove, George N. 86
Doyle, Sir Arthur Conan, Sherlock Holmes 3, 13–15, 180, 183
Drury Lane books. *See* Queen, Ellery
Dubois, Page 29
Duncan Maclain series. *See* Kendrick, Baynard

Eden, Rick 138
Edwards, Martha L. 18–19
Elias, Gerald, Daniel Jacobus books 48–51
Engel, Howard, *The Memory Book* 187–91
ethnicity
   in *The Acupuncture Murders* 76–78
   in Dan Fortune books 146
   in detective fiction 6, 20, 200
   in Mo Bowdre series 45, 59 n.8
   in Nero Wolfe books 106
   in Stephen R. Donaldson books 153

Francis, Dick, Sid Halley series 142, 147–52
Fraser, Max 132
Fred Carver series. *See* Lutz, John
Fries, Kenny, and Fries Test 199–200

Galloway, Terry 65
Garland-Thomson, Rosemarie 10, 11
   misfitting 10, 19, 55, 99, 142, 145, 157, 183
   Staring 132, 134, 162
   "subjugated knowledge" 35
gender
   and blindness 43, 53
   and deafness 86–87
   and genre 91, 122, 180
   and manual impairment 141, 145, 148–49
   and mobility impairment 105, 116
genre 12, 66, 75, 86, 93 n.4, 151, 157, 174, 185
   American hard-boiled tradition 54–55, 82–83
   British country tradition 55
   community in police procedurals 115–16
   in Dick Francis novels 149
   and ethnicity 6
   and gender 91, 122
   in Lethem, *Motherless Brooklyn* 171
   and mobility impairment 117, 126
   and psychiatric impairments 166, 189–90
Gilman, Charlotte Perkins, *Unpunished* 128 n.8
Gilman, Sander 102, 106
Griffith, Nicola 199–200
Guattari, Félix 169

Haddon, Mark, *The Curious Incident of the Dog in the Night-Time* 11, 166–67, 168, 175–78, 194, 196
Hafferty, Frederic W. 65
Hafferty, Frederic W., and Susan Foster 2, 59 n.11
Hammett, Dashiell. *See* Sam Spade

hand and arm impairment. *See* manual impairment
Haraway, Donna J., "Cyborg Manifesto" 135–36
Harris, Charlaine, Harper Connelly books 168, 194
Holmes, Martha Stoddard 119
Holt, Anne, *1222* 95, 97, 127
Homeland (SHO) 197 n.11
Hoppenstand, Gary, and Ray B. Browne 1–2

Ingram, Richard 169–70

Jackson, Hialeah, *The Alligator's Farewell* 64, 87
Jackubowicz, Andrew, and Helen Meekosha 96, 99, 104
James, P.D. 134
Jay, Martin 26
Johnson, Mary 128 n.11
Johnson, Merri Lisa 9

Kayman, Martin A. 4, 6
Kendrick, Baynard, Duncan Maclain stories 36–41
Knight, Stephen 16, 52, 144
Krentz, Christopher 61–62, 63, 64, 66, 71
Kuppers, Petra 14

Laing, R.D. 169
LeBesco, Kathleen 103
Lefebvre, Henri 10
Lethem, Jonathan, *Motherless Brooklyn* 167, 168, 170–75
Levine, Caroline 142, 149
Lewis (ITV) 18
Lewis, Victoria Ann 9
Linett, Maren
  "Blindness and Intimacy" 33, 45
  "Deafness, Communication, and Knowledge" 63, 64
Livingston, Jack, Joe Binney series 64, 81–84, 165
Loftis, Sonya, Freeman 13
Longmore, Paul 2
Longstreet (ABC) 42–44
Lutz, John, Fred Carver series 95, 96, 101–02, 117–23
Lynch, Kathryn L. 131–32, 133

Macdonald, Gina, and Andrew Macdonald 20
Mad Pride Movement 169, 197 n.4
Mairs, Nancy 128 n.6, 197 n.5
manual impairment, Chapter 5
  and form 148–49, 150–51
  and gender 141, 145
  hand symbolism 131–34
  and horror 132–33, 153
  and intersubjectivity 152, 155
  phantom limb sensation 133
  and prosthetics 134, 147, 153, 154–56, 157, 159–60, 162, 163 n.10
  shape and regularity 136, 140–41, 142, 144–47, 157
  and space 139
Marcus, Laura 5, 56, 99
Max Carrados stories. *See* Bramah, Ernest
McBain, Ed, *Let's Hear It for the Deaf Man* 79–81
McHale, Brain 100
McHugh, Susan 36, 43
McRuer, Robert 9
medical model of disability 113
Memento (Christopher Nolan 2000) 11, 194, 195–96
mental illness 169. *See also* Chapter 6; *specific conditions*
  and narrative coherence 169–70
  on TV 178–79
Messent, Peter 14–16, 32, 43–44, 61, 69, 96
Midsomer Murders (ITV) 178
Milton, John, "The Reason of Church-Government" 132
Mitchell, David T., and Sharon L. Snyder, *Narrative Prosthesis* 19, 163 n.9
mobility impairment, Chapter 4
  and genre 117, 126
  and intersubjectivity 105–07, 109, 114–15, 125
  and prosthetics 120, 124–26
  and space 100–01, 105, 120–21, 126
Mo Bowdre series. *See* Page, Jake
Monk (USA) 16, 127 n.2, 175, 179–86
Moretti, Franco 15, 23 n.4
Munt, Sally R. 5, 53, 96, 134
Murder, She Wrote (CBS) 41, 127 n.2
Murray, Stuart 177, 178

Naomi Blake mysteries. *See* Adams, Jane A.
narrative prosthesis 22 n.2
Nero Wolfe series. *See* Stout, Rex
neurodiversity 21. *See also* Chapter 6

O'Brien, Mark 128 n.10
OCD/obsessiveness. *See also Monk* and *Poirot* 16–17
Oedipus myth 18–20
Olney, Ian 153
Ott, Bill 47

Padden, Carol 91
Page, Jake, Mo Bowdre series 44–49
Panek, Leroy L. 115–16
paralysis 52. *See also* mobility impairment; Chapter 4
  in Carlon, *The Whispering Wall* 107–11
  and communication 109, 111, 113–16
  in Deaver novels 112–17
Peacock, James 172
Pepper, Andrew 5–6, 57, 100
Pepperney, Justin 132
Perception (TNT) 170, 179, 194–95
Plain, Gill 135, 147, 150
Poe, Edgar Allan 3, 4, 6, 99
Porter, Dennis 122
Price, Margaret 6, 23 n.5
prosthetic devices
  and manual impairment 134, 147, 153, 154–56, 157, 159–60, 162, 163 n.10
  and mobility impairment 120, 124–26

Quayson, Ato 19–20, 124, 145–46
Queen, Ellery, Drury Lane books 68–75

Rear Window (Alfred Hitchcock 1954) 96
Reddy, Maureen T. 91
Rée, Jonathan 62–63, 85
Ritchie, Simon, *Work for a Dead Man* 134, 158
Rodas, Julia Miele 27
Romdenh-Romluc, Komarine 187
Rosemary and Thyme (BBC) 41
Roth, Marco 174
Rushing, Robert A. 7, 23 n.11, 94 n.15, 96, 182, 198 n.14
Rzepka, Charles J. 4, 6, 15, 18, 117, 127 n.1

Sacks, Oliver, *Hallucinations* 133
  afterword to Engel, Howard 187, 188, 190
Sam Spade
  as loner 42
  as shape-shifter 61
Samuels, Ellen 23 n.7, 57
Savarese, Ralph James 165
Sayers, Edna Edith 65, 74–75, 83, 94 n.13, 94 n.14
Scaggs, John 5, 16, 28–29, 83, 185
Schlossberg, Linda 135, 150
Schor, Naomi 198 n.15
Shapiro, Karl, "The Leg" 163 n.2
Shildrik, Margrit 9, 40, 136
Sid Halley series. *See* Francis, Dick
Siebers, Tobin 23 n.7
Smith, Lesley 179
Snyder, Sharon L. 100
Snyder, Sharon L., and David T. Mitchell, *Cultural Locations* 129 n.14, 170
social model of disability 2
Soitos, Stephen 6
space 7–11, 29–30, 35, 62, 100–01, 110, 115, 117, 120–21, 126, 155, 168, 172, 177–78, 186, 193, 201
Stagg, Clinton H. 30–35
Stearn, Queenie 64
Stephens, Reed. *See* Donaldson, Stephen R.
Steward, Dwight, *The Acupuncture Murders* 76–79, 94 n.12
Stout, Rex 129 n.14
  Nero Wolfe series 102–07
stroke. *See* mobility impairment
Sue Thomas: F.B.Eye (PAX) 64–65
  memoir *Silent Night* 64, 86, 92–93 n.3
Symons, Julian 61, 79–80, 129 n.14, 153

Thornley Colton stories. *See* Stagg, Clinton H.
Thoutenhoofd, Ernst Daniël 67
Todorov, Tsvetan 93 n.4, 126
touch 173–74
Tourette syndrome 167. *See also* Lethem, Jonathan, *Motherless Brooklyn*
Tremain, Shelley 67
Trench, John, Martin Cotterell books 139–42

Van Dover, J. Kenneth 105

Warner, Penny, Connor Westphal series 64, 65, 66, 88–91, 199
Weiner, Henri, *Crime on the Cuff* 136–39, 141–42
West-Pavlov, Russell 8
Woodcock, Kathryn, and Miguel Aguayo 62, 87–88, 92

Zimmerman, R.D., trance novels 51–57
Zola, Irving 2, 168